How steam locomotives really work

The sight and sound of steam locomotives working hard was always most impressive. Here two former-GWR locomotives battle up the 1 in 100 gradient of Honeybourne Bank in October 1952. The choice of a freight train for the frontispiece is appropriate, as, in the days of steam, British Railways received twice as much revenue from freight as they did from passengers. (National Railway Museum, T. E. Williams Collection.)

How steam locomotives really work

P. W. B. SEMMENS

and

A. J. GOLDFINCH

OXFORD
UNIVERSITY PRESS

OXFORD
UNIVERSITY PRESS

Great Clarendon Street, Oxford OX2 6DP
Oxford University Press is a department of the University of Oxford.
It furthers the University's objective of excellence in research, scholarship,
and education by publishing worldwide in

Oxford New York

Athens Auckland Bangkok Bogotá Buenos Aires Calcutta
Cape Town Chennai Dar es Salaam Delhi Florence Hong Kong Istanbul
Karachi Kuala Lumpur Madrid Melbourne Mexico City Mumbai
Nairobi Paris São Paulo Singapore Taipei Tokyo Toronto Warsaw

with associated companies in Berlin Ibadan

Oxford is a registered trade mark of Oxford University Press
in the UK and in certain other countries

Published in the United States
by Oxford University Press Inc., New York

© P. W. B. Semmens and A. J. Goldfinch, 2000

The moral rights of the author have been asserted
Database right Oxford University Press (maker)

First published 2000

A catalogue record for this book is available from the British Library

Library of Congress Cataloging in Publication Data
(Data available).

ISBN 0 19 856536 4

Typeset by EXPO Holdings, Malaysia
Printed in Great Britain
on acid-free paper by
Biddles Ltd,
Guildford King's Lynn

Contents

Introduction

Although British Railways operated its last mainline steam locomotives in August 1968, there is still immense interest in the large numbers of them which have been privately preserved. Not only do these operate on the various heritage railways throughout the country, but a select few are passed to operate trains on parts of Railtrack's national system. In the museum world various working reproductions of historic locomotives have been constructed, and there is even a brand-new Class A1 Pacific being assembled in Darlington at the time of writing. (The former are correctly referred to as 'reproductions', rather than 'replicas', because they differ in numerous details from the originals, although mirroring fairly accurately their appearance. There is no way in which designs of anything getting on for two centuries old would meet today's safety standards.)

The development of the steam locomotive was an empirical process, owing little to the century-old use of stationary steam engines. As technology progressed and better materials of construction became available, the steam locomotive slowly developed in size and complexity. At the same time knowledge on how to operate them accumulated and became more widely known, but, in the United Kingdom, the training of enginemen never developed in the formal way that it did in some continental countries, notably our nearest neighbour, France. The *Handbook for Railway Steam Locomotive Enginemen*, produced by the British Transport Commission in 1957, was the first such official publication in Britain, but, even so, the training of footplate staff still largely relied on inspectors, who were themselves ex-drivers, and the 'Mutual Improvement Classes', run on a voluntary basis by the senior drivers at each particular depot.

This whole process was essentially 'hands-on', a technique often referred to in industry generally as 'Sitting with Nellie'. As a result many ingrained practices were passed on without the fundamentals of steam technology and locomotive design being taught or understood. Not surprisingly it was unusual for footplate crews to press their locomotives to the limit of their performance, or generally experiment with operational practices. In France, where crews were paid bonuses for coal economy and regaining time, they quickly got to know how to operate the locomotives to maximize their rewards.

This book is intended to provide, without fable or favour, a realistic scientific and engineering account of much of this missing background, avoiding myth and partisanship, to enable those interested in the first mechanical means of land transport to appreciate the reasons for various design features as well as the limitations of their various parts. It does not set out to instruct footplate crews on how to operate a locomotive, but is intended to provide the reasons which underlie what they are taught to do.

Because it is intended for those currently interested or involved in steam locomotive operation, we have deliberately kept the general descriptions in the present tense, although, where the development of a particular technology is being discussed, we have referred to it as a story from the past.

Virtually all steam locomotives were constructed at the time when everyone in this country used Imperial units (feet and inches, pounds and tons), and we have continued the use of these. Where appropriate we have also given the SI equivalent, but slavish use of all the decimal places in the conversion factors has been avoided. We have not, for instance, differentiated between the Imperial ton (2240 lb) and the metric one (2204 lb)—the dirt accumulating on a locomotive in service would amount to more than the difference!. For those wanting to make accurate comparisons, the table below lists the units of particular interest for our purposes, including the US ton and gallon.

There is another important way in which steam locomotive descriptions vary between different countries. This is with the notation for the layout of their wheels. In the UK the Whyte system is used for steam locomotives, in which the numbers of the leading, coupled-driving, and trailing *wheels* are listed in order from the front to the rear. For example, a locomotive with a four-wheeled bogie in front of six coupled wheels is given the notation 4-6-0. For another design with an additional trailing two-wheeled pony-truck under the firebox, this changes to 4-6-2, which is one of the wheel arrangements known by a special name, in this case 'Pacific'. Tank locomotives have a 'T' after their wheel notation, which is sometimes expanded to 'PT' for pannier tank, or 'ST' for saddle-tank. For locomotives with tenders, the wheels or axles on the latter are ignored from the notation point of view. Where there is more than one set of coupled-driving wheels, each set is shown separately, separated by a hyphen (-) if they are mounted on the same frame, or a plus sign (+) if the locomotive is an articulated one.

Different systems are used in other countries, the French notation being based on the number of *axles*, rather than wheels. A 'Pacific' becomes 231, which was then used as a prefix for the locomotive's number, together with a letter for its class, Chapelon's famous 'Pacifics' for the Nord being numbered from 231.E.1 upwards. On the Southern Railway Bulleid introduced his own version of this, the 'Pacifics' having their numbers prefixed by '21C', the letter signifying their three carrying axles, but this system disappeared in the British Railways' general renumbering after nationalization in 1948. Some other countries indicated the proportion of axles that actually drove the locomotive, a 'Pacific', for example, being referred to as 'A3/6', where A might indicate it was intended for a particular type of duty.

Conversion factors

Imperial				Metric/US		
Mile	(mile)	0.621	1	1.609	Kilometre	(km)
Yard	(yd)	1.094	1	0.914	Metre	(m)
Foot	(ft)	3.281	1	0.305	Metre	(m)
Inch	(in)	0.039	1	25.4	Millimetre	(mm)
Gallon	(gal)	0.220	1	4.546	Litre	(l)
Gallon	(gal)	0.833	1	1.201	US gallon	(US gal)
Ton	(ton)	0.984	1	1.016	Metric tonne	(tonne)
Ton	(ton)	0.833	1	1.120	US ton	(US ton)
Pound	(lb)	2.205	1	0.454	Kilogram	(kg)
Horsepower	(hp)	1.340	1	0.746	Kilowatt	(kw)
Pound force	(lbf)	0.2248	1	4.448	Newton	(N)

The table should be read from the centre column outwards. For example, 1 kilometre equals 0.621 miles, while 1 mile equals 1.609 kilometres.

CHAPTER 1

Why use steam?

What is a steam locomotive?

Although every enthusiast knows what a steam locomotive is like, to be able to understand how it works in detail we must first look at its fundamental characteristics and the physical, chemical and engineering laws under which it operates.

A steam locomotive is a 'heat engine', which converts the chemical energy of the fuel it burns into useful work hauling trains. It does this by turning water into steam, which it uses as a working fluid to drive the pistons and coupled wheels. The important thing about the efficiency of this process is not the boiler pressure, of itself, but the temperature range over which this working fluid operates. Nor is the water/steam system the only one that could be used—indeed, because the steam in a locomotive's cylinders is only slightly above its condensing temperature, the mean pressure as it expands is not as great as it would be with other working fluids.

It is the widespread availability of water throughout our planet, and the familiarity of its everyday use by humans, which made it the obvious choice of the pioneers who built the first steam locomotives empirically. Some 70 per cent of the human body consists of water, and land covers less than a third of the Earth's surface, while the maximum depths of the oceans far outstrip the highest mountains. Water does have its drawbacks, as it dissolves most solid materials to some extent, and this property often produces problems for the locomotive engineer. It is also corrosive to many common engineering metals, especially at high temperatures.

Solar energy falling on the Earth powers the natural water cycle, evaporating it from the oceans and returning it to the land as rain, where some of it can be trapped and used for various personal and technological purposes. The extent of this recycling is massive, as shown by the following example. During the build-up for the 'Rail 150' celebrations along the Stockton & Darlington Railway in 1975, among the sales items produced were tins of 'Locomotion Steam', copying the contemporary sales of similar containers of 'London Fog'. A suitable disclaimer was made on the label (in small print, of course) that the tin contained only air. However, a colleague of one of the authors came up with the information that each of the tins would actually have in it some 100 000 molecules of water whose oxygen atoms had passed through the boiler of George Stephenson's pioneering 0-4-0. During the 150 years that had elapsed since the first train trundled from Shildon to Stockton, the steam that had been discharged by that locomotive would have been spread fairly uniformly throughout the northern hemisphere, and the quantity stipulated would have been contained as water vapour when the tin was sealed. (Bonding exchanges take place between the hydrogen and oxygen atoms in liquid water, so it is only the oxygen ones we can pinpoint in this way.)

Virtually all forms of life require regular supplies of water to survive, and very early in the process of human civilization the advantages of water for cooking purposes were realized. By the 1600s the use of pots and pans to boil water was commonplace, but there was little need for vessels which could withstand any significant pressure above atmospheric, except possibly in the brewing trade. This was one of the biggest hurdles which the pioneers of steam power had to find a way of overcoming.

The origins of the stationary steam engine

The stationary steam engine pre-dated the steam locomotive by just over a century, and our examination of the way steam power has developed must therefore start back in the late seventeenth century. Savery was the first to make a 'fire engine', whose primary purpose was to pump water out of mines, a task which was far more important at that time than mechanising transport. His engine worked by admitting low-pressure steam to a vessel which had connections at its top and bottom, with appropriate valves. When the vessel was full of steam the supply was isolated and a bottom valve opened to the mine's drainage sump. As the steam condensed, the partial vacuum allowed atmospheric pressure to force water from the sump into the vessel until it was nearly filled. A change of valve positions then readmitted the steam supply to the top of the vessel, while a second bottom one opened to enable the water to be forced up the mine shaft. In the later versions there were two similar

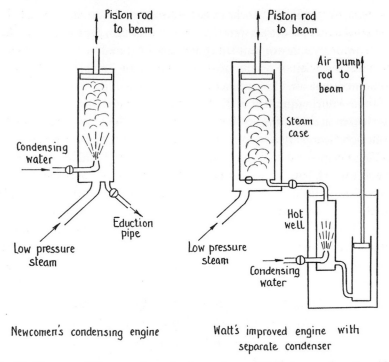

Fig. 1.1 Diagrams of Newcomen's condensing engine and Watt's improved engine with separate condenser.

vessels side-by-side to enable the system to be worked continuously. The valve operations were made automatic and the system became small enough to be used for domestic purposes.

Newcomen made the next big step forward, by using a cylinder and piston to rock an overhead beam connected to conventional mine pumps. A low-pressure boiler supplied steam to the bottom of the cylinder through a valve, and this enabled counterweights on the beam to haul the piston upwards. After turning off the steam supply, cold water was sprayed into the cylinder to condense the steam in it, and the partial vacuum that resulted caused the pressure of the atmospheric on the top of the piston to force it downwards, as shown in the left-hand diagram of Fig. 1.1. (At sea-level atmospheric pressure is about 14.7 lb/in^2 expressed in the Imperial units which were used by British locomotive engineers in the age of steam, which corresponds to 10^5 N/m^2 or 1 bar, in SI units.) The whole system operated at only slightly above atmospheric pressure, well within the limits of contemporary equipment. Because the spray cooled the whole cylinder down, a lot of the next charge of steam did no more than warm it up again, being condensed immediately it was admitted. The thermal efficiency was thus very low, but the practical mining advances that resulted were sufficient to see these engines being installed, not only in the United Kingdom, but elsewhere on continental Europe.

James Watt improved the Newcomen engine by using a separate condenser, and also applied low pressure steam to the top of the piston, both of which significantly reduced the usage of steam. (See Fig. 1.1, right.) The consequent increase in efficiency, and the corresponding reduction in fuel costs, were very important, particularly for installations that were remote from supplies of cheap fuel. The development of Watt's improved engine was a slow business, and it took him 10 years to obtain an accurately-bored cylinder and make a satisfactory separate condenser, together with the pumps required to remove the air that entered the cylinder with the steam. (To prevent

Plate 1.1 The use of massive stationary steam engines for duties such as pumping water out of mines pre-dated the steam locomotive by a century, but there is now little more than a few ruined engine-houses to remind us of them.

Plate 1.2 Although the hardware has disappeared, impressions of the size of the slow-acting mining machinery powered by stationary steam engines can be obtained from the work of contemporary artists.

'wind-logging', Newcomen found it necessary to sweep the air out of his cylinders by letting the steam drive it out through the 'eduction pipe' used to remove the condensate. A 'snifting valve' in the condensate receiver showed when all the air had been driven out.)

Another important development by Watt was his 'parallel motion', enabling the piston rod to provide a upward vertical thrust on the end of the beam, instead of relying on the Newcomen 'arch heads' which could only cope with downward traction forces. It was said that he took more satisfaction from his invention of parallel motion than the separate condenser.

Watt also pioneered the 'rotative' steam engine, a machine needed to supplement the horse-powered 'gins' used to haul minerals out of the deeper mines made possible by the new pumping engines. With this there were difficulties because the idea of a crank-lever to transmit the forces to the driving shaft had been patented, so he adopted the 'Sun and Planet' arrangement, which also had the benefit of doubling the speed of the flywheel which was needed to even out the cyclical forces from a single cylinder. He also developed a double-acting engine, with steam being used to move the piston in both directions, which doubled the power available.

It was Richard Trevithick who championed the use of 'strong steam', initially with stationary engines. The first of these was built in 1800, and soon became popular in Cornwall and South Wales. Their operation depended on relatively high-pressure steam forcing the piston backwards and forwards against atmospheric pressure, and exerting a force which could be transmitted via a crank to the drive shaft with its flywheel. Because his steam was saturated, to avoid any loss of pressure from unnecessary condensation, he kept his single cylinder warm by housing it inside the boiler. As well as doing away with a cumbersome condenser and the need for a supply of cooling water, it was much faster to operate, since the start of each stroke was no longer delayed until the contents of the cylinder had started to condense. As the piston approached each end of the double-acting cylinder, one valve opened to discharge the exhaust steam to atmosphere, while another then admitted steam from the boiler to drive the piston in the opposite direction. Because of the higher boiler pressure the required output could be obtained from smaller cylinders and pistons, which also reduced the size of the other equipment. On the other hand there was an increased risk of explosion, and much public criticism was made by Watt and his business partners of every such mishap that took place with their rival's high-pressure engines. It is somewhat ironic that Murdock put forward ideas for a high-pressure steam engine in 1784, but his partner, James Watt, disapproved.

Adapting the steam engine for locomotion

A lot of development work was needed to adapt the principles of the stationary steam engine to enable it to become a prime mover for the transport of goods and passengers. Because of the size and weight of the early steam engines, their first use was for waterborne transport, Symington and Müller building a paddle-wheel steamer in 1788.

It was Trevithick who first mechanized land transport, adapting his high-pressure steam principles, and beginning with experimental models. One of these had a spectacular end after he and his companions had adjourned to a nearby hostelry to celebrate one of its trials. They parked it in a nearby shed but failed to ensure that the fire had been doused. After the water remaining in the boiler had evaporated, the model, as well as the shed, caught fire, and both were destroyed. Undeterred, he built three high-pressure steam carriages, but the state of

Some early steam locomotives

Plate 1.3 The working reproduction of Richard Trevithick's Penydarren locomotive of 1804. When Trevithick won the wager with the original, he *walked* in front of it, using the controls at the far end. By modern standards this is considered too hazardous, so the driver of the reproduction rides on the rudimentary tender, and operates the vital controls from there.

Plate 1.4 *Locomotion* was built by George and Robert Stephenson for the opening of the Stockton & Darlington Railway in 1825, which was the first public railway to own and operate a steam locomotive. This is the 1975 reproduction, built by Mike Satow, seen standing outside Darlington North Road Museum.

the roads at that time prevented anything worthwhile being developed. In 1804 a wager by an industrialist in South Wales prompted him to mount one of his static high-pressure engines on wheels, and this first cumbersome locomotive made its way along the Penydarren plateway in 1804, hauling a load of 10 tons along the $9\frac{1}{2}$-mile route. The weight of the locomotive was too much for the lightly-constructed permanent way, and the engine was returned to its static duties. His final locomotive was *Catch-me-who-can*, which ran on a fairground-like

Plate 1.5 In advance of the planned opening of the Liverpool & Manchester Railway in 1830, the company held the Rainhill Trials in 1829 to determine the most suitable locomotive design for the line, which was to be worked by locomotives for most of its length. The Stephensons' *Rocket*, with its multi-tubular boiler, won the trials. The illustration is of the reproduction, built for the National Railway Museum by Mike Satow to mark the Trial's 150th anniversary celebrations. It is shown in Sacramento, where it was taking part in the opening of the California State Railroad Museum. Thanks to the higher American loading-gauge it was running with the correct height chimney which cannot be used on most lines in Britain.

Plate 1.6 The Frenchman, Marc Seguin, visited England in 1825 and met George Stephenson while looking at the country's railways. In 1829 he built a steam locomotive, which, like the Stephensons' *Rocket*, had a number of fire-tubes in its boiler, but, instead of using the exhaust steam to induce the air for combustion, a forced draught was provided by large a fan mounted on the tender. This reproduction of his 1829 design was built and demonstrated in the late 1980s. Each cylinder only drove the wheels on its side of the locomotive, and some unusual rodding was used to absorb the 'fore-and-aft' forces produced as the crank-pins rotated.

circuit close to where Euston station is today. By selling rides to the public he hoped to popularize steam traction, but this was a failure, and, ever-ready to be distracted by new schemes, he emigrated to South America, to return and die penniless in 1833.

By this time the development of the steam locomotive had been taken up by other engineers, the most successful being George Stephenson. He continued to keep the cylinders as warm as possible, and those in *Locomotion,* which inaugurated the Stockton & Darlington Railway in 1825, were also enclosed within the boiler shell. It was only with experience, and the increasing boiler temperatures which went with higher pressures, that locomotive engineers were able to avoid the complications of keeping the cylinders warm in this way. In Stephenson's 'Planet' design the cylinders were mounted immediately below the smokebox, which provided better mechanical arrangements to transfer the forces from the pistons and cylinder covers to the drawbar, as well as providing some warmth for the cylinders, which could now be lagged.

Another major problem that had to be tackled by the designers of early locomotives was how to transmit the tractive effort from the pistons to the driving wheels. One can see variations of parallel motion on locomotives such as *Agenoria*, dating from 1829 and preserved in the National Railway Museum at York, although detailed inspection will also reveal the fracture in one of its cylinders! George and Robert Stephenson's *Rocket*, which was the runaway winner at the 1829 Rainhill Trials, was provided with slide bars and associated motion which would have been instantly recognizable by locomotive engineers 150 years later. The design of the valve-gear to control the admission and exhaust of the steam from the cylinders was much more primitive, and serves as a reminder that a railway locomotive has to be able to reverse, unlike pumping engines and many of the rotative type.

The use of rails rather than the ground to support and guide wagons goes back to the Middle Ages, when wooden ones came into use. By the 1700s there were some extensive systems in operation in the northern coalfield. The Tanfield Way which crossed Causey Arch in County Durham handled more than 200 000 wagons a year. Each held just over two tons, and was hauled by its own horse, which made its way along between the rails, with its handler walking outside. Their combined experience enabled the necessary tractive effort to be generated by the horse's hooves gripping the ballast spread between the rails. For steam locomotives to be successful they had to be capable of hauling more than a single wagon, and thus reducing the mine's manpower requirements, as well as the need for fodder, which was rising in cost during the Napoleonic wars. Most locomotives exerted their tractive effort on the rails, which introduced significantly-different demands on the track, even though the rails, by that time, were being constructed from metal. The coefficient of friction of metal-wheels-on-metal-rails was far less than hooves on ballast, and this, coupled with the higher forces needed to move the heavier loads, caused the early locomotive engineers to have to consider ways of getting sufficient grip for the wheels.

Blenkinsop, on the Middleton Railway near Leeds, introduced a cog-wheel drive outside the rails in 1812. Less successfully, Brunton built his 'Mechanical Traveller' locomotive the following year, which propelled itself with the aid of a pair of mechanical legs behind it which pressed on to the ballast between the rails. The adhesion problem was very elegantly put into proper proportion in 1813 by some experiments carried out by Hedley on the Wylam wagonway on the north bank of the Tyne. He built a wagon which was powered by four men who stood on platforms fixed to it, and turned handles connected by gearing to the driving wheels. Various numbers of coal wagons were attached behind it, and the ability of the men to move them on level track demonstrated that adhesion was capable of handling the required tractive effort from a locomotive.

The maximum tractive effort that can be provided without causing the driving wheels to slip is a function of the vertical load on them, known as the adhesion weight. If the track is capable of bearing more weight, heavier locomotives could haul larger loads, but the early cast-iron rails were not all that strong or reliable. It was only about the time when Stephenson started building the Stockton & Darlington Railway (S&DR) in 1822 that malleable iron rails, which were capable of supporting heavier weights than the previous cast-iron variety, became available. The steeper the gradient, the greater the tractive effort needed to haul a given load up it, and, by the time Stephenson was building the S&DR, his experience prompted him to use horse- or locomotive-haulage as long as the gradients against the load were no more than 1 in 300. Where the line had to be steeper than this, he resorted to incline-working with rope haulage, as at Etherley and Brusselton.

It is likely too that the early locomotives suffered some of their adhesion problems from their primitive or non-existent springing. Stephenson had tried *steam* springs unsuccessfully on one of his Killingworth designs, and also used a pair of chains to couple its wheels together to use their combined adhesion weight. Without effective springs, it was very likely that the faulty distribution of weight on the locomotive's axles as it passed over irregularities on the track could be enough to start a slip—not to mention the increased damage to the rails by overloading them. It was not until 1827 that Nicholas Wood applied steel springs to locomotive axles at Killingworth. In the light of 150 years' experience, the reproduction *Locomotion* built in 1975 was provided with springs, and was easy to drive, albeit on modern track.

The development of commercially-successful steam locomotives was thus a long business, requiring the talents of many pioneering railway engineers as well as the parallel development of new materials and techniques by experts in other engineering and production techniques. This book is not a history of the steam locomotive as such, but this short summary enables us to appreciate some of the reasons (mistaken and real) why certain features were adopted and retained on steam locomotives throughout the century and a half that they formed the primary means of traction on the world's railways.

The properties of steam and water

We must now look in more detail at the properties of water and steam, which provide the means of converting the chemical energy of the fuel into useful work.

Water has the chemical formula H_2O, each molecule containing a pair of hydrogen atoms attached to the central oxygen one, but the three atoms do not lie in a straight line. Hydrogen is the lightest of all elements, with an atomic weight of 1, while oxygen is heavier, with a weight of 16. Like any compound, water can exist in three different forms—solid (ice), liquid and vapour (steam), depending on the temperature. In strict scientific terms, steam as used in locomotives is a vapour rather than a gas, because it is at all times capable of being liquefied by the application of pressure alone. A vapour only becomes a gas when its temperature has been raised above its 'critical point'. This, in the case of water, is 374 °C, which requires the application of no less than 219 atmospheres pressure (over 3200 lb/in^2 or 220 bar) to keep it liquid.

In an open atmosphere water boils at about 100 °C. Any liquid only boils when its vapour pressure equals the external pressure to which it is subjected. If the water is contained in a pressure vessel fitted with a safety-valve which opens at 200 lb/in^2 (13.8 bar), the temperature will have to reach 198 °C before the safety-valves lift, while in the boiler of one of Bulleid's original Pacifics, with its working pressure of 280 lb/in^2 (19.3 bar) above atmospheric, the maximum temperature of the boiling water would have been 213 °C. (See Fig. 1.2.) Water molecules being very stable, they have no tendency to decompose at such temperatures. Reducing the external pressure also lowers a liquid's boiling point, which is why it is difficult to cook or make a good cup of tea on top of a high mountain.

It is the molecular structure of a liquid which determines the shape of its vapour pressure *vs* temperature curve, and the strong bonding between the adjacent molecules in the liquid form gives water a high boiling point for its mass. (Ethanol, or ethyl alcohol, with a much higher molecular weight of 46 compared with 18 for water, boils at only 78.5 °C under ordinary atmospheric pressure.) The boiling point of a particular liquid also increases if it contains any dissolved materials, although the pressure of the steam above it is no greater. As we will see in Chapter 3, there are other good reasons for keeping down the amount of dissolved

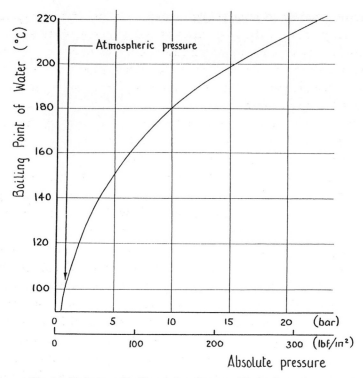

Fig. 1.2 Variation of boiling-point of water with absolute pressure.

material in a boiler. However, unless one uses distilled water as a feed, there is bound to be some build-up of solutes in a locomotive boiler.

Even when the temperature of a liquid reaches its boiling point, the boiling process may not begin immediately. Some sort of nucleation is needed to start the bubbles of vapour forming. If one heats water in clean stainless-steel saucepan or a glass beaker, boiling often commences explosively, the phenomenon being known as 'bumping'. It can be avoided by providing a suitably rough surface, and the heating surfaces of a locomotive's boiler are sufficiently rough for this purpose. Nevertheless it is possible for 'priming' to occur, when the sudden evolution of steam forms so many bubbles that liquid is carried over into the cylinders. The reasons for this are different, and will be described in Chapter 3.

When water turns into steam, it expands by a large factor—by no less than 1670 at atmospheric pressure. This in itself explains why the explosion of a boiler can be so devastating. If a high-pressure boiler ruptures, not only does one get the immediate release of the compressed steam in it, but, as the large mass of water present is all above its atmospheric boiling point, a considerable quantity flashes off as steam. As we will see shortly, a lot of heat is needed to turn water into steam at the same temperature, so this effect would cool down the water and not all of it turns into steam, although the violent boiling process would almost certainly send it all out of the fissure. Domestically the same effect takes place on a much reduced scale if a pressure-cooker is accidentally opened before being allowed to cool.

The magnitude of a locomotive boiler explosion was well demonstrated in 1935, when the crew of a PLM 2-8-2 working a Geneva–Paris express up a 15-mile bank allowed the water level to fall and uncover the top of the inner firebox. This overheated, losing its ability to withstand the pressure, and the crown sheet burst downwards, discharging the contents of the boiler through a tear in the plates which had an area of 17 ft^2 (1$\frac{1}{2}$ m^2). The whole boiler was ripped from the frames and cab, killing the crew, and causing the brake to be automatically applied as the air pipes were severed. This brought the train to a halt with the rest of the locomotive still on the track, and attached to its coaches. Fortunately the train was going round a curve at the time and the boiler's trajectory sent it off into the lineside fields. It first hit the ground, firebox first, 272 ft (83 m) from the point of the explosion, after clearing a telegraph line and a row of trees in the process. It then cartwheeled three more times, finally finishing up 512 ft (156 m) from where it had taken off.

The railway undertook a very extensive investigation, and concluded that the crew had failed to realize that the water level had become too low some 7 min before the explosion occurred. The fusible-plug warning device, which will be described in more detail in Chapter 2, had probably been blowing for 9 min, so the crew had had plenty of time to do something about it. It was calculated that the boiler contained 60 lb (27 kg) of steam and 7 tons of water, all at 200 °C and 227 lb/in^2 (15.7 bar). The water contributed all except 2$\frac{1}{2}$ per cent of the energy released, of which a mere one per cent was needed to send the boiler cartwheeling forward.

Water is used to define the basic unit of heat, which is the calorie. One calorie will raise the temperature of a gram of water by one degree Centigrade. (In these weight-conscious days we are used to looking at the calorie count of our meals, and those are kilocalories, each of which would raise the temperature of a kilogram of water by a degree, or, alternatively, the temperature of 10 grams from 0 to 100 °C.) In all probability the temperature of the water in the tender of a steam locomotive will be of the order of 15 °C, so every kilogram put into a boiler pressed at 200 lb/in² (13.8 bar) will have to be heated to 198 °C before it will even start to boil. It thus needs approximately $(198 - 15) \times 10^3 = 183\ 000$ calories, and none of that will be used, being lost when the steam is exhausted through the chimney.

This is, however, only a small part of the total loss, as even more heat is needed just to turn water into steam at the same temperature. This is known as 'latent heat', part of which represents the work required to push the atmosphere back to accommodate the vastly-increased volume of the steam. In addition, a lot of energy must be provided to overcome the attraction the molecules have for each other in liquid form. At 100 °C the latent heat of vaporization of water is 542 cal/gram, or over five times the amount needed to raise its temperature from freezing to boiling point. This is why a kettle takes a lot longer to boil dry than it has taken to reach boiling point.

Unless a locomotive is fitted with some sort of preheater, all the heat used to raise the water to boiling point and then vaporize it will be lost out of the chimney when the steam is exhausted from the cylinders. To achieve a high overall thermal efficiency, it is thus important for a locomotive to use as little water as possible. We will discuss the complex factors which determine the overall efficiency of a locomotive in later chapters, but, other things being equal, by raising the boiler pressure it is theoretically possible to reduce the amount of steam needed, which would decrease the total amount of heat lost in its evaporation.

Another important way of improving the efficiency of a steam locomotive is by the use of superheating. As described earlier, the temperature of steam in the boiler is the same as that of the water, and is determined by their pressure. If, however, the steam is completely separated from the water, its temperature can then be increased independently. As its pressure remains the same, its volume must increase, which means a smaller weight of steam enters the cylinder for each stroke. This in turn reduces the quantity needed to be boiled, thus cutting down on the amount wasted in the form of latent heat. There are other advantages of superheating, which we will discuss in Chapter 4.

Although the provision of a separate superheater is needed to achieve high superheat, a certain amount is almost always obtained, more or less by accident. At various points between the boiler and the cylinders there will be constrictions in the pipework or the regulator. These will produce a drop in steam pressure, but as no *external* work is done, there can be no loss of energy. The pressure energy lost has to be converted into some other form, and appears as superheat. If one studies the way non-superheated locomotives were worked at the end of the nineteenth century, it will be found that they were usually driven with regulators only partly open, the resulting pressure drop providing sufficient superheat to avoid undue condensation in the cylinders.

We tend to refer to the billowing white clouds of exhaust from a locomotive's chimney and from its safety valves, as 'steam'. What we see, however, are actually droplets of condensed vapour, as the steam is instantly cooled below its dew-point by the air. In hot and dry conditions, which are rarely experienced in this country, steam trains could be seen operating with no more than a haze of smoke from their chimneys, and no white plume.

There is another source of steam or water vapour, which, on condensing, can have other important effects within steam locomotives. Most fuels contain some hydrogen, which burns to water. If the products of combustion passing the heat-transfer surfaces are allowed to cool too much, water can condense out on any cool metal. This is particularly likely when the locomotive is being steamed from cold. Most fuels also contain sulphur, and its oxides emitted in the exhaust gases dissolve in any condensate, making it strongly acidic. The BR standard 9F 2-10-0 locomotives with Franco-Crosti boilers suffered 'acid-dewing' of this sort in their preheaters, which corroded and had to be removed after a short life. Blow-off from a locomotive's safety valves can also condense on the overhead roof structures of large stations, particularly in cold weather, and the subsequent drips of sooty water were not popular with passengers waiting on the platforms!

While it is the water/steam transition which most concerns the locomotive engineer, the water/ice one cannot be ignored. Unlike most liquids, the density of water does not increase all the way down to the point at which it starts to solidify. Water reaches a maximum density at 4 °C, after which it begins to expand again, and it is for this reason that lakes and rivers freeze from the surface downwards. This factor was vital to the evolution of life on earth, which was able to exist in the unfrozen water below the ice layer, but also has an adverse effect on unprotected water systems in cold climates.

Another peculiarity of water is that its volume increases by 9 per cent when it freezes. Not only do unprotected water pipes burst in cold weather, but steam locomotives experience similar problems, particularly with the feed-water connections between locomotive and tender, although cylinder damage is not unknown. The supplies of water in depots and on stations also have to be assured in cold weather, and, when steam traction was widespread, staff had to be kept available, round the clock, to ensure that the protective braziers were functioning. As with the phase change from liquid to vapour, it is necessary to supply latent heat to convert ice to water at the same temperature. This is 80 cal/gram, so represents 80 per cent of the amount of heat then needed to raise the same amount of water to boiling point. When thawing anything out it is thus worthwhile physically removing as much ice as possible as long as it can be done without causing damage.

Because ice expands on freezing, the application of pressure to it will cause some degree of melting. This is what makes ice slippery. The weight on a locomotive's wheels is normally sufficient to melt any ice on the railhead, but it is possible for sufficient ice and snow to become compacted into flangeways to cause derailments.

CHAPTER 2

Burning the fuel

Alternative fuels

The steam locomotive was originally developed for the private railways in the coalfields of Britain, and, not surprisingly, coal was used as the source of heat. Almost immediately after public railways had subsequently started to spread across the country, legislation, in response to public opinion, required locomotives 'to consume their own smoke'. Initially this was not easy to achieve with coal, and there was a wholesale switch to coke as a fuel. Coke had first been a byproduct of William Murdock's process to produce gas for illumination purposes, which he had made by heating coal in a closed retort some three decades before the first practical steam locomotive appeared. The techniques were well developed by the time railways had to conform to the new legislation, and coke manufacture took place at numerous locomotive depots around the country.

When coal is turned into coke, the volatile matter is driven off, leaving what is essentially carbon, although most solid impurities remain. Exactly the same process takes place initially when lumps of coal are added to the firebox of a steam locomotive, as the heat drives off the volatiles, which, although inflammable, burn comparatively slowly if there is no radiant heat present from a white-hot firebed. It is thus quite easy for them to be cooled below combustion point before all the carbon in them has been burnt, and smoke results. As we will see shortly, various ways were developed to overcome the problem.

After the use of coke, another solution to the 'black smoke' problem was to divide the grate area into two with a longitudinal water-filled 'feather', with some holes through it connecting the two halves. There were two fireholes, and each was used alternately, ensuring that one half of the fire was kept bright, so it could 'consume' the smoke from the other. Many small locomotives, particularly those used for shunting in factories, were never provided with brick arches, as described below, and

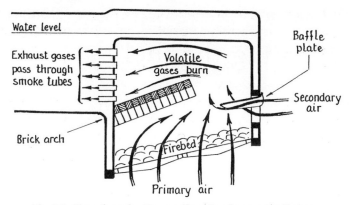

Fig. 2.1 Air and combustion gas flows in a locomotive firebox.

the same firing technique was used to keep alternate halves of the firebed 'bright'. It was rare for such locomotives to be required to produce high power outputs, so this practice was acceptable.

The final solution to the problem was developed by Matthew Kirtley, the first locomotive superintendent of the Midland Railway. In conjunction with Charles Markham, he developed a firebox suitable for burning coal in 1856. As will be described in the next section, this had a 'brick arch' (now sometimes made of concrete) at the boiler end, as shown in Fig. 2.1.

In a stream of air, carbon burns to carbon dioxide, the chemical reaction being as follows:

$$C + O_2 = CO_2.$$

Every kilogram (2.2 lb) of carbon burnt in this way liberates 8020 kcal. However, if insufficient air is present, there will only be enough oxygen to convert the carbon to carbon monoxide:

$$C + \tfrac{1}{2}O_2 = CO.$$

This is a far less exothermic reaction, producing only 2400 kcal/kg, so the chemical combination of the second oxygen atom liberates over twice the heat generated by the first. It is thus very important to avoid wasting so much of the heat in the fuel by starving it of oxygen. Carbon monoxide, however, is inflammable, and will burn given the right conditions, so it is possible to carry out full combustion in two stages, and thus liberate all the heat content of the carbon.

The discovery of cheap supplies of oil enabled this to be used as an alternative fuel for steam locomotives, and it has the advantage of being a liquid. Filling a tank in the tender with oil is a much easier task than topping one up with coal, but very different arrangements have to be made to burn it in the firebox, as will be described in due course. Oil primarily consists of hydrocarbons, with chemical formulae of the generic form $C_nH_{(2n+2)}$, which burn to carbon dioxide and water, given adequate supplies of air. It is hydrocarbons which are also driven off from coal when it is heated after being fed into the firebox, and appropriate air supplies have to be provided to burn them *above* the firebed.

Not all countries that wanted to have railways were blessed with coalfields, and oil supplies were not widely available until well into the twentieth century, so some railways were forced to use alternative forms of fuel. Many developing countries had extensive natural forests, through which their railways were to run. Adapting locomotives to burn

Plate 2.1 Wood was used as a fuel in many countries. Two wood-burning nineteenth-century locomotives are preserved at the Finnish railway museum at Hyvinkää. Inside the 'balloon' chimneys the exhaust follows an indirect path which gives more time for sparks to cool down before being discharged into the lineside forests, thus reducing the fire risk in dry weather.

wood was not too difficult, although the calorific value is lower, and the fireman has to feed the logs into the firebox by hand, rather than use a shovel. Wood-ash is much lighter than that from coal, and wood-burning locomotives working hard were inclined to emit a stream of burning sparks which could easily set fire to lineside forests and crops. To trap the sparks, large 'balloon' chimneys were used, and they came to typify the early North American steam locomotive.

Over the years many other solid fuels have also been used for steam locomotives, most of them being some sort of waste material, whose cheapness outweighs the lower calorific value. A typical example of this was on sugar plantations, where there are vast quantities of bagasse to be disposed of after the sugar has been extracted. One of the big problems with vegetable waste is normally its high water content, which absorbs heat when it is driven off, but in the tropics there is plenty of sun to dry the sugar-cane residues before they are put on the locomotive.

Dried vegetable matter is largely cellulose, which consists of long chains of molecules having the chemical formula $(C_6H_{12}O_6)_n$. The oxygen present is in combined form, so less oxygen is required from the air to convert the fuel to water and carbon dioxide. The down side to this is that the amount of heat generated is not as great is when hydrocarbons are burnt.

Many unusual fuels have been utilized for steam locomotives, but there is an oft-repeated anecdote that mummies were used in the 1850s by the Egyptian railways. The origin of this has been traced back to Mark Twain in *Innocents Abroad*, and it is not known whether there is any truth in it. The cloth wrappings and embalming oil would certainly have provided some heat, and the mummies would presumably also have had some calorific value.

One well-known experiment took place in Ireland, where peat (turf) is plentiful, and is providing about a tenth of the country's public electricity demand. O. V. S. Bulleid, who moved from the Southern Region of BR to become Chief Mechanical Engineer of the State Railway Company (CIE), converted an existing coal-fired locomotive to burn peat. He found that its low density, and its high water and ash contents, meant that it produced little heat in a firebox which had not been designed for it. He then went on to build a specially-designed peat-burning locomotive, but the development costs and falling prices of oil fuel caused the CIE to abandon the project and switch to diesel traction.

Although not strictly a fuel, electricity has been used to 'fire' a few steam locomotives. During World War II, it was very difficult to get coal in Switzerland, but hydroelectric power was available from their mountains, and many lines were electrified with overhead wires. A few steam shunting locomotives were fitted with a giant 'immersion heater' in the boiler, which was fed from the overhead wires using a pantograph on the cab roof, via a circuit-breaker and transformer.

Another way of providing a supply of steam for a locomotive is to replace the boiler with a simple receiver, which can be filled at intervals from a suitable static steam system. Locomotives of this type have frequently been used in places where an 'open' fire would be dangerous, such as an oil refinery, but some were also to be found in factories where there is a surplus of steam available, notably steel works.

Coal from different areas, and even from different seams in the same colliery, can very considerably in character. Analyses of three used by BR in the 1950s are given in Table 2.1. The figures are taken from one of the

Table 2.1 Calorific values and analyses of some coals used by British Railways in the 1950s

	Bedwas		Blidworth		Lilleshall	
	As received	Dry	As received	Dry	As received	Dry
Calorific value						
Cal/g	7805	7893	6977	7568	7031	7577
Pounds of water at 100 °C converted into steam at same temp/lb coal	14.53	14.70	12.99	14.09	13.09	14.11
Proximate analysis						
Moisture (%)	1.1	–	7.8	–	7.2	–
Volatile matter, less moisture (%)	26.6	26.9	35.0	38.0	39.9	43.1
Fixed carbon (%)	64.3	65.0	52.0	56.4	48.2	51.9
Ash (%)	8.0	8.1	5.2	5.6	4.7	5.0
Total sulphur (%)	0.65	0.65	0.78	0.85	0.90	0.97
Coke						
Volume ratio to that of coal	1.0	1.5	1.0	1.0	1.0	1.0
Character	Fairly hard, porous		Hard, porous		Hard, porous	
Ash	Buff, grey-tinted		Buff, pink-tinted		Grey, pink-tinted	

Source: British Railways' Performance & Efficiency Test Bulletin No.3, 1951

early BR Locomotive Test Bulletins, and the fuel had been chosen from three very different sources. Bedwas was a Welsh Grade 2A coal, fairly typical of the type favoured by the former GWR from the collieries they served. It was somewhat more friable than the others, and to prevent the test results being upset by varying amounts of fines, a constant proportion was weighed out into each bag put on the tender. However, it was found that, in the process of his work, the fireman caused further breakdown. For all the locomotives being tested at that time, one common type of Grade 2B hard coal was used with every class tested, and that came from Blidworth Colliery in Nottinghamshire. Another Grade 2B hard coal came from Lilleshall, in Shropshire, but was of a type which had proved troublesome in service, and was included in these tests with one particular class of locomotive to quantify how it behaved.

It will be seen that the Welsh coal was much drier than the other two, which put its 'As received' calorific value up by 11–12 per cent. We do not know what the 'As fired' moisture contents were, but, if the nature of the Bedwas lumps prevented the uptake of water, that could improve the thermal efficiency because heat is required to evaporate the moisture before coal burns fully. It also contained far less volatile matter, which would have helped prevent the emission of black smoke, for the reasons we will discuss later. In this sense it was again typical of Welsh locomotive coal of that era, which was sometimes referred to as 'semi-anthracite'. Once the volatiles have been driven off, the coal has effectively turned into coke, and, in doing so, that from some sources, such as Durham, can swell up considerably. For locomotive purposes this has to be watched, as the swelling effect can block up the air gaps between lumps on the grate. That said, the Bedwas coal expanded by 50 per cent when it was coked, which was presumably acceptable from the airflow point of view. As coke burns from its surface, the more porous it is, the greater is the area available where air can react with it, and hence increase the rate of combustion.

Combustion

The rate of combustion of a given material is highly dependent on its temperature. In a domestic environment the paper in books will waste away extremely slowly over several centuries. Many might think this deterioration was not 'burning', but the fibres are actually slowly being turned into carbon dioxide by the air. On the other hand, if a lighted match is put to the corner of a piece of paper, it will catch fire quite quickly. As those of us who used to light our domestic fires know, the best way to get the sticks alight was to roll the newspaper up so it burnt more slowly, and this heated the wood until it reached a temperature at which its combustion took place at a reasonable speed. The lumps of coal balanced on the sticks needed even longer to heat up and get to the point at which the fire became self-sustaining.

On the railways, those who have the dirty job of raising steam either use 'fire-lighters' to ignite the coal, or 'borrow' a shovelful of fire from another locomotive: in either case they have progressively to build the fire up to get it burning properly. However, when the firebox is up to temperature with the locomotive working hard, small particles of coal can burst into flame in the time between being put through the firehole and reaching the fire, so intense is the radiant heat above an ideal firebed, which is typically some 6–9 in (15–22 cm) thick.

Particle size of the fuel also has an important effect on its inflammability, and the extreme examples are the coal-burning power stations. Coal, ground in mills to the consistency of flour, is shot into the boiler's furnace by a blast of air, and burns just like a gas flame. Many organic powders and natural products which one normally considers as being non-inflammable, such as sugar, can even cause explosions if dust from them is left lying around and somehow gets ignited.

Coal being burnt on a steam locomotive grate should ideally be in lumps about the size of a fist. In the heyday of steam traction, collieries were able to produce it in large lumps. At one time in the ninetenth century many Tyneside collieries regularly got rid of their 'small coals' by burning them at the pithead, as there was no market for them. So important was the ability of a colliery to produce large lumps that they took every opportunity to show off what they could do. When the railway was opened between Darlington and York in 1841, the site engineer at Croft Bridge recorded in his diary that there were '... several large Coals on the tops of the Waggons—I measured one with 30 Cubic feet in it'. Such a block would have weighed over a ton, but, even before the introduction of mechanical coal-cutters in the mines, the average size of coal dropped considerably. The upper size for coal-lumps that can be used on a steam locomotive is determined by the dimensions of the firehole door, but one of the tools issued to every fireman is the coal-pick, or coal-hammer, which can be used to break up any lumps that are too large as they came out of the tender or bunker. Particularly large pieces of coal can also prevent the supply trimming down naturally on to the shovelling plate, much to the fireman's annoyance!

On the other hand, coal to be burnt in a locomotive must not be too small in size. Piling a injudicious quantity of 'slack' on a domestic fire can easily put it out, and, while this would probably not be quite the same with a steam locomotive, too much fine coal shovelled on to the firebed will clog the free flow of air through it, and rapidly reduce the steaming rate of the boiler. With poor quality coal like some of that in World War II, the build-up of surface clinker often had the same effect, and it had to be broken up with the pricker to let the air through. If fine coal is added in small quantities it is whisked straight through the boiler by the blast when the locomotive is working hard, and promptly wasted.

As the lumps of coal used on steam locomotives take several minutes to burn completely, there is the need for a grate to support the coal while this takes place. This contains gaps to enable a supply of air from below to support the combustion, as well as to let the ash drop out from the firebed, to avoid it becoming choked. Later in this chapter we will consider the design of the grate in more detail, and see that in steam's later years many of them were provided with means to carry out other functions as well, such as breaking up clinker. There is a limit to the amount of primary air that can be permitted to pass through the firebars, as excessive flow rates cause the fire to 'lift' and finish up in the smokebox or along the lineside.

Clearly, the material used for the grate has to withstand high temperatures without melting. The continuous flow of cold air through it significantly reduces the temperatures reached by the metal, usually cast iron. In the days of coal fires in the home, the grate in a domestic hearth could distort quite quickly if the level of ash underneath was allowed to build up and choke the air space. The firebars of a steam locomotive require renewing quite frequently, and, as the damage to them usually occurs in particular areas of the grate only, the use of a sectional design, consisting of individual firebars or groups of them, enables the cost of replacements to be kept to a minimum.

The air coming through the firebars is known as the 'primary air', and first comes into contact with the lumps that are nearly completely burnt. The volatiles driven off by the heat after each lump of coal had been added by the fireman leave the *top* of the firebed, and it is also important to have sufficient oxygen at this point to complete the combustion. This is ensured by the 'secondary air' which is normally introduced through the firehole door well above the level of the grate. A deflector or baffle plate is usually provided just inside the firebox to direct this down towards the burning volatiles as they rise from the firebed. Some latter-day North American locomotives were built with several holes through the side walls of the firebox, through which more secondary air was introduced with the use of steam injectors.

Proper mixing of the secondary air with the volatile gases driven off is vital to prevent the emission of black smoke. The final solution was that applied by Kirtley and Markham, who installed a 'brick arch' inside the firebox. (See Fig. 2.1.) This slopes upwards towards the rear, and stops any products of combustion from entering the boiler tubes until they have been swept backwards to met the secondary air. When George Stephenson developed his safety lamp, he showed that hot gases passing though small-diameter tubes are quickly cooled below the temperature at which they could ignite methane in the mines, and there is a similar effect in a locomotive boiler. The provision of a brick arch retains the gases inside the firebox significantly longer, enabling them to mix with the air while still hot, and so ensure that combustion is completed.

To achieve maximum thermal efficiency it is equally as important not to have too much excess air in the gases leaving the boiler. Air consists of just under a quarter of oxygen by weight, most of the rest being nitrogen, which takes no part in the combustion process. All of it entering the firebox is heated to a high temperature, and is ultimately discharged up the chimney, mixed with the products of combustion. Any surplus air being supplied will have to be heated to the same temperature as the rest, and thus adds to the heat losses.

Ideally, therefore, to obtain maximum thermal efficiency there should be no free oxygen in the fluc gases leaving a boiler. This is nearly achieved in the huge static boilers at power stations, with their sophisticated fuel- and air-management equipment and measuring instruments, but is impossible with a locomotive which also has severe constraints of size and weight. In practice, for maximum efficiency the fireman needs to work with about 20 per cent excess air, and a typical curve for the unnecessary heat losses from a steam locomotive as the excess air varies either side of this is shown in Fig. 2.2.

No locomotive has been fitted with an air-excess meter, so the fireman has to use some other indication to keep the quantity correct. The most

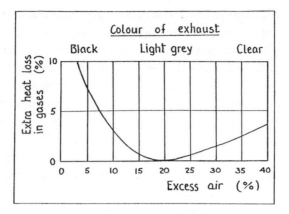

Fig. 2.2 Variation of heat losses in locomotive's exhaust gases with different quantities of combustion air.

Plate 2.2 The cab of *Evening Star*, the last steam locomotive built by British Railways. A simulated fire can be seen burning inside the firehole, where the sliding doors have been opened using the lever on the left-hand side. Above them can be seen the two water level-gauges, with their black-painted 'protectors'.

reliable way of doing this is to watch the top of the chimney. With the correct amount of air there is a light grey smoke plume, which clears completely if too much air is made available. On the other hand, if there is insufficient air, unburnt fuel is emitted, appearing as dark smoke, and the losses rise much more quickly. The curve actually only shows the effect of the production of carbon monoxide, and the losses caused by the unburnt materials in the smoke also decrease the thermal efficiency.

Too much secondary air entering the firebox has also to be avoided to prevent any cold stream impinging on the boiler back tubeplate, where it causes sudden temperature changes. The resulting contraction can produce leaks around the fire-tubes where they are expanded into the plate. Most designs of firehole doors are provided with air holes of some sort, but opening the doors fully to put coal in is bound to produce a considerable increase in the flow of secondary air. To open them and shut them by hand for every shovelful is laborious, but several railways provided a hinged flap which was pulled up to reduce the free area when the doors were open. Firemen were trained to flip it down and up for every shovelful by giving a jerk to a chain, the other end of which was attached to the back of the boiler. Sometimes an enthusiastic driver would help by operating the doors, allowing the fireman to concentrate on his shovel, but careful coordination was needed on a swaying locomotive to avoid covering the floor of the footplate with spilt coal!

Many latter-day steam locomotives in North America were provided with steam-operated firehole doors, and Bulleid adopted them on his Southern Railway Pacifics. When the fireman depressed a pedal, a steam cylinder caused the two doors to rotate sideways and upwards, opening the firehole. They were not too popular with crews, largely because the heavy doors would close rapidly as soon as the pedal was released, and could trap the fireman's hands or shovel. If the locomotive rolled at the critical moment, it was all too easy for his foot to come off the pedal prematurely.

The LNER had another arrangement to reduce the amount of unnecessary air entering the firehole, which, on their locomotives is provided with a large, oval, door which is hinged on one side. The top half contains a small, horizontally-hinged, oval flap, which can be latched open or allowed to close by gravity. If the coal is small enough to pass through this opening, the fireman normally does not open the main door, but just uses the small one. Such a technique does not enable him to place coal on specific parts of the firebed, and, to fill any 'holes'

Plate 2.3 The Royal Bavarian State Railways' Class S²/₆ 4-4-4s had twin firehole-doors, as can be seen on the preserved No. 3201 in the transport museum at Nuremberg. The locomotive briefly held the world steam speed record of 96 mph (154.5 km/h). During the latter half of the nineteenth century, numerous locomotives used in the United States also had more than one firehole in their extremely wide fireboxes, which were necessary to burn the low-quality coal available. This arrangement made it impossible for the driver to see the signals ahead from a normal cab, so he was accommodated in one perched on top of the boiler, thus prompting the nick-name 'Camelback'.

which have developed in the fire, it is necessary to open the main door and direct shovelfuls at any thin spots.

Getting coal into the corners of a wide firebox is always particularly difficult, and, at one time, it was not unknown for the rear ones on the former LMS 'Princess Coronation' Pacifics to the filled up with firebricks. Placing coal in the front corners of a long firebox is also tricky: some firemen developed the technique of bouncing their shovel on the bottom of the firehole, which caused the coal to shoot off it at speed.

It is always important for the fireman to ensure there are no 'holes' of any significant size in the firebed. If there are, a lot of cold air is drawn straight through them. This robs the burning coal of some of the air needed for its combustion, and also cools the gases entering the boiler. It is not always easy to spot holes in a white-hot firebed, but they often draw attention to themselves by producing a thrumming noise.

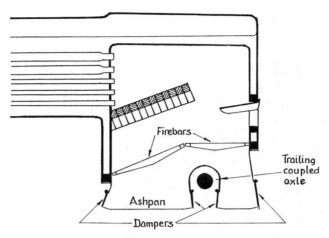

Fig. 2.3 Arrangement of ashpan and dampers on locomotive with trailing coupled axle.

Sometimes they can be spotted because the fire burns even hotter around a hole, and a fireman can improve his vision by deflecting cool air on to the suspect place by holding his shovel at the correct angle in the firedoor opening.

The fireman can control the amount of primary air entering the bottom of the firebox by means of dampers, of which there are usually two, one at the front of the ashpan and the other at the rear. With locomotives having a rear coupled axle which passes through the ashpan, as shown in Fig. 2.3, it is possible to provide an additional pair of dampers, but this complicates the operating mechanisms, which, because they operate in a particularly harsh environment, are, in any case, very stiff to move. The normal arrangement is to open the front damper(s) when running smokebox-first, and the rear one(s) when travelling backwards.

George Stephenson got over the problem of accommodating the rear axle in the ashpan with his 'Long-Boiler' locomotive designs. These had their rear pair of driving axles as close together as possible, with the firebox located behind them both, but this made it difficult to obtain a satisfactory weight distribution, and the cab was inclined to bounce rather too much.

The size of the ashpan itself can also be important, especially for locomotives which are rostered to make long through runs. If they are too small, the level of the ash can build up to the point where it significantly reduces the airflow to the grate, and so decreases the rate at which coal can be burnt. Examination of past performances showed that some 4-6-0s were particularly prone to such problems. The space in the ashpan occupied by the housing for the rear coupled-axle on locomotives of this wheel-arrangement is clearly shown in Fig. 2.3.

The larger a locomotive's grate, the more work is required from the fireman, but there are ways in which the designer can ease the effort needed. If the grate is sloped downwards towards the front, the vibration at normal speeds shakes the coal gently forward, and so reduces the proportion of shovelfuls that needed to be thrown several feet towards the front of the incandescent firebed. Such an arrangement is fairly easy to arrange with a locomotive having small rear wheels, when the line of the rearmost axle passes through the ashpan at a fairly low level. If the rear axle carries large-diameter driving wheels, it is not possible to arrange for the grate to slope uniformly, as shown in Fig. 2.3, which depicts a typical layout for a British mixed-traffic 4-6-0.

Professor W. A. Tuplin of Sheffield University carried out many studies on the maximum power outputs of British steam locomotives. In 1956 he showed there was a definite relationship between the maximum power output and the grate area. Higher outputs were possible over short periods, but the figures fell off as the duration of the high-power demand increased. For periods of 5 mins, a maximum of 49 equivalent drawbar horsepower (EDHP) per square foot of grate area could be sustained, but the output dropped to 38 and 36 for periods of 30 and 60 mins, respectively. In SI units these figures become 3.4, 2.6 and 2.5 kW/m², respectively.

It must be emphasized that not every locomotive design can achieve this, as the boiler and motion might well prevent such high outputs. Dr Tuplin commented pithily on the demands such efforts made on the fireman: 'Careful placing of eight shovelfuls of coal per minute in the face of about 100 radiant horsepower from white flame at 2500 °F (1400 °C) just inside the firehole tends to put off any fireman who is not really enthusiastic about record-breaking'. (See Table 2.2.) Some locomotive engineers, furthermore, managed to provide built-in obstacles to output, by making the shovelling-plate on the front of the tender lower than the bottom of the firehole-door. As a result every shovelful of coal had to be lifted through that height—a not-inconsiderable additional task with the quantities involved.

One of the highest power outputs quoted by Professor Tuplin took place on a notable World War II run from Darlington to York with the

Table 2.2 Approximate fire temperatures

Colour of fire	Approx temperature (°C)
Red (just showing)	550
Red (dull)	700
Red (bright)	975
Orange (deep)	1100
Orange (bright)	1200
Yellow	1325
White	1425
White (intense)	1550

Average temperature of fires

Fuel	Approx. temperature (°C)
Coal (hand-fired)	1025
Liquid	1325
Coal (mechanically fired)	1450

streamlined Gresley A4 Pacific *Capercaillie*, when its sustained power output between Otterington and Poppleton (now Skelton) Junction was nearly a third higher than the normal 'best' figure for a 20-min run. In BR days a test run with a dynamometer car showed that a rebuilt 'Merchant Navy' using Bedwas coal was capable of producing 2000 indicated horsepower at 90 mph, which required a continuous firing-rate of 1.7 tons of coal per hour. Similar, if not higher, rates were also achieved with the LMS 'Princess Coronations' and the solitary BR Class 8 Pacific, No. 71000.

Probably the finest example of sustained firing ever recorded was that carried out by *Chauffeur* Marty of the Paris–Orlèans Railway in the early 1930s, when he was involved with the tests of Chapleon's 4-8-0 No.4701. On one particular run he put no less than four tons of coal into its firebox *in one hour*. Nearly 40 years later, in conversation with one of the authors, M. Chapelon was still talking about the feat. But *Chauffeur* Marty came from a hard school, having formerly been a stoker on a French naval torpedo-boat, when his life could have depended on it being able to get away quickly from hostile warships!

In some countries mechanical firing equipment has been fitted to many large coal-burning locomotives. This normally takes the form of a scroll feeder which brings the coal, which has a fairly small size range, from the bottom of the tender to the front of the cab. Another, shorter, scroll then lifts the coal to the level of the firehole door, where it is delivered on to a firing-plate. Several controllable steam jets are provided, which enables the fireman to direct streams of coal to whichever parts of the firebox need it. The overall coal supply is controlled by varying the rate of rotation of the scroll conveyor, which is powered by its own small steam engine. There were a few trials of such equipment in this country, but coal consumption was usually higher for the same work output, and the equipment got in the way of hand-firing. In the United States, however, every locomotive with a grate bigger than a certain size was required, by regulation, to be fitted with mechanical firing. Quite apart from considering the well-being of the firemen, such a rule was also justified because it enabled full use to be made of the locomotive's potential.

Firing a steam locomotive with a liquid fuel requires a very different layout inside the firebox, because it is virtually impossible to contain a liquid on a firebed like a solid and still allow air to pass through it. The nearest to this was the arrangement adopted by James Holden of the Great Eastern Railway at the end of the nineteenth century. His system was based on that developed by Thomas Urquhart to enable Russian locomotives to use petroleum refuse. Holden's intention was slightly different, and started as a means of solving the environmental problem of disposing of liquid tar produced as waste from the manufacture of gas in the railway's works at Stratford. The fireboxes of the adapted locomotives were fitted with sprays to feed the fuel, using a jet of steam, over a thin coal fire, which had been started in the usual way. Once steam was raised, the coal was levelled out and covered with a layer of broken firebrick. This provided a support for the burning liquid, yet still permitted the primary air to enter the firebox in the usual way. The locomotives could also use fuel oil if it was available, and the crew were able to regulate the boiler pressure accurately by controlling the fuel flow from the two longitudinal storage tanks on top of the tender. To mark the success of the work, one of Holden's 2-4-0s was named *Petrolea.*

With the development of oil-firing technology, later oil-fired locomotives had straightforward burners, using steam for atomizing. Some oil-fired locomotives have used fuels that needed to be heated to reduce their viscosity sufficiently for them to flow to the burner. In the late 1940s, the GWR converted a number of its locomotives to burn oil at a time when the country's coal supplies were short. They used heavy fuel-oil, and heating coils were needed in the tender tanks, as well as a steam jacket on the supply pipe where it passed under the footplate. The burner was mounted at foundation-ring level at the front of the firebox, facing the rear of the locomotive. The oil flowed over a weir on to a ribbon of steam which atomized it for burning, the flame being projected slightly upwards into the firebox. The firehole door was normally sealed, although it could be opened if required when the burner was turned off. The system was later adopted in other areas of BR, but never extensively used because of foreign-exchange problems with oil fuel.

An external steam supply is needed for lighting up, and is obtained either from another locomotive or from the shed installation. Originally such a system would have needed an external steam supply to get the boiler up to pressure, but the Army's Royal Engineers used air from a commercial compressor in the depot to light up its oil-fired locomotives at the beginning of their shift. The preserved Ffestiniog Railway today uses the same system. Originally their conversions were made so it could use waste oil collected by society members, and so save purchasing coal, but the change also eliminated any dangers of lineside fires from sparks. When 'Health & Safety' rules restricted the use of waste oil in this way, it was still worthwhile switching to gas oil, which additionally has the advantage of a uniform composition. It is also a mobile liquid, which, like the Great Eastern's fuel of a century earlier, will easily flow from the tender to the burners without having to be preheated.

Oil burns very differently from coal or coke, as a consequence of its chemical composition, and, because of the concentrated flame coming from burners, it is necessary to protect parts of the firebox from direct impingement by using suitable refractory linings or walls. Oil has a calorific value getting on for 50 per cent higher than a good coal, so less is needed to generate the same amount of heat. Whereas coal mainly burns to carbon dioxide, a lot of water vapour is produced from oil, and about a third more oxygen is needed to ensure complete combustion. These factors, as well as the different flame characteristics, all have to be taken into account when converting or designing a locomotive to burn oil fuel.

Earlier reference was made to the solid impurities in coal, most of which are left behind in the firebox or ashpan. The big exception to this is sulphur, which normally occurs as small quantities of metallic sulphide ores. With the heat and plenty of oxygen, this is converted to sulphur dioxide (SO_2), which can easily be recognized by its sharp and irritating smell. In higher concentrations it quickly becomes choking, and that from the ash thrown out from one of the 'Britannias' doing a quick turn-round at Liverpool Street station in the 1950s could be extremely unpleasant for nearby passengers. When absorbed in water, sulphur dioxide forms sulphurous acid (H_2SO_3), which is corrosive. Given the right circumstances, it can be oxidized further to sulphuric acid (H_2SO_4), which can severely attack any steel parts of a locomotive with which it comes into contact. Any prolonged formation of dew on the internal parts of a locomotive's boiler has always be avoided, and since oil fuels also contain sulphur, they can be even more troublesome because of the additional water, compared with that from coal, produced during combustion.

The simplicity of handling oil fuel enabled the Southern Pacific Railroad in the western United States to build a remarkable family of steam locomotives which were used for almost 50 years on its line from Sacramento to Truckee. Rising almost 7000 ft (2130 m) in 100 miles (160 km), this stretch presented a huge obstacle for freight trains taking Californian produce to markets in the eastern United States. Progressively larger locomotives were introduced, but problems arose with the numerous tunnels, where the confined exhaust made working conditions impossible for the footplate crews. Experimentally operating one of the locomotives tender-first demonstrated that this would protect the crew from most of the fumes, and the idea was worked out for what was to become the railroad's famous 'Cab-in-front' design. The tender was hitched to the front buffer-beam (now at the rear), and the rear of the cab, now leading, was boxed in, with windows to give the crew an excellent view. Engineer and fireman sat in seats at either side, with all the controls to hand, while the 400 °C exhaust was blasted out yards behind them.

Oil fuel from the tender was easily fed through a pipe to the controls in the cab, and then to the firebox just behind it. Because of the steep gradients it was necessary to pressurize the fuel tank slightly with air from the compressor, to force the oil uphill to the front during the climbs. In the type's final form, one of the 4-8+8-2 Articulated Consolidations weighed over 290 tons, and had a tractive effort of 124 300 lb.f (5530 kN). The final survivor of the AC-12sf class today forms an appropriate centre-piece in the California State Railroad Museum at Sacramento.

Effects of high temperature

The interior of the firebox is by far the hottest part of a steam locomotive. Important steps have to be taken to ensure that its materials of construction can withstand the temperatures involved, and to check that they do not waste away too quickly. The problems facing the locomotive designer are compounded by the fact that the shape of a firebox required for adequate combustion is not ideally suited to cope with the stresses caused by the pressure in the boiler.

The ideal shape for a pressure vessel is a sphere, since the stresses in all directions act circumferentially, and they are thus contained within the shell, which therefore has no need for any internal staying. From the locomotive designer's point of view, a boiler of this shape is not easy to accommodate, and the next best arrangement is to use a cylinder with domed ends. Circumferentially these are every bit as satisfactory as a sphere, but, depending on the exact shape of the ends, some form of internal staying might be needed to withstand the pressure. In later practice the rear and front tubeplates, which form the ends of cylindrical part of a steam locomotive's pressure vessel, are flat, and just a few longitudinal stays are needed to support them, in addition to the strengthening effect of the flue tubes.

The only latter day type of boiler with a cylindrical firebox was the so called marine type, although many early locomotive ones took this form as can still be seen on preserved locomotives such as *Locomotion* and *Agenoria*. With the 'marine' type, the firebox consists of a large-diameter tube which is placed in the lower half of a cylindrical boiler. There is an internal horizontal grate just below its mid-point, and the lower part of the firebox has to act as the ashpan. Only a relatively small number of locomotives was built with this type of boiler, and all of them were of types not required to produce high power outputs.

When larger fireboxes were needed, it was not possible for them to be cylindrical, and interior and exterior surfaces of complex shape appeared, and some sort of internal support was therefore required. Locomotive fireboxes are always liberally supplied with stays connecting the internal and external plates, while there is sometimes need for others which passed laterally right across the water-space. The gap between the inner and outer plates is closed at the bottom, below the level of the grate, by the solid 'foundation ring', to which both plates are riveted and/or bolted.

In Britain it became customary to make the inner firebox out of copper, as that metal's superior ductility gives it an advantage over steel. This enables it to deform slightly to relieve any high stresses that arise when rapid changes of temperature occur. A higher tensile strength is obtained using copper which has been alloyed with a small quantity of arsenic. The production of this is, however, now frowned on for environmental reasons.

Many different firebox shapes have evolved, but in this country they can conveniently be divided into two main types—round-topped and Belpaire. With the former, the top wrapper-plate externally continues the shape of the boiler itself. Where the side plates are extended downwards towards the foundation ring, they became more or less flat, and are shaped to fit snugly between the main frame-plates.

Up to the turn of the century, most British locomotives had fireboxes of this type, but in 1902 Ivatt fitted one with a wide bottom above the trailing wheels of one of his C1 Atlantics on the Great Northern Railway. This was possible because these wheels were of small diameter, and the same arrangement would not have been possible had that axle carried driving wheels. This move increased the grate area from 24.5 to 31 ft^2 (2.28 to 2.88 m^2). After being fitted with high-temperature superheating, these 'Large Atlantics' worked many top-link expresses on the LNER main lines well into the 1930s, including the 'Yorkshire Pullman'. Most British Pacifics also benefited from wide fireboxes, as did Gresley's V2 2-6-2s, which became known as one of the classes of 'locomotives that won the war'. His smaller and lighter 2-6-2 design (the V4s) also had wide fireboxes, and the second of them was fitted with a thermic syphon, as discussed later in this chapter.

The Belpaire firebox, named after its inventor, the 1850 chief mechanical engineer of the Belgian State Railway, has a flat-topped wrapper-plate, with raised front corners which give it a characteristic appearance. Many locomotives with this type of firebox collect their steam from these corners, rather than from a dome. With both types of firebox, the lower part of the inner box is similar in shape to the outer sheets, but the crown-sheet is usually flat, and well below the outer firebox to allow plenty of space for the steam to collect. To give more space for the steam there is usually a larger gap between the inner and outer firebox top-sheets compared with those on the sides.

Fireboxes are provided with numerous straight stays, pitched at about 4-in (10 cm) centres, linking the inner and outer plates, which provide the strength to prevent them distorting under pressure. In may cases, particularly with round-topped fireboxes, complicated girder-stays are needed to support a flat crown-plate from the cylindrical top of the wrapper. The straight stays are threaded at each end, and the threads for the outer sheets are slightly larger in diameter than those at the other end. This enables the stay to be inserted from the outside, and both threads tightened together. A nut is screwed on to the end of each stay protruding into the hotter parts of the firebox, to protect it from the heat, or, alternatively, the end is riveted over. In the course of service, the threads become worn, and many railways had systems for recutting them in standard-sized increments to extend the life of the box as long as possible. Alternatively, the holes in the plates can be drilled larger and screwed bushes inserted.

The inner and outer fireboxes can move relative to each other as steam is raised and temperatures rise. In certain parts of the box this differential expansion puts a lot of lateral stress on the stays, giving them a tendency to break. To overcome this, flexible ones are used in the more vulnerable areas. Some are quite simple in design, merely having part of their length turned down to a smaller diameter, enabling them to flex more easily. In the very large fireboxes on many North American locomotives, a totally different type has had to be used because of the greater relative movement. They are not screwed directly into the outer plate, but had a spherical end which rested in an external cup which was threaded so it could be screwed into the plate. To make the assembly steam-tight, a cap was screwed on to the outside of the cup. Stays can be made of copper or steel, the former being more flexible but subject to fatigue, while the latter are stronger. An alternative material sometimes used is a copper/nickel alloy called 'monel metal'.

It can be difficult job to check if any stays have fractured, as there is no way of looking at all those located in the narrower water-spaces. However, with experience, a boilersmith can usually tell whether a stay is intact or not by hitting its end with a hammer inside the firebox, during one of the locomotive's routine inspections. This technique may not locate a partly-fractured stay, and, to compensate for the possibility of any breaks being undetected or occurring before the next boiler inspection, British practice has been to put them at a closer pitch than strictly necessary if they could be guaranteed to remain intact. In some countries a different system was adopted, and each stay had a narrow hole bored through most of its length. Since the exterior of the firebox was not covered with cladding, if a stay developed a deep crack, a tell-tail wisp of steam from the end of the hole immediately indicated what had happened. It was thus possible to use less stays, and still maintain the same safety factor. The first cost, as well as maintenance, would be reduced by installing fewer stays, although thermal losses are somewhat higher from the unlagged firebox which was sometimes a feature of this arrangement, and, on raised British platforms, the radiant heat from them would have been unpleasant. On some American locomotives the stays were drilled through their whole length, and it was possible to see the glow of the fire through the hole! Danish practice was to bore the stays from the outside as far as the point where they entered the inner firebox, and holes were provided in the cladding to permit the escape of steam from a cracked stay to be seen.

Heat reaches the water surrounding the firebox in two ways. In the first instance, the mass of burning coal lying on the grate radiates heat energy, which behaves in much the same way as the radiant light from the same source. It travels in straight lines, and impinges on the firebox back- and side-plates, as well as the rear portion of the crown-plate, heating all of these strongly. It also shines on the brick arch, which also becomes very hot, and itself radiates heat back into the firebed, helping to promote even more vigorous combustion.

In the second instance, the primary air becomes hot as it passes through the firebed, and both it and the secondary air are heated still more as the volatile gases they carry with them also burn. This hot mixture begins to give up its heat energy to all surfaces of the firebox by conduction, including those which are not directly exposed to direct radiant energy from the firebed. The residual heat in these gases as they leave the firebox is dealt with in other ways, as described later.

It will be apparent that the fiercest heat impact is on the lower sides and rear of the firebox, and it is around these parts that the greatest transfer of heat to the water takes place. Traditionally the inner firebox in this country is constructed of copper. This has a higher thermal conductivity than steel, and it is corroded less by water. On the down side, copper melts and softens at lower temperatures than steel, its tensile strength is less, and the technique of welding rather than riveting plates together was developed rather later with copper than with steel. As a pure metal, copper melts at 1083 °C, compared with 1535 °C for iron. While alloying will change these figures somewhat, they indicate the significantly lower temperature for copper. As the temperature in parts of a firebox can reach 1400 °C, it is extremely important for the copper plates to be kept adequately 'cooled' by the water behind them, which can only be at a maximum of 213 °C, even for a boiler operating at 280 lb/in² (19.3 bar). Even in ideal circumstances it is only the fact that the hottest part of the fire is not actually against the copper plates that prevents the surface from melting.

In practice it is necessary to take into account many other factors. The violent boiling of the water on the outside of the plate leads to the production of bubbles, which can become superheated and thus at a higher temperature than the water before they move off into the body of the liquid and collapse. Even more significant is the effect of an insulating deposit of scale, with its markedly lower heat-transfer coefficient, which forms on the water-side of the plates. Figure 2.4 shows that, while there is still a linear temperature gradient through the copper plate, the much steeper one through the scale means that more of the copper is at a higher temperature. The LMS, when it was considering the construction of a super-Pacific in the late 1930s, did a lot of work to

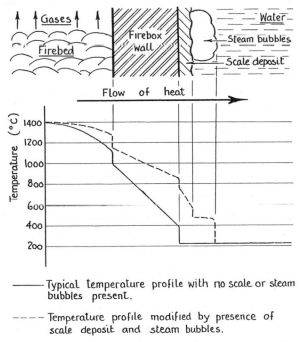

———— Typical temperature profile with no scale or steam bubbles present.

– – – – Temperature profile modified by presence of scale deposit and steam bubbles.

Fig. 2.4 Heat-transfer from fire and combustion gases to water surrounding the firebox.

examine this matter. It was concluded that the heat flux being handled by the copper plates was getting high, but had not yet reached a dangerous level, as long as the recommended boiler washing frequency was maintained to limit the maximum thickness of scale that might accumulate.

Scale deposits build up on all surfaces where water actually boils, which includes the water-side of the inner firebox and in the water-spaces around it. It is necessary to be able to remove these solids, either by washing them out or using descaling rods. Access is needed to do this, so wash-out plugs and mud-holes are provided to enable all vulnerable places to be reached. The plugs usually have tapered threads to ensure proper sealing, and a square head to enable sufficient torque to be applied to drive them home. Mud-doors are oval, and fit inside oval openings, where they are held in place by the steam pressure. They are inserted narrow-ways-on, and then rotated and pulled against the inner surround of the hole with a sealing gasket in place. A clamp is bolted on to the mud-door, and bridges the outer surround.

Water does not always circulate freely in the space around the firebox. With a deep one, when a locomotive is being lit up, it is possible for the foundation ring to be cold enough to touch, even when the boiler has started to make steam. One of the ways of reducing the stagnant space above the foundation ring, and improving the water circulation in the top of a firebox is to use 'thermic syphons'. These were invented by Nicholson, an Englishman, but were first fitted extensively to locomotives in North America during the 1930s, In this country they were introduced in 1941 by Gresley on the second of his V4 2-6-2s, which was provided with a single syphon, and at about the same time by Bulleid with his 'Merchant Navy' Pacifics, all of which were provided with a pair of them.

In essence a thermic syphon is a triangular funnel, the top of which is attached to the crown-plate. For most of its length it consists of two parallel longitudinal plates about 3 in. apart, and supported by internal stays. At its bottom end, the syphon curves to become a circular pipe, which is welded to the lower front wall of the firebox. An upward flow of water is induced inside by convection, rising at a rate of about 4 ft/sec ($1\frac{1}{4}$ m/sec), and this ensures a rapid circulation of water around the inner firebox, as well as providing more heating surface. The fairly large discharge area at the top prevents the water being shot out like a fountain, which might cause spray to be carried over with the steam.

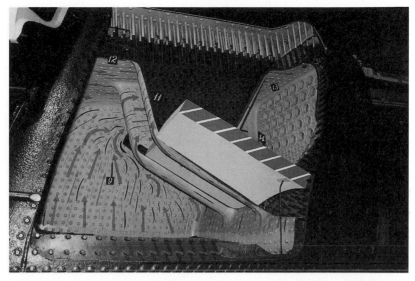

Plate 2.4 The upper part of the firebox of the sectioned 'Merchant Navy' locomotive in the National Railway Museum, showing the rear tubeplate on the right, with the small-diameter smoke tubes and the larger flues for the superheater elements. The nearer of the two Nicholson 'thermic siphons' (11) has also been sectioned to show the internal stays, as has the area above the crown of the inner firebox, where the change in colour on the stays indicates the working water-level. On these locomotives the brick-arch (14) was supported by the siphons as well as the sides of the firebox.

Thermic syphons are completely different from the 'arch tubes' used in the nineteenth century, which were mounted transversely across the firebox, and had the primary function of aiding the support for the brick arch.

As well as having to cope with differential expansion between parts of the firebox, the whole boiler expands as it heats up, and provision has to be made to deal with this. As the main steam pipes feeding the cylinders are at the front end, this is where the boiler is fixed rigidly to the frames and cylinders. The expansion thus occurs at the firebox end, and a support has to be provided to permit it to move backwards and forwards while taking its weight. This can take the form of either slides, or a transverse vertical support-plate which can flex in the longitudinal direction.

To help protect the firebox from overheating and collapse if the water level falls below the level of the crown-plate, fusible plugs are provided in the latter. These have an alloy core which melts at a somewhat lower temperature than that at which the copper would soften. In the absence of water to keep them below the alloy's melting point, the core runs out, allowing a jet of steam to enter the inner firebox. This is not sufficient to put the fire out, but is intended to alert the crew to the state of affairs. Unfortunately the warning can be missed, and, in the case of the French boiler explosion referred to in Chapter 1, neither of the crew took any action, although the plug must have been blowing for nearly ten minutes. The footplate of a steam locomotive at the head of an express train is a noisy place, and it could be difficult to detect the blow from a fusible plug inside the firebox if the firedoor is closed. There were also cases of the partial collapse of the crown-plates of LMS Pacifics, when the crew failed to note that the fusible plug was blowing. No. 6224 *Princess Alexandra* was involved twice, in 1940 and 1948.

In the latter days of steam in North America, the railways were suffering a lot from boiler explosions, and a separate low-water alarm was installed on many locomotives. It had a tube which dipped into the water as far as the lowest permitted level, and exterior cooling caused it to become filled with condensate. If the water level dropped, and the end came out into the steam space, the condensate flowed out, allowing steam to take its place. The resultant rise in temperature caused differential expansion between two parts of the alarm, which made a whistle sound in the cab. Even with this equipment at least one explosion took place after the alarm had been heard from the lineside some distance beforehand, and the driver was seen to be taking no action. It is possible that the equipment gave too many false alarms, and this caused the driver to ignore it, a perennial problem with any warning device.

Ash and clinker

Most solid fuels contain some non-combustible material, and most of this is left behind when it is burnt. Ideally these impurities will have a small particle size, and so fall between the firebars to be caught in the ashpan. In the UK these gaps are usually $\frac{3}{8} - \frac{5}{8}$ in (10–16 mm) wide, but coal often contains some lumps of incombustible material, or forms clinker which is not small enough to be got rid of in this way. Hopefully the journey can be completed without having to get this rubbish out of the firebox, but it, as well as any unburnt fuel remaining, has to be removed when the crew 'dispose' the locomotive at the end of the day. Long-handled shovels are carried for this purpose, but the job of manoeuvering considerable quantities of hot materials out of the firehole, and then through the door of the cab, is a thankless task for the fireman. To speed up the disposal process, some locomotives are fitted with 'drop grates'. Part of the firebars can be unlatched and swung down, enabling any residues to be simply pushed out into the ashpan.

The ash in some types of coal has a low fusion point, and turns into semi-molten slag at the temperatures found in the firebed. The more mobile forms of this work their way down through the fire, and, when the cooler firebars are reached, they can solidify into clinker. In the worst case the clinker sticks to them—a process known as 'going for the bars'. This can get bad enough to cut down the amount of air for the fire, and steaming then suffers. While supplies of high-quality steam coal were readily available up to World War II, the railways could not always get what they wanted from then onwards, and it became necessary to modify the locomotives to deal with the residue from the less suitable types.

The outcome was the fitting of rocking grates. (See Fig. 2.5.) These are made in two halves, longitudinally, each with its own rocking gear. The firebars are fixed in sections to pivoting rockers, which can be worked from the cab. Sticking up from the floor either side of the firehole door are two stubs, and the fireman has an extension lever to place on top of them. Moving this backwards and forwards causes the components of the half-grate to shake backwards and forwards through about 10 degrees, which breaks up any clinker and gets rid of much of it with the ashes. A forked catch has to be swung up to enable the lever to be moved, and a second one, with a wider gap, can be lifted in the depot when the locomotive is being 'disposed'. This permits the sections to be

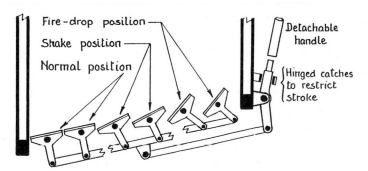

Fig. 2.5 Rocking grate.

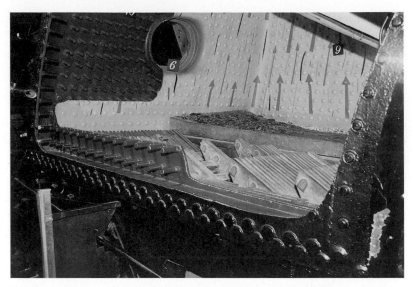

Plate 2.5 The lower part of the firebox interior of the sectioned 'Merchant Navy' locomotive in the National Railway Museum, showing the rocking-grate in the foreground, and a simulated firebed on the far side. The arrows on the walls indicate the directions in which the flames and hot gases move. The firehole is indicated by the figure (6). The numerous stays between the inner and outer fireboxes are shown by the sectioning on the left.

moved through 45 degrees, dumping everything left on the grate straight into the ashpan. Clearly, the fireman must take care which catches are released, otherwise he could be in the embarrassing position of dumping his entire fire 'on the road'! Such equipment materially speeds up the job of 'putting the locomotive to bed' at the end of the day, as well as enabling its performance to maintained in traffic if it has received some poor coal.

Finally the ashpan has to be raked out into the depot's ashpits. This, again, is a dirty, hot and arduous job, but some modern locomotives have the ashpan in the shape of a hopper with bottom-doors which can be opened to allow the accumulation of ash to fall clear.

During the burning process, small particles of coal can be lifted off the firebed by the draught, and carried through the boiler-tubes in the flow of hot gases. A lot of these particles will burn in the process, turning into small bits of char. Ideally these will be trapped in the smokebox, the function of which will be dealt with in more detail later

In the days of steam traction on main lines, it was necessary to reduce the risk of lineside fires during the summer, and the permanent-way gangs regularly cut the vegetation on railway property, then getting rid of it by controlled burning. With mechanized track maintenance there is no pool of manpower to do this, and the operation of preserved steam locomotives on Railtrack's lines was at one time banned during the summer months, just when most people would wish to join such excursions. During the writing of this book success was achieved to eliminate the problem by fitting wire-mesh screens to the locomotives which prevent the emission of sparks, not only from the chimney, but also from the ashpan. Lineside fires can also arise from sparks produced by an electric train's brake-blocks. Towards the end of the long descent in Switzerland from the Lötschberg Tunnel, towards Brig, there is a water-main alongside the track, with taps at intervals, each with a plastics bucket to enable the crew to douse any fire that might be started.

CHAPTER 3

Raising steam

Heat transfer

The boiler, usually constructed integrally with the firebox, is the largest single component of a steam locomotive, and dominates its appearance. However, it contains few moving parts, and from an engineering point of view is a relatively simple unit. It nevertheless requires conscientious servicing and maintenance, and a good grasp of its technology is vital for anyone wanting to understand all the workings of the steam locomotive. Diagrams showing longitudinal- and cross-sections of small and large locomotive boilers appear in Figs 3.1 and 3.2.

When the hot gases leave the firebox, they still contain a lot of the heat generated by burning the fuel. As much as possible of this needs to be recovered, and this is the main function of the boiler, which is primarily a heat exchanger, but also serves as a water and heat reservoir. After various earlier, but less successful, boiler designs, when the Stephensons built *Rocket* for the Rainhill Trials, they put a bundle of small-bore tubes inside a cylindrical pressure vessel. This not only set a pattern for most steam locomotive boilers, but also provided the prototype for many of the gas/gas, gas/liquid and liquid/liquid heat exchangers used today in power stations and processing industries.

The boiler begins at the front of the firebox, the front plate of which is pierced with a pattern of holes to take the smoke-tubes. At the other end of the boiler, the shell of which is cylindrical or provided with a slight conical taper, there is another corresponding tubeplate, and a bundle of tubes about 2 in (50 mm) in diameter is fitted between them. As the hot gases flow through the tubes, they pass much of their remaining heat through the metal into the water surrounding them. In more recent British practice, the surface area of tubes provided for heat transfer is approximately ten times the area of the internal firebox walls, the ratio reflecting the much smaller temperature difference between the gases

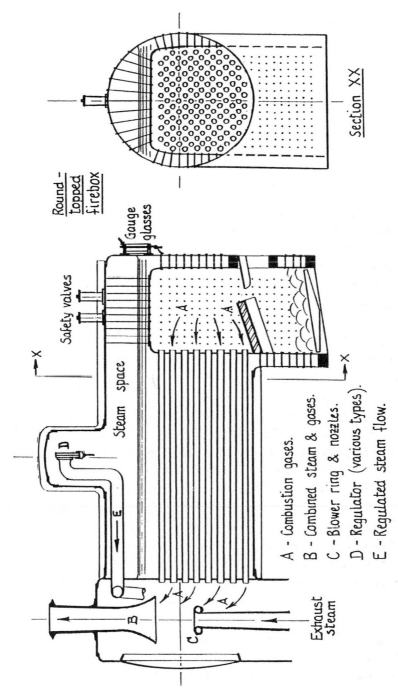

Round-topped firebox

Section XX

A - Combustion gases.
B - Combined steam & gases.
C - Blower ring & nozzles.
D - Regulator (various types).
E - Regulated steam flow.

Fig. 3.1 Longitudinal cross-section of a small parallel boiler without superheater.

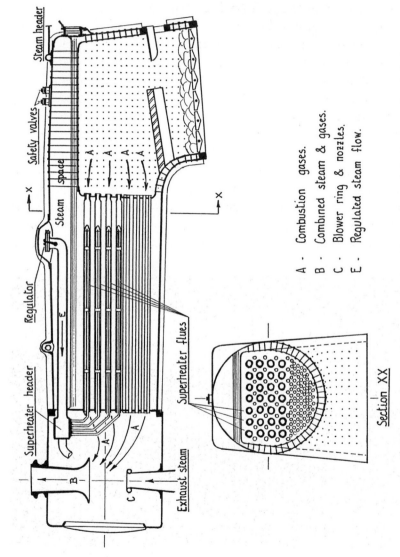

Steam header

Safety valves

X

Steam space

Regulator

Steam

Superheater header

Superheater flues

Exhaust steam

A — Combustion gases.
B — Combined steam & gases.
C — Blower ring & nozzles.
E — Regulated steam flow.

Section XX

Fig. 3.2 Longitudinal cross-section of a large taper boiler with superheater, Belpaire-top, and wide firebox.

and the water as the former become progressively cooled. All boilers have these so-called 'small tubes', but, if the locomotive is superheated, there is also a lesser number of large tubes or 'flues'. These are usually about 5 in (250 mm) in diameter, and carry inside them the superheater elements, which will be described later. The ratio of the number of small to large tubes is determined by the amount of superheat required. The large tubes also contribute to the heating surface for the water, and the ratio of their heat-transfer area typically varies from 50 to 200 per cent of that of the small tubes. (The surface area of the superheater elements themselves depends on other factors, and will also be discussed later.)

Each railway company or locomotive manufacturer had its own views about the layout of the different-sized tubes in the tubeplates. One of the factors affecting this is the need for inspectors to be able to see inside the boiler to carry out the periodic examinations which necessitate a visual check being made of the whole boiler shell. It is relatively easy to remove a small tube, and in any case they need renewing fairly frequently, but replacing the superheater flues is much more expensive and time-consuming. Because of their size and greater thickness they have to be

Plate 3.1 The boiler of the sectioned 'Merchant Navy' Pacific at the National Railway Museum, showing the smoke-tubes and larger superheater flues (22), with the superheater elements (29) inside them. The regulator (26) is mounted in the dome (25), and the steam to the superheater header passes through the large-diameter main steam pipe (27). The working water-level is indicated by the change in paint colour at the top of the boiler.

screwed into the firebox tubeplate, rather than just being expanded with a suitable roller tool.

In some locomotives the tubeplate at the firebox end may be brought forward within the boiler drum by a foot or two (300–600 mm), to provide a 'combustion chamber', which gives more space and time for the volatile material driven off from the fuel to complete its burning process. If this is not complete, some of the potential heat in the fuel will not be released for transfer into the water.

Because of the high surface area of the small tubes, as the gases pass forward along them, their temperature quickly drops below that at which combustion can continue, and much of any unburnt material which may be present is deposited as soot. The quenching effect of small-diameter tubes was used by George Stephenson in his famous 1815 safety-lamp which dramatically reduced the number of methane explosions in northern coal mines. It is easy to see how fuel easily turns to soot using a candle and a test-tube full of cold water. If the latter is inserted *into* the flame it quickly becomes covered with soot, but when the glass surface is kept well above the top of the luminous part it remains bright and the water quickly heats up.

Occasionally industrial steam locomotives, which generally had relatively short tubes, could be seen with flame belching from their chimneys after the regulator was closed. This only occurred when quantities of unburnt gases were being generated in the firebox and were inadequately cooled in their passage through the tubes. These could be reignited by something like a particle of entrained red-hot fly-ash at the exit of the chimney where they came into contact with a new supply of oxygen.

The smokebox is attached to the front of the boiler, and is primarily an empty shell. In earlier practice it consisted of a rectangular steel box with a rounded top to match the shape of the boiler, and an opening door, or doors, at the front, to provide access to the tubes for cleaning. In the centre is the blast-pipe, taking the exhaust steam from the cylinders and discharging it through the chimney, and, at the same time, producing a partial vacuum which draws the combustion air through the firebed at the other end of the boiler. Later the so-called 'drum-head' type of smokebox was adopted, which was circular in cross-section, and looked like an extension of the boiler. As well as being easier to fabricate, this design makes it easier for the fireman, at the end of operations, to remove the ash which is carried through the tubes and deposited in the

Plate 3.2 The smokebox of the sectioned 'Merchant Navy' locomotive in the National Railway Museum, showing the multiple Lemaître blast-pipes (41) and the petticoat leading to the chimney (43). The conical screen between them is to prevent large cinders being blasted out of the chimney. The superheater elements can be seen curving upwards from the flues to join the header (28), from which the three main steam pipes convey the steam to the cylinders.

smokebox. Ash is corrosive, so the less that is left behind the better. In addition to the blast pipe, the smokebox also contains the chimney entry. The proportions of these two components are a vital part of the design of every locomotive, and will be discussed in detail later.

In some locomotives the regulator, or main steam valve, is mounted in the smokebox, rather than under the boiler dome, and those fitted with superheating also have the to be provided with space in the smokebox for the headers or manifolds to which are fitted the tubes which loop in and out of the large flues.

Having outlined the main features of a locomotive boiler, we now need to look as the detailed processes by which the heat in the products of combustion are transferred to the water. The principles have already been discussed in the chapter on the firebox, but the constraints differ from those in the boiler. Because the tubes transmit less heat than the inner firebox plates, less scale is deposited on the water-side of them. On the other hand, as the gas temperatures are lower, and the tubes run horizontally, soot and ash can collect in them. This not only impedes the transfer of heat from the gases to the water, but in extreme cases some tubes can become blocked, and thus completely useless.

While operating a train, care should be taken to avoid the production of dark smoke. Not only is this a visible sign of wasting some of the calories in the fuel, but it indicates that soot is being allowed to build up in the tubes. The regular servicing work on a steam locomotive involves cleaning the interior of the small tubes, and this normally forms part of the fireman's duties when 'disposing of the locomotive' at the end of its duty. Usually this is done through the smokebox door with the aid of a cylindrical brush on the end of a long rod, which is inserted into each of the small tubes in turn, pushing any deposits through into the firebox. The process is not so easy with the large tubes, because of the superheater elements inside them, but there is usually room to get the brush down beside the elements and remove a lot of the deposits. The Great Western Railway adopted a different cleaning practice; all their locomotives had a steam pipe with a stopcock mounted on the front ring of the smokebox. A steam lance, with a flexible connection, was screwed on to this by the fireman and the cock opened, enabling him to dislodge any soot and ash with a jet of steam.

Sometimes special equipment is fitted to enable the tubes to be cleaned while the locomotive is in steam and even working. Oil-fired locomotives are more likely to suffer from soot deposits, and a favourite trick is to insert a small amount of sand through the firehole door when the locomotive is working hard. The colour of the exhaust changes instantly in a spectacular fashion, and care has to be taken to choose the right places for the operation to avoid complaints from those living beside the line! The quantity of sand used also varies considerably, depending on the scale of the problem. The 0-4-0ST *Prince* on the Ffestiniog Railway used to receive its dose of sand from a baked-bean tin, but a more robust technique was used in West Germany at the end of the steam era. Some of their last regular steam workings were by oil-fired Class '043' 2-10-0s on 1760-tonne ore trains running northwards from Rheine. The driver would wind the reverser into full gear while the fireman tipped *half a bucket* of sand into the firebox. The resulting black cloud over the flat countryside was still visible from the cab many miles further on, but there were only the grazing Friesian cows to complain! Some North American locomotives were fitted with a sand-gun on the firebox back-plate and this enabled sand to be directed at the chosen parts of the rear tubeplate using a jet of steam as propellant.

However, sand can be somewhat abrasive, and so may damage the firebox tubeplate and tube ends, especially when propelled by a steam jet, so some railways used a steam 'soot-blower' as an alternative. This behaves much as does a sand-gun, but relies on the steam jet itself to dislodge the soot. Out on the road its use was recommended once an hour, with a final sweep just before the end of the journey.

Many boilers have been provided with two large openings, one on the top and the other at the bottom, although in BR practice the latter was not fitted. Where a bottom door was fitted, it was provided for access when inspections were being made, or work done on the interior. Strict precautions have to be taken whenever this is used, as the oxygen level in the boiler space can become too low for survival. Even if air has been present, any exposed steel surfaces in a closed vessel can remove sufficient of the oxygen by rusting to make the atmosphere fatal for anyone entering it without breathing equipment.

Most locomotive boilers have a large hole in the top to take the dome, and many of them have their regulator, or main steam valve, in this fitment, with access being usually obtained by means of a bolted cover. The purpose of the dome is to provide a take-off point for the steam that is as far removed as possible from the boiling surface of the water. This ensures that the quantity of water droplets carried over is reduced to a minimum as they can cause damage if any significant amount builds up in the cylinders or can reduce the efficiency of the superheater.

In the early days of railways, boilers were of relatively small diameter, enabling very tall domes to be provided. As the size of locomotives increased, so did boilers, and the height of the dome had to be reduced to keep within the loading-gauge, bringing the take-off point for steam nearer the level of the water. Railways which use fireboxes of the Belpaire type can choose to transfer the take-off point to the high front corner of the outer box. As an alternative, locomotives can be fitted with an internal arrangement of blades which induce a rapid circular motion to the steam as it leaves the area above the water surface. A series of slots then separates any water droplets flung out of the main steam flow by centrifugal force, and returns them to the boiler, letting the relatively dry steam pass on to the superheater or the cylinders.

The main steam valve used by the driver to control the flow of steam from the boiler to the cylinders is called the regulator, and numerous different designs have been developed. (See Fig. 3.3.) When starting a train from rest, it is necessary for the driver to be able to control

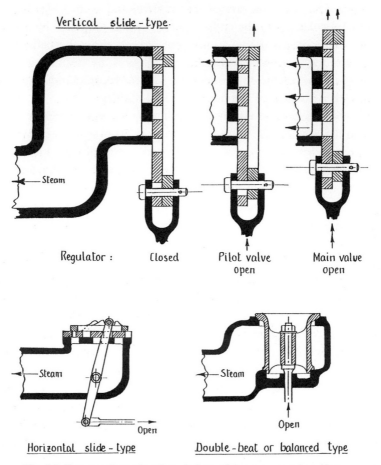

Fig. 3.3 Cross-sections of various designs of dome-mounted regulators.

accurately the delivery of a small amount of steam to the cylinders to avoid the locomotive slipping. To achieve this the regulator should be easy to work and provide a wide range of openings. On the other hand, when the locomotive is running at speed, and full power is needed, the regulator should not restrict the steam flow. When the regulator is first opened, the opening mechanism will be subjected to the full boiler pressure on one side of the valve ports, and a relatively low one on the other, and this will cause a lot of friction which the driver has to overcome. It is not easy to provide lubrication for the moving surfaces, although this was frequently attempted in the days when boiler pressures and steam temperatures were low.

A dome-mounted regulator is normally operated by a rotating rod passing through the firebox back-plate, with the control-lever moving in the plane across the cab. Some engineers alternatively fitted a push–pull rod, which enables the driver to open the regulator by pulling backwards a lever pivotted high-up on the back-plate. In both arrangements a steam-tight gland is needed where the operating rod passes into the boiler, and that inevitably produces an appreciable amount of friction, making it harder for the driver to adjust the opening accurately. A third system uses an external push–pull rod which actuates a crank close to the dome, where the gland has to be provided in the boiler drum.

With the advent of superheating, the regulator was sometimes repositioned in the smokebox, where it is mounted across the upper part of the front tubeplate. This increases the length of the control rod from the cab. In this position the need for an opening in the boiler shell, with its glands, is avoided, but other difficulties sometimes occur due to expansion. If the regulator handle is stiffer to move than the actual regulator, as the boiler warms up and increases in length, the regulator may start to open. To overcome this an intermediate rocking-lever can be mounted midway along the boiler, and any expansion in the two halves will then be counterbalanced.

The ease with which regulators can be operated does not necessarily decrease with the size of the locomotive. Many of the steam locomotives in the United States were far larger than any which ran in Britain, but their regulators, known there as 'throttles', had quite short handles and were extremely sensitive. As part of the celebrations when the California Railroad Museum at Sacramento was opened in 1981, regular performances were given of the 'Song of the Iron Horse'. As well as the singing and dancing by the human performers, various steam locomotives made their own way on and off the set. In the finale, two of the largest present shot forward towards each other, stopping a short distance apart like the Eurostars did in Coquelles at the inauguration of the Channel Tunnel in 1994. On the final Californian performance, one of the authors was on the footplate of the preserved Union Pacific 'Challenger' 4-6-6-4, which, with its tender, turned the scales at just under 300 tons. As the show reached its climax, the 'engineer' was able to adjust the throttle so the locomotive was moving forward at about a foot a minute until the stage-crew whipped aside the screens and we shot forward on to the set.

On another occasion he observed the preserved Norfolk & Western Class J 4-6-4 No. 611 setting back its 15-coach train, weighing some 1000 tons, into the remains of Chattanooga Terminal. It moved so slowly over the last quarter-mile of the complicated layout that passengers could easily alight, with their luggage, while the train was still under way. Both incidents provided a remarkable insight into the controllability that had been developed with North American locomotives.

Withstanding the pressure

The boiler shell has to be strong enough to withstand the steam pressure inside it, and this is why, from the early days of steam locomotion, most of them have been circular in cross-section. In the first half of the nineteenth century large steel plates were not available, and a boiler would be constructed from numerous relatively small, wrought-iron, ones, riveted together. This made it difficult to ensure that the cross-section was a true circle, and, if it was not, the shell flexed slightly when steam was raised or it cooled down, which caused grooving near the joints. If this was not detected, or ignored, the result could be catastrophic, but the resulting explosion took a totally different form from that when the crown of a firebox collapsed. Much or all of the shell was destroyed, but the tube-bundle was often left more-or-less intact, as shown by the illustration of the remains of the Great Western 2-2-2 *Achaeon*, (Plate 3.3) which blew up at Gloucester in 1885. The detailed design of boilers was changed to avoid the problem, making use of the availability of larger steel sheets, better textured steels, and improved methods of rolling the material into cylindrical form. Wide lapping sheets are used to join adjacent boiler plates, and adequate numbers of rivets provided. When it became possible for the rivet-holes to be drilled rather than punched, that alone increased the strength by ten per cent.

The strength of a boiler decreases slowly in service for a number of reasons. Corrosion reduces the thickness of the metal, and this does not take place uniformly. High temperatures can also alter the microscopic-structure of the metal, again weakening it. These processes are relatively slow, and internal regular boiler examinations can be timed to reveal weakening of the structure before it can possibly become dangerous. Much more serious is fatigue cracking, which can develop very rapidly when a component is subjected to cycles of varying stress. While a

Plate 3.3 The result of an 1850s' boiler explosion, after the boiler-shell had become grooved or notched because it was not truly circular in cross-section. The result of such an explosion was very different from one caused by too low a water-level over the crown of the firebox. (*GWR Magazine*)

locomotive boiler is, at most, only lit-up daily, the effects of vibrations from its movements over the track are far greater. Not only are there the thrusts of the pistons, but rail-joints used to be placed every 20 yards ($18\frac{1}{4}$ m) or less along the line. It is not difficult to amass the 1×10^7 or so stress cycles, at which point fatigue-cracking begins to be significant, but this can be avoided by ensuring that the stress-raisers, such as those produced by punching the holes for rivets, are designed-out, or at least evaluated very carefully.

With the development of electric-arc welding processes, and X-ray examination techniques to examine the results, joints between individual plates can be simplified, which reduces the weight/strength ratio of those boilers to which these techniques are applied. Suitable grades of steel are needed as well, and it was only Bulleid, on his Pacifics, who adopted this to any extent in the UK for boiler shells, but it was used extensively overseas. UK practice was also to use arsenical-copper plates for the inner firebox, as this was more resistant to corrosion than steel, but in many other countries steel was the normal material used.

Steel is cheaper than copper, and has a higher tensile-strength/weight ratio, although the latter is ductile and conducts heat better. In contrast to what was done on the boiler shells, copper welding is widely used this country, particularly when making major repairs to fireboxes. These techniques require the use of an inert atmosphere, usually provided by argon.

The taper boiler came into fashion early in the twentieth century, with its diameter decreasing towards the front. Its adoption was made possible by the introduction of improved rolls for shaping the boiler plates. There are several advantages from the use of this shape, which reduces the weight of the boiler and the amount of water required to fill it, as well as occupying less space. The reductions in weight and space occupied take place at the front of the locomotive, and this enables larger and heavier cylinder castings to be used. As less of the heat in the combustion gases remains to be transferred at the front end of the boiler, the rate of steam generation is matched by the volume of water available. In addition, a smaller-diameter front-end to the boiler and smokebox improves the driver's vision.

The tube-plates at both ends of the boiler are flat, and are thus are not ideally shaped to withstand the internal steam pressure. The small boiler tubes (and any large ones, if fitted) help to stiffen the plates, but are not present in the area above the water level, as is shown in the diagrams of the cross-sections of boilers. Longitudinal stays are therefore fitted, either running from front to rear of the boiler, or attached to the cylindrical boiler shell by anchor pads, or 'palms'. The stays are then tensioned by bolts on the outside of the tubeplates.

Structurally boilers are designed so they will provide an economic life in service before being scrapped, and will only require a reasonable amount of overhaul effort during this time. The designers thus have to balance the likely amount of corrosion that may occur against extra thickness (and therefore weight) of the boiler plate. The rate at which corrosion occurs can be faster at higher boiler pressures, with the consequent higher temperatures. Increasing the boiler-pressure will thus have a double effect on the strength needed, both to deal with the increased stresses, and also to ensure that any extra corrosion will not reduce the economic life of the boiler.

The increase in weight with boiler-pressure can be quite marked, as shown in Table 3.1 by the figures for those provided for the Gresley Pacifics, all of which had comparable total heating surfaces.

Table 3.1 Changes in boiler weights with increased boiler pressure

Class	Date	Working pressure		Weight (empty)		Total heating surface	
		lb/in^2	bar	tons	tonnes	ft^2	m^2
A1	1922	180	12.4	23.9	24.3	3455	321
A3	1927	220	15.2	26.6	27.0	3327	309
A4	1935	250	17.3	28.0	28.5	3325	309

It will be seen that there were significant increases in empty weight, although the actual percentage increase was less than the corresponding ratio of pressures, thanks to other design refinements.

There are two fitments on every boiler which are so vitally important for safety reasons that their provision is mandatory by law. These are the safety-valve(s) and the water-level gauges. Although safety-valves were used on the very early steam locomotives, many of the designs then used were not reliable, or their efficient operation could be circumvented by the locomotive crew. Odd though it might seem, many crews wanting to get just that little bit more out of their locomotive considered it a reasonable risk to interfere with the safety-valve, frequently with fatal results.

In its earliest form the safety-valve consisted of a weight on a long lever, which applied a force nearer the fulcrum to keep the valve closed. Not only was it extremely easy to increase the pressure by adding an extra weight—or just leaning on the lever—but irregularities in the track relieved the force on the valve, which emitted a series of puffs of steam, as has often happened with the reproduction locomotives built in the last quarter-century. Although fitted to these new locomotives in the interest of authenticity, safety-valves of this archaic design have to be supplemented by the lock-up type, the setting of which cannot be tampered with by any unauthorized person.

Springs could be used in place of weights on the lever, but these too could be irregularly adjusted. In 1856 Ramsbottom got round this problem with his well-known design of twin safety-valves. These were kept closed by a central spring between them, using a lever across the top to apply the pressure, with a long 'tail' extending into the cab. If any improper weight was applied to this, it increased the loading on one of pair, but relieved the closure force on the other, making it lift at a lower

Every boiler has to be fitted with at least one safety valve to prevent it being over-stressed and bursting. Various different designs were used during the steam era, the most common being shown in these photographs

Plate 3.4 The simplest form of safety-valve consists of a tapered circular disc, held on to a conical seat by a weight mounted on a lever. An example of this arrangement can be seen on the 1934 sectioned reproduction of *Rocket*. When the boiler was almost up to working pressure, irregularities in the track could cause the weight and lever to bounce, making the valve emit puffs of steam.

Plate 3.5 An example of the directly-sprung safety-valve developed by Hackworth at Shildon. One of these can also be seen on the 1934 *Rocket* reproduction. (Plate 3.3)

Plate 3.6 The safety-valves on Midland 'Single' No. 118. Sealed external springs have replaced the weight used on *Rocket*, but levers are still used to apply the necessary force to the valves situated in the top of the dome.

Plate 3.7 An example of Ramsbottom safety-valves, as fitted to the preserved Lancashire & Yorkshire 2-4-2 tank, No. 1008.

Plate 3.8 Although Ramsbottom's design of safety-valve prevented any easy way of 'holding them down' to increase the boiler pressure beyond its safe limit, they were much larger and heavier than the later Ross 'pop' valves, such as this pair fitted to one of the Southern Railway's 'Schools' class 4-4-0s. Unfortunately 'pop' valves can open suddenly without warning, the resulting loud noise sometimes being quite frightening in the confines of a station.

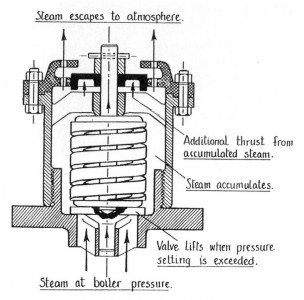

Fig. 3.4 'Pop'-type safety-valve.

pressure. In the early days the crew was encouraged to pull down on the lever from time to time check that the valves were working properly. Although Hackworth had used a pile of leaf-springs in the early part of the nineteenth century, it was the later availability of reliable coil-springs which enabled more compact designs of safety-valve to be produced. In time these became standard, and it was possible to design them in such a way that the tension of the spring could not be altered without breaking a seal or undoing a lock.

The straight-forward type of spring-operated safety-valve has a conical seat, so its discharge orifice rapidly increases as the pressure rises by only a small amount above the setting, keeping the excess boiler pressure within a small range. It must clearly be designed so that it can release the full flow of steam to ensure that the safe working pressure of the boiler is not exceeded. As the pressure falls, the valve similarly closes progressively, but, as there is only a small pressure differential to force it shut at the moment of closure, it sometimes fails to seat tightly, thus wasting steam.

To overcome these potential losses, the 'pop' design of valve was invented by Ross. (See Fig. 3.4.) This is arranged so that, as soon as it lifts, there is a increase in the area of the valve subjected to the steam pressure, and the valve instantaneously opens fully. With latter-day safety-valves of this type, the name is a considerable understatement, as, without warning, the valve can suddenly emit a loud roar from the escaping high-pressure steam, much to the discomfort of those nearby. When the pressure drops, this type of valve closes instantly, which ensures that it seats better, avoiding any continuous loss from a 'feathering' valve. There is a down side to these valves, however, as there is a significant differential between the pressure at which they open and close, so every time one lifts, a lot of steam, water, and heat is lost from the boiler. When one of the LNER V2 2-6-2s was tested on the Swindon plant in 1952 it was found that the safety valves lifted at 225 lbf/in^2 (15.5 bar), but did not reseat until the pressure had dropped to 205 lb/in^2 (14.1 bar), which discharged so much steam that it made conditions in the building hazardous. A calculation done in 1953 showed that, on a typical British Pacific, the opening of one of the pop valves would cause the boiler pressure to drop from 250 to 240 lb/in^2 (17.2 to 16.5 bar). The heat lost was equivalent to the burning of more than 16 lb (7.3 kg) of coal. At one time it was not unknown for firemen to receive a day's suspension if they allowed their safety valves to lift!

It was always desirable to have more than one safety valve as an insurance against failure, but as locomotives became more powerful, and maximum steaming rates increased, it became necessary to install more than one valve just to ensure that the steam can always be discharged more rapidly than it can be generated. There are, for example, many circumstances when the driver has to shut the regulator unexpectedly while the locomotive is working at full power. Any such an event must not be allowed to cause any over-stressing of the boiler by the pressure rising above that for which it was designed. Most modern locomotives thus have two separate safety-valves, but the largest Pacifics can require as many as four. The normal practice is for each of them to be given a slightly different setting, so that as pressure builds up they will open in sequence. In practice this happens anyway as there are bound to be slight differences between their settings. Before a newly-overhauled locomotive is passed to run on any railway, one of the checks carried out by the boiler inspector is to ensure that the safety valves operate at the correct pressure, and that all of them lift when the steaming rate is high.

There will also be similar periodic checks during the currency of its operating certificate.

Steam discharged from a safety-valve is hot and moving at a high velocity, so a locomotive is never deliberately stopped under any close overhead structure, particularly a footbridge in a station. The valves have to be mounted well clear of the maximum water-level normally reached in the boiler to avoid any water entrainment, but this can nevertheless occur in unusual circumstances, such as when the water foams. This is known as priming, and cause of the phenomenon will be discussed later in the chapter. If it happens while a locomotive is blowing off, a shower of dirty water-drops spreads over a large area, to the considerable annoyance of those caught by the resulting unexpected fall-out.

While the number of safety valves is determined by the maximum steaming rate, regulations stipulate that *every* locomotive must have two independent means of determining the water level in the boiler. Most railways provided two 'gauge-glasses' of the types to be described, but the Great Western only used one, supplementing it with a pair of 'try-cocks', as fitted to the earliest locomotives in the first decades of the nineteenth century. These are simple 'on–off' cocks, mounted at different heights on the boiler, one above and the other below the normal operational water-level. Normally the upper one emits steam when it is opened, while the other spouts water, but if both discharge steam the water level is too low. On some of the early locomotives these cocks could not be reached from the footplate, those on the Stephensons' *Rocket* being on the side of the boiler near the front. The reproduction locomotive built in 1979 has a conventional gauge-glass above the firebox, and its pair of try-cocks in the authentic position are mainly used to make pots of tea when it is stationary. This impresses the onlookers, but the quality of the water is such that none of the crew has ever actually drunk the resulting brew!

A conventional gauge-glass consists of a straight glass tube about $\frac{1}{2}$ in (15 mm) in diameter, mounted between a pair of fittings, which incorporate three cocks. (See Fig. 3.5.) The first two enable the gauge-glass to be isolated from the boiler, and the third then enables the water and steam in it to be discharged via a pipe leading down below the footplate. By emptying the glass in this way, and then refilling it, the crew can be sure that none of the pipes is blocked and the gauge is displaying the true water level in the boiler. These cocks are fully opened

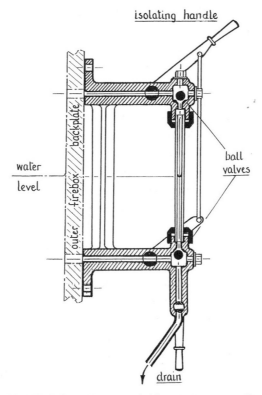

Fig. 3.5 Boiler water-gauge (with protector removed).

or closed by being turned through 90 degrees, and the position of their straight handles immediately indicates whether they are open or not.

The glass tubes can shatter without warning, and two different items of equipment are provided to protect the crew if this should happen. Automatic cut-off valves are provided in the top and bottom arms, taking the form of ball-valves which are pushed shut by the escaping water or steam. Sometimes the upper valve is replaced by a heat-resisting spring which is closed by the escaping steam. Between them these cut-off devices reduce the flow of steam and hot water, and the smaller quantity escaping (together with any pieces of shattered gauge-glass) is kept away from the crew by a 'protector'. This has armoured glass on three sides, with a perforated metal plate nearest the boiler to allow the steam and hot water to escape without enveloping the crew.

Some gauge-glasses are of different design, known as the reflex type. These consist of a flat glass plate, which is mounted in a holder facing the footplate. The internal surface of the glass has prismatic grooves in it. As glass and water have similar refractive indices, where there is water inside them they look dark, but the prisms reflect the light when only steam is present. These glasses are very much stronger and do not break even if accidentally hit with one of the footplate tools, so protectors are not needed. This type of gauge-glass was more extensively used on locomotives in countries other than the UK, but was adopted by Bulleid on his Pacifics. This design enabled them to be illuminated at night by the electric lighting in the cab roof. The normal type of gauge-glass needs illumination alongside it, which is normally provided by an oil-lamp.

The reflex type of gauge-glass also appeared in this country on the American 2-8-0 freight locomotives brought into England in preparation for the 1944 invasion of Europe. They had the North American arrangement of *screw* cocks for the gauge-glasses, each of which needed several turns to open it fully, and so ensure that the gauge read correctly. The failure to do this properly, together with the unusual dark and light indication of the water-level, caused three incidents when the fireboxes partially collapsed after the crew had mistakenly allowed the water level to get too low.

At times it is not particularly easy to read the level in a normal gauge-glass. It is possible to confuse one that is empty with a full one during a quick glance, and the glass can also get sufficiently dirty to obscure the water level partially. The LNER pioneered the use of a plate with diagonal black and white stripes at the back of the protector. Seen through a column of water in the gauge-glass, which acts as a convex lens, the angle of the stripes is reversed, thus providing a clear indication of the water level.

The gauge-glass normally has to be positioned in the cab to enable the crew to see it. Being at one end of the boiler, the indication can alter considerably with changing gradients, which has some important safety implications. For instance, the glass on one of Gresley's A4 Pacifics is $6\frac{1}{2}$ in (165 mm) high. On level track, with water in the bottom of the glass, there is a covering of $4\frac{3}{4}$ in (121 mm) over the back of the inner firebox, which corresponds to only $2\frac{1}{4}$ in (57 mm) over the fusible-plug at the front. However, on a rising gradient of 1 in 57, with the water-level at the same point in the glass, the cover at the front of the firebox decreases to zero. So, when climbing such a gradient the crew has to ensure that the water level is kept well above the bottom of the glass, which would be a safe minimum on level track.

On rack railways, where the gradients are not only very steep, but also change frequently, it is customary to mount the gauge-glass in line with the dome, in the middle of the boiler where the indications do not change with the gradient. At the speeds reached it is not too difficult for

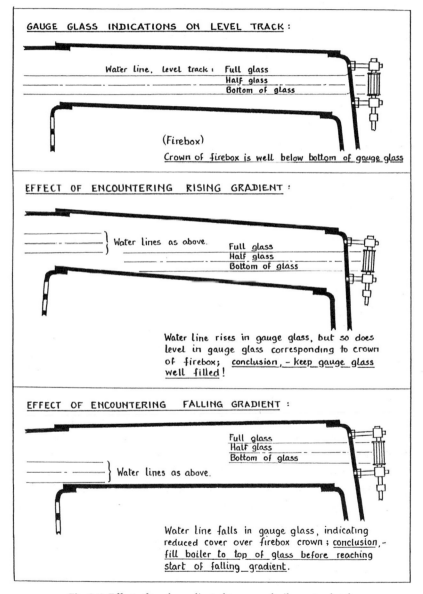

Fig. 3.6 Effect of track gradient changes on boiler water-level.

the crew to see what is happening in the water-level even with the gauge several feet away. However, they still have to remember that the water-level over the firebox will change as the gradient alters.

Because it takes time to inject a significant amount of water into a boiler, it is vital that the locomotive crew know what changes in gradient lie ahead, and control the water-level in anticipation. Fig. 3.6 illustrates the reasons for this.

For efficiency and aesthetic reasons most boilers are lagged and provided with cladding, which is usually supported on light metal hoops. In the past, various different materials have been used for the lagging, including blue asbestos, which, if still found to be present, requires the locomotive being put into 'quarantine' for it to be removed by specialists if there is any risk of exposure, whether or not it is being restored to operating condition. Nowadays fibreglass is the acceptable lagging material.

Providing the draught

The earliest locomotives relied on tall chimneys to provide, by convection, the draught to burn enough fuel for them to carry out the work needed to be done. By the end of the 1820s, however, the exhaust steam from the cylinders was being injected into the chimney near its base to increase the draught which had previously only provided by convection. It is said that this beneficial effect was discovered by chance after the exhaust had been turned into the chimney to reduce the locomotives' noise, which was frightening animals, particularly the numerous horses used for riding and transport. Whatever were the original reasons, this arrangement is particularly useful, because, whenever more steam is being used, the draught also increases and more steam is generated. The system is therefore self-governing, and matches the heat production in the firebox with the power required from the cylinders.

It soon became apparent that a separate space was needed at the front of the boiler, not only to improve the mixing arrangements, but also to collect the fine ash which tended to be pulled through the tubes by the increased draught. This took the form of a 'smokebox', consisting of a box, rounded to match the shape of the boiler, with the chimney mounted on top. Although later smokeboxes became an extension of the boiler, in the early days they often remained on the locomotive's frames when the boiler was removed for overhaul. At one time the Stephensons recommended enclosing the inside cylinders in the bottom of the smokebox to keep them warm, but this complicated the removal of the ash which was deposited in the smokebox when the velocity of the combustion products dropped after they had emerged from the tubes. A door is needed to enable these deposits to be removed at intervals, as the quantity would otherwise build up sufficiently to block the exit of the lower tubes. The ash also becomes corrosive when it gets wet, quickly attacking the bottom plates in the smokebox. For this reason the base of today's smokeboxes is sometimes lined with firebrick, or cement. A further change was made for the exhaust steam from the cylinders, which, instead of being conveyed in separate pipes to the two sides of the chimney, was combined and discharged through a blast-pipe, situated in the bottom of the smokebox, separated from the chimney but in line with it.

In the course of time numerous different experiments were tried to improve the effectiveness of the way the exhaust steam induced the flow of gases through the boiler. The efficiency of the process depends on two main factors. The first is the surface area of the jet of steam at the point where it entrains the exhaust gases from the boiler. The second is the velocity of the jet, but unfortunately a high-velocity jet means that the steam leaving the cylinders is still at a relatively high pressure, which leads to a lower cylinder efficiency. The need for a low back-pressure during the exhaust stroke of the pistons therefore leads to the designer having to limit the blast-pipe velocity. Clearly a compromise is needed, based on a full understanding of the conflicting factors. As with so many parts of the locomotive, at the design stage there has to be a trade-off between conflicting requirements.

The first comprehensive examination of smokebox performance was carried out by Professor W. F. M. Goss of Purdue University in the United States, using a testing plant built in 1891. By 1908 he was able to recommend the front-end proportions shown in Fig 3.7, to be used with a cylindrical, or drum-shaped, smokebox. Mounted in the bottom, on top of the cylinder castings, is the blast-pipe, which must be accurately centred under the petticoat which forms the entry into the chimney. In the version shown, there is a baffle plate between the ends of the tubes and the blast pipe, which tends to equalize the velocity of gases in the different tubes, combining the flows to be picked up equally by the jet. Such a fitting has to be removable as it prevents access to the tubes for

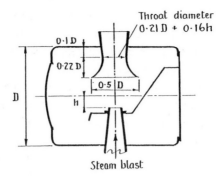

Fig. 3.7 Front-end proportions recommended by Goss in 1908.

cleaning, and it was not adopted elsewhere in the UK until the 1950s, when it was fitted as part of the smokebox 'self-cleaning' equipment, as described later in this section.

On the Great Western Railway, Churchward adopted the Goss principles, and that railway's locomotives were renowned for their steaming capabilities during the early part of the twentieth century. As the size and power output of steam locomotives increased during their final years of their traction supremacy, a lot of work was carried out to improve draughting arrangements. Work on the Swindon and Rugby test plants, combined with road testing, provided a lot of useful data, and enabled changes in detailed design to be objectively evaluated. Some startling improvements in the maximum steaming rate of some locomotives resulted. It was even possible to improve further the steaming rate of some GWR designs which had benefited for so long from the Goss layout.

The most spectacular increase was with the Ivatt Class 4MT 2-6-0s designed for the LMS just before nationalization, the first of which were fitted with double chimneys and blastpipes. It was found that this arrangement had no advantages, and the later members of the class were fitted with a single chimney. Work on the test plant showed that, as originally built, the continuous maximum steaming rate was only 9000 lb/h (4090 kg/h), but after modifying the single-chimney draughting arrangements, this almost doubled to 17 000 lb/h (7730 kg/h). The latter figure was still some 2000 lb/h (920 kg/h) below the limit imposed by combustion on the grate. When an LNER V2 2-6-2 was sent to Swindon for testing in the early 1950s, it was found that the self-cleaning equipment fitted had reduced the maximum steaming rate to 14 000 lb/h (6350 kg/h), but modifications to the draughting raised this to over 30 000 lb/h (13 600 kg/h).

The draughting system has to operate under widely-varying conditions. As the locomotive starts from rest, steam will be admitted to the cylinders for nearly the whole of the piston stroke. Under these conditions, when the exhaust valves open to exhaust, the steam will still initially be at a high pressure, but this will fall quickly, so the usual very loud, discrete, 'chuff' ensues. At the same time the flames above the grate elongate instantly as more air is pulled though the firebed, and then subside again, the process being repeated, in the case of a twin-cylinder locomotive, four times for every revolution of the driving wheels. At these speeds the overall average use of steam is quite low. When the train is moving fast, even with the valve-gear 'linked up' to maximize the expansion of the steam, the flow rate to the blastpipe will be higher, but with lower peaks in the pressure. The discharge from the nozzle then becomes more or less continuous, rather than being divided into separate 'chuffs'.

When a locomotive is accelerating from rest, or 'slogging' its way slowly up a steep gradient, the high rate at which steam is flowing to the blastpipe during each exhaust beat will increase the back pressure in the cylinders, thus decreasing the efficiency. To reduce this, some railways fitted blastpipes with variable orifices. In one form the size of the orifice could be increased or decreased by means of a rod from the cab, but this was found to be an unnecessary complication, and crews could well be tempted to restrict the orifice to give better performance, at the expense

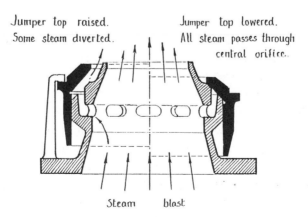

Jumper top raised.
Some steam diverted.

Jumper top lowered.
All steam passes through
central orifice.

Steam   blast

Fig. 3.8 Automatic 'jumper-top' for blast pipe, showing the two alternative positions.

of efficiency. An alternative arrangement was extensively used in this country by the GWR, and by some other companies as well. This was to fit an automatic 'jumper-top', as shown in Fig. 3.8. When the pressure inside the blastpipe increased beyond a certain point, the separate portion on the top of the nozzle lifted, increasing the discharge area, and thus reducing the back pressure. All sorts of dirt gets deposited on the outside of the blastpipe, and oil spray from the cylinders, carried through with the steam, is often carbonized by the heat in the smokebox. All this unwanted 'rubbish' can jam a jumper-top in either position, and thus render it 'wrong' for at least some of the time. With the fitting of larger superheaters, the higher steam temperatures made the oil even more likely to decompose, and, with the development of draughting arrangements that were better proportioned for operating conditions, in BR days many of these fitments were removed as unnecessary.

Numerous different ways of increasing the contact area between the steam jet and the combustion gases have been tried. The simplest is to fasten a metal rod across the top of the blastpipe, thus splitting the jet into two. Such an arrangement was known as a 'jimmy', and many of these were fitted unofficially over the years by crews who saw them as a way of avoiding poor steaming. Officially they were not permitted, for several good reasons. There was a distinct possibility that in time they would work loose, which could have unfortunate results. For example, if the piece of metal were blasted out of the chimney it could cause a lot of damage if it landed on something or somebody close to the line. Alternatively, if it fell down the blastpipe, it could work its way into the valve-gear and cause a lot of damage. There was also always the point that the need for such an item offended the sensibilities of the locomotive's designer because they tackled the symptom rather than the cause of bad steaming.

Many formal ways of achieving the same effect were tried over the years, and some of these are illustrated in Fig. 3.9. As early as the 1890s Adams on the London & South Western Railway introduced his 'vortex' design of blastpipe. The exhaust steam emerged through an annular slot, and could thus entrain the gases on the inner and outer surfaces of the jet. The lower part of the blastpipe was bifurcated to enable the smokebox gases to reach the centre of the vortex.

An obvious development is to provide twin blastpipes and a double chimney, and many large locomotives were successfully fitted with this arrangement as the century progressed. Although the Ivatt 2-6-0s were

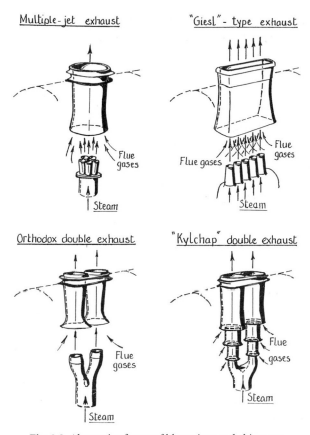

Fig. 3.9 Alternative forms of blast-pipes and chimneys.

too small to benefit from such an arrangement, double chimneys proved invaluable with the largest locomotives. With multiple-cylinder designs, the steam from all the cylinders has to be combined and then split between the twin blastpipes. The alternative arrangement of having separate exhaust systems does not work, because alternate blasts out of the separate chimneys permit air to be drawn in through the one which is not discharging, thus reducing the smokebox vacuum.

One of the most successful arrangements has been the fitting of Kylchap cowls between the blastpipe and base of the chimney. These consist of a series of small petticoats, containing internal splitters, which progressively divide the steam jet into separate streams, and so increase the entrainment, but without raising the back-pressure on the cylinders. The name is derived from MM. Kylala and Chapelon, the Finnish and French railway engineers who designed and patented the arrangement.

In Britain Gresley fitted Kylchap exhausts and double chimneys to four of his streamlined A4 Pacifics in 1936, including *Mallard*. This country's railways had a long-standing aversion to paying royalties for the use of other companies' patents, and, in spite of *Mallard's* world record, no more of the class were given the same improved draughting system in LNER days. It was not until the late 1950s, when commercial speeds started to rise on the East Coast Route, that double chimneys and Kylchap exhausts were fitted to the remaining A4s, as well as to some of the non-streamlined A3s, markedly increasing their capabilities. By that time, however, the patents had expired, and the actual cost of making and fitting the equipment was minimal!

There were also some exhaust arrangements which used multiple blastpipes, although these tended to be referred to as 'nozzles'. The first of these to be used in Britain was the Lemaître exhaust, invented by an engineer on the Nord Belge Railway in the 1930s. In its original form the blastpipe consisted of a variable central nozzle, with five others surrounding it, the combination discharging through a large-diameter chimney. In Britain it was adopted by Bulleid after he had moved from the LNER to the Southern in 1937, and first used when he successfully redesigned the front-ends of the 'Lord Nelson' 4-6-0s. It later appeared on some of the other existing Southern designs, as well as on his own Pacifics and the wartime Class Q1 0-6-0s.

The other multiple-jet exhaust system which appeared towards the end of the steam era was the Giesl Ejector, which consisted of an array of exhaust nozzles arranged in a rectangle, with twin rows side-by-side. The shape of the chimney reflected this layout in plan view, making locomotives fitted with this equipment instantly recognizable from their resulting, far-from-elegant, appearance. The Austrian railways claimed that the Giesl system increased the power of locomotives by a third while reducing the coal consumption, but it was never quite clear how efficient had been the draughting it replaced. One of the features stressed by the Austrian inventor was that the steam leaving the nozzles should not be travelling at supersonic speed, but this was not necessarily a special feature of his design. The petticoat was long and narrow, which prompted one commentator in this country to say that the main advantage of the Giesl arrangement was that it provided better access to the front tube-plate for cleaning! In the main this form of draughting came too late to exert any major influence on steam traction, but it was tried on a few British locomotives, including one on the Talyllyn Railway, the first preserved railway in the world.

The final discharge of the exhaust takes place through the external chimney, an item which dominates the whole appearance of a steam locomotive. The external contours were thus very important to get right, and there were strong family resemblances between different locomotives designed by the same chief mechanical engineer or coming from a particular railway. Quite small changes in the external proportions of the chimney could make a lot of visual difference. Both the LMS and the GWR shortened the height of those on some of their 4-6-0s in the 1930s, with the successful aim of making them look more impressive. From the performance point of view, the 'vital statistics' are hidden inside it, but externally the chimney often provided the opportunity to ornament the locomotive with brass or copper bands. In some cases the locomotive's number was even displayed in brass numerals on each side, while others painted their country's national colours round them in bands! Other railways went for the simplest possible design, consisting of an unadorned, straight-tapered 'stove-pipe', which was lighter, and much cheaper to manufacture.

Some locomotives were provided with a raised front lip to the chimney, known as a 'capuchon' by analogy with a similar item on the cap of a military uniform. Its purpose was to prevent down-draughts entering the smokebox when the locomotive was coasting with the regulator shut. If this occurred, the flames from the firebox could suddenly erupt from the firehole door—a dangerous situation for the footplate crew. A capuchon only gave limited protection against such a happening, the first line of defence being the installation of a 'blower'. Provided with a separate supply of steam, controllable from the cab, this creates sufficient vacuum in the smokebox to keep the gases flowing through the boiler in the normal way. A blower consists of a ring of holes, either in a tube surrounding the blastpipe, or in the petticoat, which discharge jets of steam up the chimney. It is standard drill to turn the blower on before the regulator is shut when a locomotive is moving fast, and also when it enters a tunnel. The use of the blower is also vital to liven the fire, and thereby increase the steam pressure, when the locomotive is stationary. As was found out with the National Railway Museum's reproductions of *Locomotion* and *Rocket*, which do not have blowers, it can sometimes be very difficult even to raise steam if the wind is blowing in the wrong direction!

Plate 3.9 Many locomotives were fitted with smoke-deflectors to lift the exhaust clear of the driver's sight-line, as on this Southern Railway Class N 2-6-0. Although large in area when viewed from the side, it will be seen that, end-on, they did not significantly obscure the driver's view ahead. The streamlined front-end of Gresley's A4 Pacifics was also very effective at lifting the exhaust, as can be seen in Plate 3.11.

As boiler diameters increased, the height of the chimneys correspondingly decreased to keep within the railway's loading gauge. By the 1920s the very short height permitted had begun to cause another problem. When the locomotive is travelling at speed with a small regulator opening, the momentum of the exhaust only lifts it a short distance above the top of the boiler. With a side wind there can be an area of lower pressure on the latter's down-wind side, and this can drag the exhaust down into it, effectively blocking the crew's ability to view the signals ahead. To overcome the problem, many locomotives were provided with smoke-deflectors alongside the smokebox, helping to move the passing air upwards. Many different designs were tried, and one of the advantages of the 'streamlined' front-end adopted by Gresley for his A4s was that the sloping wedge helped lift the exhaust.

The provision of streamlining at the front-end of a locomotive complicates the provision of another vital fitment—the smokebox door.

This is vital for access to permit cleaning and ash disposal. With an ordinary cylindrical smokebox it is easy to hinge a circular door on one side of the front for this purpose. It is important for the door to remain airtight, to avoid loss of draught on the fire, so latter-day designs consist of one-piece dished pressings. Such a stout construction enables them to be secured shut by means of a central dart on an external handle, which engages with a removable cross-member inside the smokebox. A second handle on a screw enables the door to be tightened up, the pair of them looking like the hands of a clock. Some railways in Britain used a series of clamps to secure the door around its circumference, but this is an unnecessarily complicated arrangement which takes much longer to open and close. Gresley's A4s have a fairly conventional smokebox door inside the streamlined outer casing, and access to this is obtained via a panel in the front which is opened upwards using a mechanism operated by a crank-handle.

The 'char' deposited in the smokebox still contains some combustible material, and it is possible for it to catch fire if air is allowed to enter the smokebox, the most obvious entry-point being gaps around a badly-fitting door. When this happens it is referred to by enginemen as 'having a fire at both ends', and the results can be seen afterwards by the patch where the paint on the outside has been burnt off the bottom of the door by the internal heat.

In BR days many smokeboxes were modified to make them 'self-cleaning', with the aim of cutting down the daily task of removing char from them. This involved the fitting of a plate behind the chimney, very similar to that recommended by Goss. By directing all the gases leaving the tubes past the bottom of the smokebox, it ensured that the rapid flow there would pick up any char and sweep it out of the chimney. A gauze plate was mounted similarly in front of the chimney to prevent any dangerously large lumps of material being projected into the air, but care has to be taken not to make the holes in this too small, as it is possible for them to be closed by particles of ash becoming stuck to them. For this and other reasons, these arrangements often adversely affected the maximum steaming rate, but changes in the blastpipe and chimney design sometimes overcame the problem. As mentioned earlier, the former LNER Class V2s were a case in point. They suffered badly from poor steaming when the self-cleaning plates were first installed, but a redesign by Swindon doubled the maximum steaming rate.

Plate 3.10 Chute fitted to preserved Finnish Railways 4-6-0 No. 555 to simplify removal of ash from the smokebox.

Superheating

In Chapter 1 the relationship between steam pressure and the temperature of the water in the boiler was discussed, and we saw that the two had a fixed relationship, determined by water's chemical and physical properties. However, once steam has been separated from water, its temperature can be raised further without altering its pressure, simply by adding more heat. This is known as superheating, and adding extra energy in this way can improve the thermal efficiency of a steam engine. We will be considering the reasons for this in more detail in Chapter 4, but it is helpful to outline them here, before describing how superheating is carried out.

It is steam pressure which forces the pistons along the cylinders, and to reduce the amount used, the inlet valve is closed well before the piston reaches the end of its travel. The steam in the cylinder then expands for the rest of the stroke, its pressure and temperature dropping in the process. Once the point is reached where the steam temperature corresponds to the boiling point of water at that pressure, some of it will start to condense. The contents of the cylinder then enter the 'wet' area of the temperature/pressure diagram for steam, which will result in the pressure dropping more quickly, aggravated by a greater rate of heat transfer to the cylinder walls. This reduces the thrust on the piston, and hence the tractive effort being exerted to haul the train. By using superheat, the point at which condensation starts is delayed, and the 'mean effective pressure' in the cylinder is raised.

As the steam passes through the superheater it also expands, and this means that, with the same valve events, a smaller mass of steam enters the cylinder at the start of each stroke, reducing the amount of latent heat that has been used to generate that amount of steam. This latent heat represents energy which is inevitably lost by any steam engine when its exhaust is discharged to atmosphere.

On a steam locomotive in Britain superheating is normally carried out in cold-drawn, seamless tubes with an internal diameter of about $1\frac{1}{2}$ in (38 mm), although different systems have been used in other countries. In the usual UK arrangement, four lengths of tube are connected, using forged return-bends, and bundled together to form an 'element', each of which is housed in one of the boiler's superheater flues. The ends of the two pipes projecting into the smokebox are bent upwards so they can be attached to headers, one supplying saturated steam from the boiler, and the other taking the superheated steam for delivery to the cylinders. The superheater thus has to operate in a hostile environment, the return bends nearer the firebox being subjected to the impingement of both hot gases and ash. Various different layouts have been adopted by railway companies to give the greatest practical surface area without extending the tubes all the way back to the firebox.

The elements have to be removed when the corresponding boiler flue has to be changed, usually as part of a major overhaul, or if one of them should develop a leak. This need constrains the design and positioning of the headers in the smokebox. Two main methods of fixing the tubes to the header have been used. Some are held on by bolts, the ends of the tubes being spherically-ground to prevent the alignment being critical when the joint is made. The alternative is to expand the elements into the header, but this requires the removal of a cover and the application of a special roller tool with its head at right-angles to the operating handle—a difficult piece of gear to use effectively in those conditions.

Typically superheaters in the UK raise the steam temperature by 200–350 °F (110–200 °C), giving cylinder inlet temperatures in the range 600-700 °F (330–390 °C). Even though the return bends at the firebox end are located at least 1–2 ft (300–600 mm) into the boiler from the back tubeplate, the temperature there can be sufficient for them to reach a dull red heat.

When superheating was being introduced at the turn of the century, there was concern that the elements could get too hot when the locomotive was coasting with the regulator closed and no steam passing through them. Some locomotives were accordingly fitted with flue dampers in the smokebox, which stopped the flow of gases through them when the regulator was closed. They were operated by a small external cylinder, but this arrangement was found to be an unnecessary complication after better materials had been developed for the elements.

A 'snifting', or anti-vacuum valve has to be fitted somewhere between the saturated steam header and the cylinders, to enable air to be drawn through the elements and the cylinders when the locomotive is coasting, and to remove the risk of char being drawn into the blastpipe. The LNER fitted its design of snifting valves prominently just behind the chimney, on top of the saturated steam header, where they enabled air to be drawn through the superheater elements on its way to the cylinders. This cools the elements, and the resulting heated flow does not cause such a large thermal shock when it reaches the valves and cylinders. Snifting valves in this position close with a characteristic noise when the driver opens the regulator.

Water impurities

Even before rain reaches the ground it has absorbed gases from the atmosphere, and the solution process continues as it percolates through the soil or runs over the surface of the Earth until it reaches the sea. Every compound has a different solubility in water, so the quantities and nature of dissolved material vary, depending on the geology of the area. There are also various animal and industrial effluents which can be picked up by water. As a result, the quality of the large quantities needed by steam locomotives in their heyday could vary widely within even quite a small area.

Nowadays the average steam locomotive working a mainline charter will be provided with water from a local fire brigade or other

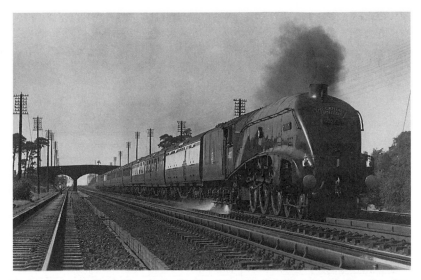

Plate 3.11 Streamlined Class A4 Pacific No. 60027 *Merlin* picks up water from Langley Troughs towards the end of its non-stop run from Edinburgh to King's Cross with the southbound 'Capitals Limited' in June 1952. There was always a certain amount of spray produced, but the real trouble occurred if the tender was overfilled, when the leading coaches would be deluged with water discharged from the high-level vents. As much as 2000 gallons of water could be picked up while passing over a trough. (Photo: D. A. Dant)

organization, which has probably filled its tanker from a water board's mains, and will have been selective in choosing its source. Preserved railways, however, are probably more constrained to make use of local, non-mains supplies, whatever their quality and suitability.

As we will consider in Chapter 7, the amount of water needed in the heyday of steam traction was immense, and the railway companies, like other large industries, could not afford (and had no need) to use potable domestic supplies, which are treated to remove bacteria as well as being obtained from sources which do not contain any toxic chemicals. Many of the latter are not fatal to a steam locomotive as they would be to a human, and traditionally much lower-quality supplies have been used by the railways.

There are nevertheless many dissolved materials in water which can cause difficulties for a locomotive. This is because any dissolved solids are not removed in the steam produced, but remain in the water where their concentration builds up steadily. Every compound has a maximum solubility in water, and once that is reached, any further increase in

Plate 3.12 To cope with poor water quality, many Chinese locomotives, such as the British-built 4-8-4 preserved at the National Railway Museum, were fitted with blow-down valves on the side of the firebox, operated by a lever from the footplate. There was also an additional blow-down from the bottom of the boiler, used when the locomotive was stationary.

concentration causes precipitation to start, either in suspended form or as a solid deposit on a surface. To get some idea of what happens, we will consider a boiler containing 5000 gallons (22.7 m³) of water. During a day's work such a locomotive can well consume a further 15 000 gallons (68 m³). The dissolved solids in a total of 20 000 gallons thus become concentrated in 5000, a four-fold increase. If the locomotive runs for two weeks between wash-outs, the concentration factor rises to 43, quite sufficient to cause some of the incoming impurities to start separating out if the water supply is not a good one.

In practice, the rate of concentration increase is not quite as high as this, because there are inevitably small water leaks from the boiler, and these contain the current concentration of the solutes, which is higher than that in the feed water. Various systems take advantage of this effect by purging relatively small quantities of water from the boiler on a regular basis, which removes a disproportionate quantity of the impurities. At one time some North American railroads had a special area at the exit from their depots, where every locomotive paused while the driver opened the blow-down cock for a few seconds. Baffles contained the high-pressure jets of boiling water which were discharged on either side. At the opening of the Californian State Railroad Museum in 1981, the locomotives in steam did no more than potter up and down the riverside track, but, even so, the Union Pacific 'Challenger' used to blow down every few days, discharging a jet of water half-way across the Sacramento River! On the scenic Durango & Silverton Railroad in Colorado, every train does a quick blow-down as it crosses a bridge over a canyon, producing spectacular effects, including rainbows.

Boiler-water quality was not always managed as well as this in the United States, as in 1917 the Interstate Commerce Commission reported there were no less than 389 accidents caused by boiler failures, resulting in 52 deaths and over 450 injuries. In 1934 the boiler of a 2-10-2 locomotive on the Denver & Rio Grand Western Railroad blew up and was flung 212 feet (65 m) ahead of the locomotive, with part of the cab going even further in the opposite direction. The official report stated that the accident was '... caused by foul water which was not in condition to absorb heat with sufficient rapidity to maintain the heating surface at a safe temperature. It is further evident that failure to wash the boiler as often as water conditions require was the primary cause of the accident'. A Federal rule required all boilers to be washed out at least every month, but the D&RGW prevented it being carried out any more frequently, regardless of the water quality.

In a country as crowded as Britain, blow-downs of the type described above are not possible, but the LMS achieved a similar effect by adopting a continuous purge system. A special valve on the back-plate of the firebox allows 1–2 gallons (5–10 kg) of water per minute to escape from the boiler, and is automatically opened by a steam supply which is turned on either whenever the regulator is opened or the injectors are operating. Originally the water was discharged on one side of the 'four-foot', but over a number of years it was found that there was an increase in rail fractures on that side of the track. The system was accordingly changed so the blow-down took place into the ashpan.

These continuous blow-down valves are mounted some distance above the lowest point in the boiler, so will not remove any sludge that might accumulate. This is deliberate, as the rate-controlling orifice in them has to have a very small diameter to limit the flow-rate, which can thus easily be blocked by any solid material. Intermittent blow-downs usually discharge from a much lower point in the boiler so they can flush out any build-up of sludge.

For those who live in areas which have 'hard' water, the resulting problems are well known. As well as making soap difficult to lather, it also affects domestic kettles, furring them up quite quickly, a problem

Plate 3.13 The container for slowly-dissolving water-treatment chemicals fitted in the tender water-space of some of the Southern Railway Pacifics.

shared with locomotive boilers. Hardness is caused by the presence of magnesium and calcium salts. Officially some 60 per cent of the piped water supplies in the UK are classified as 'hard', with just under half being 'very hard'. The latter are to be found in areas where there is a lot of chalk and limestone, such as south-east Britain. For this reason, the Southern Region and its predecessors used to suffer from the effects particularly badly in steam days. East Anglia, particularly south-east Essex, was also bad for water hardness as far as railways were concerned, while other areas were not immune. The LMS, for example, had a policy of building softening plants at many major depots and water-trough installations. In these treatment plants, by adding chemicals in controlled amounts the compounds producing the hardness were precipitated as a sludge, which settled out and was dumped.

Other railways followed a policy which exploited chemical technology using materials which dissolved slowly in a locomotive's tender. They cause any hardness to precipitate as a sludge in the boiler, which can then be purged using the blow-down system, rather than a scale adhering to the internal surfaces. The container for such materials can be seen in the tender of the sectioned Southern Railway locomotive at the National Railway Museum in York.

Organic matter getting into a locomotive's boiler can cause a totally different problem. Under certain conditions it can produce a layer of foam on the boiling surface, which can build up sufficiently to cause 'priming', when water can be carried over into the cylinders or out of the safety-valves. The latter can spray water over a large area, making it unpopular for anyone caught in the fall-out, but any accumulation of water in the valves and cylinders, where there should only be steam, can easily cause serious damage. If priming occurs on a large scale the foam can induce a sufficiently rapid flow of water through the regulator to make it difficult or impossible for the driver to stop the problem by closing it.

As we will see in the next chapter, at the end of each stroke the piston compresses the steam remaining in the cylinder, increasing the pressure to match that available from the boiler as soon as the valve opens to admit steam for the return stroke. Water, compared with steam, is almost incompressible, so if any is present during this compression phase, 'hydraulic-ing' can take place, increasing the pressure very rapidly and to far higher figures than the steam ever reaches. Although locomotives have relief valves at each end of their cylinders, these may not be able to open sufficiently to clear the accumulated water in the extremely short time available. In extreme cases cylinder covers can be blown off, or the sudden blockage to the piston's movement can produce a force sufficiently large to damage the big-end bearings, or even bend the connecting rods.

Dissolved material in a locomotive's water supplies can also cause problems with scale formation and corrosion, as we will see in the next two sections.

Scale on surfaces

When the concentration of a dissolved substance increases beyond the point corresponding to its maximum solubility, the excess starts to separate out. The resulting solid can appear in various forms. In a boiler, the least troublesome way this can happen is for it to form small particles in suspension, which circulate around the boiler without adhering to any surface. Unfortunately, when the boiler stands idle, any such precipitate will slowly settle, and can deposit as a layer on the various upward-facing surfaces in the boiler, just as dust does in a house.

Most substances have a higher solubility in hot water than in cold, so, if solids of this sort have started to precipitate out in a working boiler, more of it will separate out when it cools down. The extra material is likely to appear where there are any similar compounds to act as nuclei, thus cementing them together. Other compounds have a negative solubility coefficient, which means their solubility decreases with a rise in water temperature. They are thus likely to be precipitated where the water is hottest—on the outside of the inner firebox plates. As shown in Chapter 2, the build-up of scale at such points can significantly alter the temperature gradients across the plates, and thus reduce the output of a boiler by as much as a quarter, as well as causing the firebox plates to overheat. It is thus important to remove as much of this scale as possible at frequent intervals when servicing the locomotive, as described in Chapter 7.

Even so it may not be possible to remove it all, as regularly experienced with steam locomotives working in one of the worst areas for build-up—southern Essex. For this reason, when the 'Tilbury Tanks' used to be taken to Derby for periodic attention, they invariably received a 'general overhaul', which called for the boiler to be removed and sent to the boiler shop. There the tubes were removed to deal with scale in places which could not be reached through the various access points. So bad was the water in the area traversed by the London, Tilbury & Southend line that, after all the tubes and flues had been removed, the resulting pile of scale often filled the bottom half of the boiler shell. The front tubeplate was then removed, as this provided the easiest and quickest way to get such a quantity of scale out of the interior of the boiler.

Corrosion

The presence of certain materials in the boiler feedwater can also increase corrosion in the boiler. Chloride ions are particularly troublesome, and their presence in sea water has always made it difficult to maintain the boilers of steam-powered ships. The rate of corrosion, like most chemical reactions, increases with rising temperatures. The boilers in Brunel's *Great Britain* only operated at 10 lb/in² (0.7 bar) and a correspondingly relatively-low temperature, so were able to use sea water. Even so the build-up of solids had to be limited by a relatively large blow-down rate. If a particular solute is capable of attacking any of the boiler materials, the higher its concentration in the boiler water, the more rapid will be the corrosion.

As mentioned in the previous section, scale on the water-side of the firebox plates can significantly increase the temperature of the plates themselves. This can accelerate the rate of corrosion on the water-side, and, at the same time, by increasing the temperature on the firebox walls, it will aggravate the corrosion/erosion caused by the flames and hot gases.

Feed-water systems

For a steam locomotive to run for any length of time, arrangements have to be made for sufficient water to be added to the boiler to make up for that used as steam, or lost in any other way. All such feed water has to be forced into the boiler against the pressure within it, and two different methods are used: feed-water pumps and injectors.

In the earliest days of steam, the only method available was with a feed-water pump, a simple reciprocating device which, on early locomotives, was often mounted for convenience alongside one of the cylinders and driven off the crosshead. When any fluid is to be compressed or has its pressure raised by a reciprocating pump, inlet and discharge valves have to be provided. These can be of a simple 'flap' or 'non-return' variety, and no complicated valve gear is required to operate them, in contrast to that controlling the steam inlet and exhaust for the cylinders driving a locomotive's wheels.

The bicycle pump (Fig. 3.10) provides such an example, and its two valves are formed by the cup-shaped piston in the pump itself, and the non-return one attached to the inner tube. The former allows air to pass around it as the handle is pulled back, but seals on the forward stroke to force the air into the tyre. Air is, however, compressible, and for maximum efficiency there must be very little clearance volume when the piston is at the end of its compression stroke. A liquid like water is much less compressible, and it is not necessary to minimize this clearance volume with a water pump, so a simple plunger can be used instead of a piston, as also shown in Fig. 3.10.

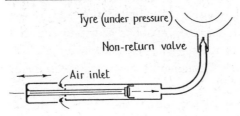

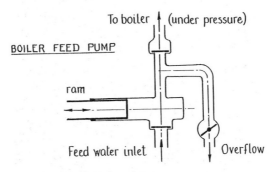

Fig. 3.10 Air and water pumps.

When the feed-water pump is connected to the locomotive's motion, in theory it would be possible to match the amount of water delivered each stroke with the corresponding quantity of steam used each time the wheels do a complete revolution. Unfortunately the amount of steam used per revolution is not constant. It depends on the inlet valve cut-off, not to mention discrepancies caused by any used to drive auxiliaries (for example, brake pumps or ejectors), to provide train heating, and being lost through the safety valves. It is thus necessary for the pump to deliver sufficient water per stroke to cover the maximum demand of all these. This means that for much of the time the boiler would get too full. Some means of stopping or reducing the pump's output has to be provided, and this is usually done by a providing a valve which allows some or all of the high-pressure water on the delivery side to bypass back to the suction. It clearly has to be mounted on the pump side of the delivery valve, unless a second non-return valve is provided at the inlet to the boiler. (see 'clack valve' mentioned below). On some early locomotives, such as *Agenoria,* the stroke of the pump could varied mechanically when it was stationary.

Plate 3.14 The feed-water pump on *Agenoria*, built in 1829 for Shutt End Colliery, can be seen mounted on the side of its boiler. It is driven off one of the overhead beams used to transmit the piston forces to the driving wheels, and provision was made for the length of the pump stroke, and hence the quantity of water delivered, to be adjusted fairly easily by moving the stirrup along the pump lever.

Even when a locomotive is standing, the non-propulsion demands for steam still occur, and a problem then arises if the feed-water pump is directly coupled to the main drive motion. At traction-engine rallies it is very common to see the flywheels on these machines turning over for long periods when the engines are stationary. While this helps keep the cylinders warm, the main reason is to top up the boiler with the feed pump. These road machines are designed so that, when stationary, the motion can be disconnected from the drive to the wheels, a facility which is not normally provided on steam locomotives. In the early days it was not unknown for a locomotive to be uncoupled from its train and run light up and down the track for some minutes to refill the boiler.

The practice even continued as late as the 1930s with the LNER steam railcars, which had feed-water pumps as well as injectors, and, unfortunately, the latter were inclined to be temperamental, as will be described later. As short, self-contained, vehicles, these railcars could usually be driven up and down in the length of the platform during a station 'stop' to refill the boiler if needed. Passengers waiting to continue their journeys were, however, somewhat puzzled by these goings-on! The feed-water pump is a relatively straightforward device, and a self-powered steam version could have overcome these limitations. They were, however, not common in the UK, no doubt because designers never liked to provide additional equipment which needed servicing and maintenance unless it was unavoidable.

Injectors provide a much simpler solution, but they rely on a supply of cold water, not always available on locomotives which were provided with condensing equipment for use in tunnels. For instance, when the GWR fitted ten of its Pannier Tanks with condensing equipment to work trains over London Transport's 'Widened Lines', from Paddington to Smithfield Market, they provided a steam-powered feed-water pump on one side of the running plate alongside the smokebox. Looking rather like the Westinghouse pumps used to power compressed-air braking systems on steam locomotives, these consisted of two cylinders, linked together, one for steam and the other for water, with their pistons connected by a drive rod. A simple valve gear caused the pistons to oscillate whenever the crew required more water in the boiler. Injectors are also more temperamental with high-pressure boilers, and feed-water pumps were more common on locomotives in North America for this reason.

It was not until 1859 that a French engineer, H. Giffard, invented the cone injector, which then rapidly replaced the feed-water pump. It does not have any continuously-moving parts, although it inevitably contains a number of valves of different sorts. A supply of steam enters it and this can raise water from the tender and inject the combined stream into the boiler, which makes it appear to be lifting itself up by its own bootstraps or even providing perpetual motion. This is obviously not so, but, as its mode of operation is hidden from the eye of the observer, this deepens the mystery. As a result there are many erroneous descriptions of the principles on which it works (the same applies to the vacuum ejector). To understand them we have to begin by describing some fundamental properties of fluids in motion.

FLOW THROUGH PIPES

In I, fluid flowing through parallel pipe loses
pressure at steady rate (A → B → C)

In II, fluid loses more pressure as it accelerates
into throat, but recovers in part as it
reaches larger section (D → E → F)

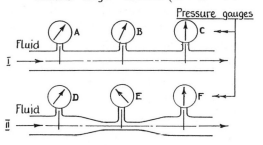

SIMPLE INJECTOR

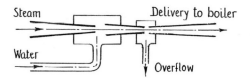

Fig. 3.11 Flows of fluids and a simple injector.

The first diagram in Fig. 3.11 shows a fluid (gas or liquid) flowing along a constant diameter pipe to which are attached three pressure gauges. The overall pressure drop between A and C will depend on the diameter of the pipe, the viscosity of the fluid, the friction caused by the roughness of the walls of the pipe, and the rate of flow. The pressure at B will lie between those at A and C. In the second diagram the central section of the pipe is narrower, which means the velocity of the flow here increases. Overall the pressure drop between A and C will increase slightly, but the pressure at B can be much *lower* than either! This is because the kinetic energy of the moving fluid increases in the narrower bore, and, as there is no energy input from outside the system, the pressure energy must decrease by the same amount. If the change of velocity, and therefore the drop in pressure, is great enough, it would be possible to admit another flow through a side connection.

Plate 3.15 One of the injectors on Stirling's GNR No. 1 4-2-2, mounted low down between the driving and trailing wheels. The control wheels for the water and steam are mounted on the tops of the two vertical rods rising through the foot-framing. The brake-block in front of the trailing wheel can also be seen, together with the adjustment device for the one on the driving wheel, as described in Chapter 8.

For practical purposes a pair of internal cones is used to cause the changes in velocity, as shown in the third diagram. The first of these is the reducing cone and the second the expanding one. The initial flow is provided by steam from the boiler, and the partial vacuum between the cones is sufficient to lift water from the tanks or tender to the side connection through a height of several feet. Traction engines and steam rollers used to be fitted with a similar device to refill their tanks by dropping a hose connected to the side branch into a handy roadside ditch or stream.

Plate 3.16 On BR standard locomotives, both injectors were mounted below the right-hand side of the cab, where the fireman could easily check the water-overflow pipes from his seat. In addition to a live-steam one, the Class 9F 2-10-0s, such as No. 92220 *Evening Star*, were provided with a combined exhaust/live steam injector, the former feed coming from below the blast-pipe via the largest of the brass pipes sweeping down from underneath the foot-framing. The water controls are the rods coming down vertically from the cab, while the live-steam supplies are provided from the auxiliary steam manifold via the cocks in front of the cab window.

A practical injector, as shown in Fig. 3.11, contains an intermediate cone, in which the water and steam to combine, the latter condensing in the process. This liberates its latent heat of evaporation, which is converted into kinetic energy, so increasing the velocity of the water at this point. When the water passes through the expanding cone its pressure rises in the usual way, and, because of the extra velocity imparted by the condensation, the discharge pressure from the injector can be higher than that in the boiler. This enables the stream of water from the delivery to be injected into the boiler. It passes through a non-return valve, which prevents water and steam flowing back out of the boiler. Because of the noise this valve makes when it shuts, it is known as a 'clack' valve.

Plate 3.17 Various important items of boiler-mounted equipment on the 1875 North Eastern Railway 2-4-0 No.910 can be seen in this illustration. The boiler feed-water clack valve delivers water approximately half-way up the diameter of the boiler. The bolt on its top was used to hold the valve shut when anyone was working on the injector with the boiler under pressure. The valve near the top of the boiler admitted steam to the exhausters for the 'simple' vacuum brake. (See Plate 8.1.)

As the additional energy comes from the latent heat of the steam, it is not even necessary to use live steam from the boiler, and injectors can be designed to operate from the low-pressure steam being exhausted from the cylinders. Such an arrangement recovers heat which would have otherwise been lost up the chimney, although, because there will be a reduction in draught, the locomotive's steaming ability, and hence its power output, will be reduced slightly. These are known as exhaust-steam injectors, but those used in this country were usually of the 'combined' type, capable of operating from live steam as well, with the change-over taking place automatically either way as the regulator is opened or shut. To improve the reliability of the change-overs, the latest design of exhaust-steam injector also incorporates a continuously-running supplementary jet of live steam.

Unfortunately the exhaust steam from the cylinders also contains oil, which, if permitted to get into the boiler, could be deposited on the metal surfaces, and reduce the heat transfer. An oil separator is therefore inserted in the exhaust steam pipe. All this extra equipment made exhaust steam injectors much more complicated, and they were only used on locomotives likely to benefit from long runs with the regulator staying open. There was never a case for providing them for shunting locomotives.

Operating an injector is something of an art. It is necessary to match the flows of steam and water. If there is too much steam the injector 'blows back' with steam coming out of the overflow, while, if there is not enough steam, water is wasted by a continuous flow from the same point. The end of the overflow pipe was usually positioned to enable the fireman or driver to see it by putting his head over the side of the cab. A properly running injector makes a characteristic 'singing' sound, which can be heard above the usual clatter on the footplate of a moving locomotive.

Injectors can fail to work for a variety of reasons, such as dirt or scale on the cones, air leaks or obstructions in the water supply, as well as the water being too hot. As mentioned, earlier, hot water will not condense the steam in the combining cone, so there no energy is released to increase the delivery pressure. As already mentioned locomotives fitted with condensing equipment have to be provided with feed-water pumps, but the same problem can arise if steam is allowed to blow-back through the water pipe into the tender of an ordinary locomotive. (In *very* cold weather it is nevertheless sometimes necessary to keep the water temperature in the tender above freezing point in this way, but the amount of heating has to be carefully controlled.) For the reasons mentioned, an injector is never completely reliable, and it is therefore customary to fit two to every steam locomotive.

The water supply for the 'slacker pipe', used to damp the coal in the tender and keep down the dust on the footplate, comes from the injector delivery, which is why it is always hot.

Various different practices were adopted for the actual injection of the water into the boiler. The feed is inevitably at a lower temperature than the water already in the boiler, and sudden severe temperature gradients can occur when an injector or feed-pump is started, with the danger of stressing parts of the structure. Some railways, the GWR, as well as the

In a number of factories where there were either inflammable gases or a surplus of high-pressure process steam, 'fireless' locomotives were used

Plate 3.18 Instead of a boiler, the fireless locomotives had a large pressure-vessel which could be filled with steam through a flexible hose connection at the front, via a stop-valve.

Plate 3.19 In the cab the equipment was very simple. A regulator on top of the boiler permitted steam to be released into the cylinders, which were provided with appropriate valve gear, as described in Chapter 4, operated by the vertical reversing lever. The driver had to keep his eye on the pressure gauge to make sure there was enough steam left to get the locomotive to the nearest recharging point.

Plate 3.20 The cylinders were normally at the cab end, and the exhaust was discharged via a pipe up the back of the cab. Because of heat losses the exhaust steam was inclined to be 'wet', so a drain was fitted to the end of the pipe to avoid water being sprayed about.

LMS in Stanier days, used the 'top-feed' system. With this the water from the injectors is added through the steam-space at the top of the boiler, and then falls on to longitudinal trays in the steam-space. The incoming water spreads along these, running off them over a considerable area, which minimizes stress gradients. An alternative system was used by the LNER, where the injectors are on the firebox back-plate, but their delivery pipes run well forward through the water-space in the boiler, enabling them to act as heat-exchangers. By the time the water enters the boiler itself, its temperature had been raised sufficiently to avoid any local over-stressing of the boiler shell.

Steam for auxiliaries

Not all the steam from a locomotive's boiler is used in its cylinders for propulsion, and there are other important uses for some of it, both on and off the locomotive itself. This section describes some of these, and outlines their need for steam supplies, although the details of ways in which the main items of equipment operate are given in Chapter 8.

A single take-off point on the boiler is usually provided for the steam used for all these auxiliaries, and is fitted with a main isolating valve.

Many companies sited this inside the cab, on top of or on the front-plate of the firebox, but on the BR standard locomotives it was mounted on the boiler, just in front of the cab, with the main valve being operated by a handle inside the cab, using a long spindle. After this main isolation there is a manifold leading to however many control valves are needed for the various items of steam-operated equipment. Not every locomotive will be fitted with all those described below, and individual layouts vary considerably.

Injectors

As described in the preceding section of this chapter, steam is needed to operate the injectors providing the feed-water for the boiler. While some locomotives are able to benefit from the use of exhaust steam from the cylinders when the locomotive is running, 'live steam' is still needed as a standby when the regulator is closed, as well as to supplement the operation of the exhaust-steam injector(s). Each injector has its own steam control valve, and these will be fed from one of the branches off the main manifold. If the locomotive has a boiler feed pump rather than injectors, that also will require its own supply of steam, unless it is driven from the motion.

Brakes

Most latter-day steam locomotives in Britain are provided with steam brakes operating on their driving wheels and those on their tenders, even if the train is equipped with a vacuum or air brake system. The driver's brake valve thus requires a supply of steam. The majority of steam-hauled trains on UK main lines were braked by vacuum, which was created by steam ejectors. Although the control system differed in some earlier designs, the final arrangement is for the driver to have a single brake handle, which will operated the brakes on both locomotive and train. By moving it in opposite directions he can apply or release the brakes on the train, and the system also produces a corresponding application of the steam brake on the locomotive. Some designs, including the BR Standard types, have an additional control for the steam brake on its own.

The vacuum ejector works on the same principle as the blastpipe, with a jet of steam entering a converging cone. The air entrained on the surface of the fast-moving jet comes from the main vacuum-brake pipe, through a 'check' (non-return) valve to stop the inrush of air if the steam is shut off. The scale of the equipment is much smaller than the blastpipe, and most brake systems have two, different-sized, ejectors. The small one operates continuously to maintain the vacuum in the train-pipe while the train is running, but the large one is only used intermittently, when the driver needs to release the brakes quickly. While some large injectors are brought into action by moving the brake handle to the 'release' position, others have a separate control. The small injector has its own steam supply, with a valve which is turned on by the driver before moving the locomotive. Some companies used a vacuum pump on one of the cylinder crossheads rather than a small ejector, for reasons which will be described in Chapter 8. Locomotives fitted with these still require a large ejector to 'blow-off' the brakes when the train is standing.

Air-braked locomotives and trains were used in some parts of Britain in the steam era, and this is increasingly likely to become the norm when preserved steam is used on our main lines. Locomotives for such workings are fitted with a steam-operated pump (compressor), usually of the Westinghouse type, normally mounted close to the front of the boiler, to enable the exhaust to be led into the smokebox, and discharged through the chimney. These pumps have automatic governors which start them operating whenever the pressure in the main reservoirs falls below the set figure, and then switches out again when it has risen to the normal operating level. The pump needs its own steam supply from the boiler manifold, with an isolating valve.

Steam heating

In the days of steam traction on BR, any heating needed in the train had to be provided by steam from the locomotive's boiler. Every locomotive which was required to haul passenger carriages, and occasionally specialized freight wagons for exotic loads such as bananas, had to be fitted with a system to supply steam at about 60 lb/in^2 (4 bar) to the train-pipe which conveyed it to each vehicle in the train. There is a reducing valve in the cab which ensures that the pressure in the heating supply does not get high enough to damage the on-train equipment, the most vulnerable items being the flexible hoses between vehicles. A relief (safety) valve is fitted on the train side of the reducing valve, and the crew can hear this start to discharge if something goes wrong, helping to ensure there is no damage from too high a pressure in the train-heating system.

The other auxiliary uses for steam previously described only required a small proportion of the boiler's output, but in cold weather the train-heating requirements could be as much as 10 per cent of its steaming capacity. If the locomotive was not steaming well it was not unknown for the supply to be turned off, or its pressure reduced by the footplate crew, if they were in danger of dropping time! Hopefully they would remember to restore the setting to normal when the next down-grade was reached. (There could be other causes for the failure of steam to reach some or all of the coaches. Unlike the vacuum connections between vehicles, each of the flexible steam ones had to be fitted with an on–off cock to stop steam escaping from the one at the rear of the train. Sometimes one of these along the train was not turned on, which isolated all the vehicles behind it from the heating supply.)

Various traps are fitted to the train-heating system to dispose of the water produced in the condensation process. Water in these and the main steam pipe can freeze in very cold weather and prevent the system operating, particularly if the train is left standing overnight without a locomotive attached. Once ice forms, the application of steam at one end of the train only was a waste of effort, so stock for commercially-important trains was at times kept warm overnight in the carriage sidings by a shunting locomotive, and in some places static preheating steam supplies were provided.

Warning devices

Every locomotive has to have the means to provide an audible warning to draw the attention of anyone on the track to the approach of the train. With steam locomotives this normally takes the form of a steam whistle, which can be mounted in a variety of positions. It is often just in front of the cab, or on its roof if the loading gauge permits. Alternatively it is sometimes fitted behind the chimney or alongside the smokebox. Steam from its own valve on the boiler manifold passes through a control valve actuated either by chains stretching across to both sides of the cab, or by levers. If either member of the crew sights anyone on the track he can grab one of these and sound the whistle, which also has to be used when approaching crossings.

Whistles are also used before a train starts to move, and traditionally also provided a means of communicating with the signalmen. There were various general, as well as local, codes to convey specific information, such as the required routing for the train. If a train was stopped at a signal not provided with a berthing track-circuit, the driver was required to sound his whistle immediately. Some of those working crack trains were inclined to whistle their annoyance with the signalman if they even sighted a 'distant' at caution! Whistle signals also provide communication between the train engine (at the front) and banking engine(s) used at the rear to assist heavy trains up steep gradients.

Various different designs of whistle have been fitted to different classes, and listeners with a musical ear can sometimes identify the class or origin of an unseen locomotive from the sound of its whistle. Most whistles produce just one main note, having a chamber which resonates primarily at a single frequency. In later years 'chime whistles' were introduced, which have three, or sometimes four, separate resonators, each tuned to one of the notes of a chord. Similar arrangements have now been introduced for the air horns of some British top-link electric locomotives, although the standard arrangement for diesel and electric traction is to provide pairs of horns, which the driver sounds alternately when a warning is required. This system was introduced by the GWR after the introduction of their diesel railcars in the 1930s, which were originally fitted with just a single horn. Staff working on the track near main roads found it difficult to differentiate between the approach of a train and the passage of a nearby road vehicle.

Great Western steam locomotives also had two whistles of different pitches, the one with the lower note being known as the 'brake whistle'. This was used if an unexpected situation arose when the driver of an 'unbraked' freight train needed the guard to apply the handbrake in his van at the back of the train.

In North America there are large numbers of 'open' level crossings, over which trains have right of way. As a train approaches one of these, the crew has to 'crow' the whistle or horn, and then hang on to it until the train actually starts to occupy the crossing. The horns and whistles have to be very powerful, so much so that care is taken by crews to keep their heads inside the cab when they are sounded. Another North American requirement is for a bell to be sounded continuously when a train is moving within station-limits, producing its characteristic doleful sound. While this used to be rung by pulling a cord from the cab, when locomotives got larger steam-operated bells were provided.

Mechanical stokers

As described in Chapter 2, some countries fitted mechanical stokers to many of their locomotives, and a few were tried experimentally in the UK. Their delivery scrolls are powered by a small steam engine, and jets of steam, controlled by the fireman, direct the flow of fuel entering the firebox. Such a fitment requires its own supply from the boiler, with appropriate controls for the fireman to use.

Electric generators

When Bulleid introduced his Pacifics, he provided them with an electric generator and lighting system. The usual oil lamps used on the Southern Railway on the front and rear of locomotives to indicate the train's routing were replaced with electric ones. The cab was also fitted with electric lighting, and another electric light was provided near the injector overflow to help the fireman see what was happening at night. These installations were retained when most of these locomotives were rebuilt by R. G. Jarvis from 1956 onwards.

Before that, a move was made to provide many other BR locomotives with a steam-operated electric generator to power a lighting system to replace the oil lamps used to indicate the class of train. The generator was mounted on the front of the foot-framing, powered by a small steam turbine on the same axis as the generator, with the exhaust being led into the smokebox.

Lubricators

It is extremely important to provide good lubrication for the valves and cylinders of a steam locomotive. They represent the largest areas where rubbing occurs, and operate at high pressures and temperatures. For the lubricant to be delivered under every condition, its pressure has to be as high as that produced by the boiler, so one of the simplest ways of doing this is to use an auxiliary supply of steam for this purpose. Various designs of hydrostatic displacement lubricators have been used, which condense the steam and use the resulting hot water to propel the oil into the cylinders. These will be described in more detail in Chapter 5, together with the alternative type of mechanical lubricators. Although the later do not require steam to make them operate, a supply is still needed to keep the oil delivery pipes warm in cold weather, and to atomize the oil when it reaches the cylinder block. The first movement of the regulator lever on most Great Western Railway locomotives was arranged to open the steam supply to the lubricators, and the driver did not move it to the fully-shut position until the locomotive had come to a stand. On other railways there were separate steam controls for the lubrication system.

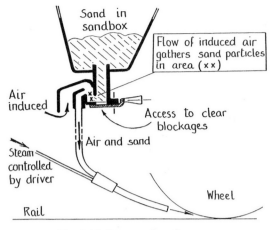

Fig. 3.12 Steam and sanding-gear.

Sanders

Although the application of sand by gravity had been used to improve the adhesion of locomotives from their early days, the invention of the steam-sander in the late nineteenth century enabled several designers to revert to single-wheelers for top-link passenger work. Sand delivered by gravity inevitably falls on the rail well ahead of the wheel concerned, and can then be blown away before the wheel reaches it. Steam-sanders blast it right into the narrow gap between the rail and the wheel. The steam jet works through an ejector similar in principle to that used for the vacuum brake, which induces a flow of air through a port close to the bottom of the sandbox, as shown in Fig. 3.12. The flow of air picks up the sand, taking it down the pipe to the ejector, which then applies it to the rail. In some countries the sand-boxes are mounted on top of the boiler, and look like another dome, but they can be identified by the characteristic shape of the air inlets and pipes leading down from them. In this position the sand is more likely to be kept dry, but any spilt during filling will fall straight into the motion, where it is unwelcome.

The blower

The importance of the blower to stop back-draughts blowing flames from the firebox out into the cab has been mentioned earlier in this chapter. The steam valve for it is accordingly always mounted within easy reach of the driver's position on the footplate.

CHAPTER 4

Using the steam

Principles of valve gears

The vast majority of steam locomotives have made use of the steam generated in their boilers in two or more cylinders. There it drives the pistons backwards and forwards, and the thrust so generated is transferred via the connecting rods to crank-pins on the driving wheels and/or the driving-wheel axle. Clearly, some way of programming the steam supply to the two ends of each cylinder is needed to obtain the required reciprocating motion, and this is the function of the valve gear.

The simplest form of valve-gear was that used by Trevithick for his 'strong-steam' industrial engines, one of which was mounted on wheels to power the world's first steam-hauled train over the Penydarren Tramway in 1804. As shown diagrammatically in Fig. 4.1, it is possible for a two-way cock to supply live steam from the boiler to one end of the single cylinder, and exhaust the 'used' steam from the other. As the piston reaches the end of its stroke, a lug on the crosshead turns the valve from one position to the other, admitting steam to the opposite end of the cylinder and exhausting that already present in the first end. Other early locomotives used a similar system, as does the 1970s reproduction of Trevithick's

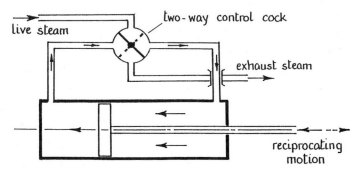

Fig. 4.1 Valve-gear of type used by Trevithick. Dotted line indicates alternative position of two-way cock.

Plate 4.1 On Trevithick's Penydarren locomotive the piston drove a crosshead which moved on two horizontal rods, one of which can be seen in this illustration of the working reproduction. (The second oil reservoir indicates where the other rod is located.) A vertical bracket on the crosshead has a hole in the top through which is threaded the valve-control rod. The position of the two-way control cock is changed each time the bracket hits either of the adjustable stops at end of each stroke. Off the plate in the top right-hand corner is the handle used to operate the valve gear manually.

locomotive, and it works in either direction of travel, giving it the advantage of simplicity as no reversing gear is needed.

However, there is the serious disadvantage that the driver does not know in which direction the locomotive will move when he opens the regulator: that is unless he has made a careful examination of the position of all the parts of motion beforehand. To enable the locomotive to be started in either direction, the automatic valve-change system can be overridden using the hand controls also provided, which enable the driver to do this, albeit with some difficulty if the system has stopped with the crank close to dead-centre.

To overcome the directional problems, as well as to enable the locomotive to restart from whatever position it may have come to rest, two or more cylinders have been provided on virtually every subsequent design. In the interests of symmetry, one would have expected the cranks of a twin-cylinder locomotive to be phased at 180 degrees to each other, but such an arrangement can result in the locomotive stopping with *both* cranks at dead centre—with the connecting rods in line with their cranks. In this position the pistons cannot exert any turning moment on the wheels, regardless of which end of the cylinders steam is admitted. To overcome this, the universal arrangement for twin-cylinder locomotives is for their cranks to be phased at 90 degrees to each other. With double-acting cylinders this gives four power strokes for every revolution of the driving wheels. Later in this chapter we will consider the arrangements adopted with locomotives that were built with three or more cylinders.

Whole books have been written about locomotive valve gears and the development of the earliest locomotives. We cannot go over either story in detail here, but a short account of the way in which these systems developed in the first half of the nineteenth century will provide an insight into their function and operation, as well as the development of various important features.

In 1825, when George Stephenson was building *Locomotion* for the Stockton & Darlington Railway, each of its two cylinders was provided with its own twin-headed valve, capable of admitting and exhausting steam at both ends of its cylinders under the action of the valve-gear. It had been realized that the movements of the valve needed to be phased at around 90 degrees to its piston, and that was achieved by means of an eccentric on one of the axles.

The way an eccentric operates is shown in Fig. 4.2. It is essentially a means of deriving reciprocating motion from the rotation of the axle, which can also be done by a crank (also shown), but, although the latter can provide a longer stroke, it requires a lot more lateral space, and is more difficult to apply if it has to be placed part-way along the axle. An eccentric is a circular disc clamped to the axle, with its centre off-set by

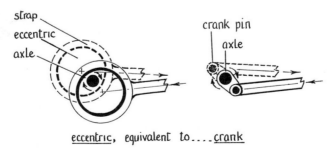

Fig. 4.2 Eccentric and its crank equivalent for converting rotary into reciprocating motion.

half the amount of reciprocating travel needed. Around the periphery of the eccentric a 'floating' strap is located, and is constrained to move only in the required radial direction. As the axle rotates, the output rod attached to the strap moves backwards and forwards, once per revolution of the axle. Unlike a crank, which can be used to transmit thrusts to and from the rod to which it is attached, an eccentric cannot readily be used to make an axle revolve by applying reciprocating forces to its rod. This is because there is a much greater loss of effort through friction between the eccentric and its strap than between the crank-pin and rod.

On *Locomotion*, and its sisters, a very unusual arrangement was adopted, as there were two take-offs from just one eccentric, situated at right angles to each other. In this way each of them was able to operate the valve-gear of one of the cylinders, which were phased with the usual 90 degrees between them. This was an elegant solution, which partly made up for all the complications of mounting the cylinders inside the top of the boiler to keep them warm in the mistaken interest of avoiding the steam in them condensing. This supposed problem had worried the early locomotive engineers, from Trevithick onwards. By the time the Stephensons built *Rocket* for the Rainhill Trials in 1829, the whole layout of locomotives had been simplified by mounting a cylinder on each side of the boiler, although the valve-gear for each still effectively shared a single eccentric on the driving axle.

The eccentric on *Locomotion* is of the 'slip' variety, and is not keyed rigidly to the axle. Its freedom to rotate is, however, limited to half a revolution by 'stops'. Letting the eccentric move through 180 degrees relative to the pistons reverses the valve events, and thus the locomotive's direction of travel. However, the driver has no means of manually moving it from one stop to the other, and the reversal of the valve events only takes place after the locomotive has moved half a wheel-turn in the new direction! Normally the only way round this quandary is for the driver, from his place on top of the boiler, to disconnect the valves and operate them by hand to get the locomotive moving in the new direction. Immediately it has moved the necessary few feet, the valve gear can be re-engaged and allowed to operate normally. (When demonstrating the reproduction locomotive, the ideal operational track is purpose-built with a short rising gradient at each end. After coming to a stand, the locomotive is allowed to roll back by gravity in the opposite direction, which neatly reverses the valve gear!)

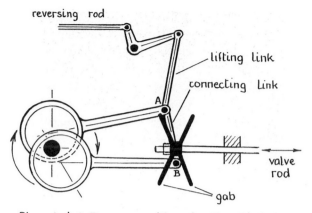

reversing rod

lifting link

connecting link

A

valve rod

B

gab

Pins at A & B engage with gab alteratively, according to direction of travel desired.

Fig. 4.3 'Gab' reversing gear.

Rocket suffered from the same problem, in spite of being fitted with a much more sophisticated valve gear, but the Stephensons quickly went on to adopt the valve-gear known by their name, which was widely used on railways all over the world throughout the steam era. The development took place in two stages. The first move was to provide each cylinder with a pair of eccentrics, one set for 'forward' travel, and the other at some angle greater than 90° from it, for 'reverse'. Neither was directly connected to the valve, but, depending on the direction of travel required, the rod ends were moved vertically so the appropriate one engaged the 'gab' on the valve spindle, as shown in Fig. 4.3. Some time after this arrangement had come into use, the idea occurred to do away with the double-sided gabs, and connect the ends of the two eccentric rods with a curved link. This contained a die-block which operated the valve-spindle, and by raising or lowering the link from the cab, the locomotive could readily be reversed. A general arrangement diagram of the Stephenson gear is shown in Fig. 4.4.

In due course two variants of the Stephenson gear were developed by Gooch and Allan, and known by their names. They varied in the way in which the die-block and link moved vertically relative to each other as the direction of travel was reversed. Gooch moved the die-block rather than the link, and Allan moved both simultaneously, in opposite directions, but the basic method of operation is the same for all three types of valve gear, and all three achieved the same overall effect, albeit with detailed differences in the valve-events obtained.

Plate 4.2 In the United Kingdom, Stephenson's valve-gear has traditionally been installed between the frames of a locomotive, and is thus difficult to photograph. However, it was simple and effective enough for wider use. This example is on a winch manufactured by Clarke Chapman of Gateshead-on-Tyne, and fitted to the preserved Baltic ice-breaker, *Sankt Erik*, dating from 1915. The link is driven by two eccentrics mounted on the main shaft behind the drum on the right, the winch being easily and quickly reversed by moving the link up and down by means of a lever on the cross-shaft.

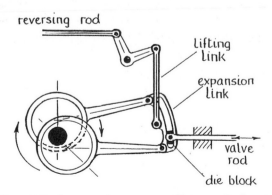

Fig. 4.4 Stephenson valve-gear as used between the frames.

Plate 4.3 An example of Gooch's valve-gear on a Spanish 0-4-0T shunting locomotive displayed outside the new station at Cordoba. The link, with its concave side towards the cylinder, is pivoted at its centre, while the reversing gear moves the valve rod and die-block vertically. The drive for the link is unusual, with one eccentric and one return crank.

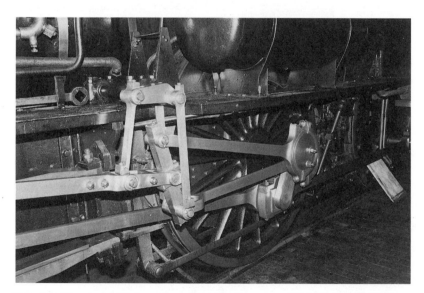

Plate 4.4 Allan straight-link motion as fitted to the preserved Danish Class C 4-4-0 No.708. The link and die move in opposite directions as the gear is reversed. Twin eccentrics mounted on a return-crank are used to drive the gear.

As we will see in more detail later, the introduction of the link provides an infinitely variable transition from full forward to full reverse via mid-gear, at which point there is relatively little movement of the valves. This enables drivers to make significant improvements in

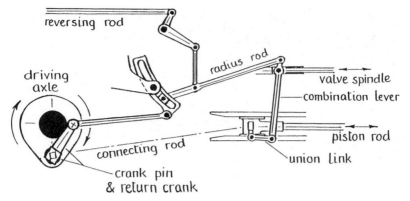

Fig. 4.5 Walschaerts' valve-gear as used outside the frames.

efficiency, by limiting the proportion of the piston stroke for which steam is admitted to the cylinder. When the valve shuts, the steam already present in the cylinder expands and continues to provide thrust. Although the pressure falls somewhat in the process, the effect is to improve the locomotive's overall thermal efficiency. For this reason the link is normally referred to as an 'expansion link'. This will be discussed at greater length in a later section.

As early as 1844, Egide Walschaerts of the Belgian State Railways became dissatisfied with the motion derived from the Stephenson arrangement, and invented his own gear, which more precisely synthesized the valve motion which was required. In its later form, as shown in Fig. 4.5, this has an expansion link which can be driven by a single eccentric, but, as normally used on outside-cylinder locomotives, the eccentric is replaced by a return crank bolted on to the main crank-pin of the driving axle. The die-block is raised or lowered to reverse the locomotive, but the radius rod it operates is not directly connected to the valve spindle, but is joined to the 'combination lever'. The latter is connected, at its bottom end, via a 'union link' to the cylinder's crosshead, and, as its name implies, it combines the motions of the radius rod and crosshead, applying the result to the valve spindle. Walschaerts' gear has been widely used throughout the world, particularly on locomotives with outside cylinders, being rugged in construction and capable of providing the steam inlet and exhaust events required for high cylinder efficiencies.

Many different types of valve gear have been used at different times on steam locomotives, but lack of space makes it necessary to concentrate

Plate 4.5 Walschaerts' valve-gear as used on the WD 2-10-0 *Longmoor*, seen on exhibition in the Utrecht Railway Museum. As referred to in Chapter 5, two five-feed syphon oil-boxes can be seen on top of the foot-framing, as well as the corks sealing the twin oilers on the top of the combination lever.

our further studies on the Stephenson and Walschaerts' types, plus Joy valve-gear, as well as certain of the poppet-valve designs, one of which was used on a number of LMS and BR Standard locomotives towards the end of the steam era in the UK.

Slide-valves

We must now look at the design of the actual valves used to admit steam to the cylinders and then exhaust it to the blastpipe. For our point of view there are two main types of these—slide-valves and piston-valves—the two designs being compared in Fig. 4.6.

Although piston-valves were used occasionally in early locomotives, there were manufacturing reasons why slide-valves were used more extensively until the beginning of the twentieth century. In its simplest practical version, the slide-valve has a cross-section like an inverted U, the two legs having the equivalent of serifs on them, as shown in the upper diagram of Fig. 4.6. When the valve is in its central position, the width of these serifs completely covers the ports, which are connected to the two ends of the cylinder. The valve is contained in the valve-chest, which is filled with live steam when the regulator is open. Movement of the valve in one direction will thus admit steam to one end of the cylinder and allow any in the other end to escape to atmosphere via the

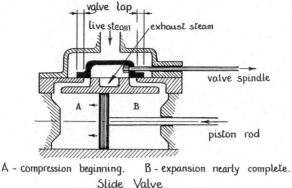

A - compression beginning.   B - expansion nearly complete.

Slide Valve

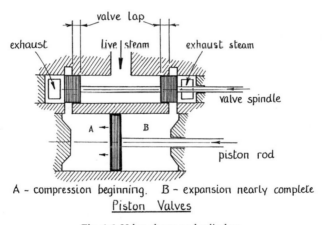

A - compression beginning.   B - expansion nearly complete

Piston Valves

Fig. 4.6 Valve-chests and cylinders.

blastpipe. Originally the valves were dimensioned to work as on Trevithick's locomotive, with steam being admitted to the cylinder for the whole of each piston stroke without any expansion, and immediately allowed to escape as soon as the piston reversed. This made it highly inefficient.

To improve the efficiency of using steam in the cylinders, the outside edges of the 'serifs' are extended to provide 'lap', as shown in the upper diagram in Fig. 4.6. This ensures that, after the valve has stopped admitting steam to the cylinder, the release of the steam to atmosphere is delayed, enabling advantage to be taken of its expansion. To compensate for the period when the lap prevents steam entering the cylinder, the stroke of the valve has to be increased. An efficient valve gear thus has a

Plate 4.6 The sectioned cylinder and valve-chest of the reproduction *Rocket* built for the Science Museum in the 1930s. To avoid the generation of excessive pressures between the valve faces, the lengths of slide-valves are quite short. This necessitates long steam passages to the ends of the cylinders, which can cause inefficient heat losses between the alternate flows of live and exhaust steam.

long lap and long travel relative to the width of the cylinder's ports. In addition, the angle of the eccentrics driving the Stephenson valve gear has to be advanced materially from 90 degrees to ensure that the admission of steam still takes place at around dead-centre.

When a locomotive with 6-ft (1800 mm) diameter driving wheels is travelling at 60 mph (100 km/h), they are rotating at nearly five revolutions a second. This means that the steam has to enter each end of the cylinder in a fraction of a tenth of a second. To build up the steam pressure in the cylinder quickly at the beginning of each power stroke, the lap dimension is reduced without making any corresponding alteration in the valve-gear dimensions, which initiates the process fractionally before the piston reaches the end of its travel. This is called *lead*. A corresponding modification, called exhaust clearance, is occasionally applied to the exhaust side of the valve, and is sometimes erroneously referred to as 'exhaust lap'.

The working face of a slide-valve is kept in contact with the cylinder casing by the steam pressure on the steam-chest side. With the regulator fully open, there is thus a considerable force on the 'back' of a slide-valve, which increases the wear on it as well as on the port-face of the steam-chest. The force needed to move the valve to and fro is also increased, putting an extra load on the valve-gear. On occasions the reversing gear can clatter quite badly as a result of these forces, which can be transferred back to the cab. It is thus standard practice for the driver of a slide-valve locomotive to shut the regulator before any alteration is made to the reverser's setting. This is particularly important when the gear is reversed by a lever, rather than a screw, there being a

Plate 4.6A As will be seen from Plate 4.6, the piston of the 1930s *Rocket* reproduction was fitted with a number of beautifully-machined, wide metal rings. Sixty years later the remains of the original locomotive were examined in detail at the National Railway Museum, and it was found that the pistons consisted of nothing more than a pair of metal discs, the gap between them being filled with turns of some sort of rope!

Plate 4.7 The right-hand cylinder of the sectioned 'Merchant Navy' locomotive in the National Railway Museum, showing the double-headed piston-valve and the more direct steam ports between the valve-chest and the cylinder possible with piston-valved locomotives. Originally these locomotives were provided with a chain-driven valve-gear mounted between the frames. This moved the outside-admission piston valves by means of a rocking-arm between the heads. When the locomotives were rebuilt, the hole in the inside surface of the steam-chest for the drive to the valves was sealed with a square-headed plug. The valves were then driven through conventional glands in the valve-covers.

possibility that the driver may not be strong enough to cope with the forces involved once he has lifted the catch holding the lever stationary.

Slide-valves do have the slight advantage that they will be lifted off their faces if the pressure in the cylinder rises too high, if, for example, water becomes trapped. This allows it to escape, albeit with the risk of bending the valve spindle! Various ways have been tried to overcome these disadvantages of slide-valves, but the complications were not worthwhile, particularly after the development of the piston-valve, which provides a much more satisfactory arrangement.

Piston-valves

As shown in Plate 4.7, the modern piston-valve is shaped like an overgrown 'dumb-bell' that was once used for body-building exercises. It has a number of 'split-rings' on each head to provide the necessary steam-tightness, and these work in the same way as the piston-rings in a car. Piston-valves have several advantages over the older slide-valves. To start with, the surfaces exposed to steam pressure are balanced, so there is no increase in the forces required to move them when the regulator is opened to admit steam to the valve-chest. The heads can also be fixed well apart, thus shortening the length of the steam passages that lead into the cylinder ends, and, at the same time, making them more direct. This reduces the pressure-drop as the steam enters and exhausts. The resulting smaller surface area of the passages also reduces the exchange of heat between the two flows. This is an advantage because the colder steam being exhausted after expansion removes heat from the surrounding metal, which, in turn, cools the incoming steam at the start of the next stroke, thus wasting energy and reducing the cylinder's thermal efficiency.

With slide-valves, the spindle used to operate them has to enter the steam space in the valve-chest, and so has to pass through a stuffing-box capable of withstanding full boiler pressure. Piston valves are normally arranged for inside-admission, so the stuffing-boxes at the end of the valve-chests only need to withstand exhaust-steam pressures. However, in their rebuilt form, the Bulleid Pacifics have retained the outside-admission piston valves which were originally provided, when they were operated by rocker arms between their heads in the centre of the steam-chest. This arrangement avoided the need for stuffing-boxes in the end covers, so outside-admission was adopted. When the locomotives were rebuilt it was considered undesirable to change the steam-passages in the cylinders, so the same piston valves were used, but were moved by spindles from the orthodox Walschaerts' valve-gear, which still provided outside admission. Modern forms of packing used in the stuffing-boxes have satisfactorily prevented losses of steam.

Piston-valves have the disadvantage that they cannot automatically 'lift', like the slide variety, to release any trapped water. Cylinders thus have to be fitted with relief-valves on their covers, and drivers must assist the process by using the manually-operated drain-cocks if they become aware that this is occurring. (If the steam-operated type is fitted, they will be forced open automatically.) Piston-valves have in the past been

Stephenson's valve-gear for inside cylinders

Clearances often make it difficult to accommodate Stephenson's valve-gear for locomotives with inside cylinders, and various different solutions have been adopted to solve the problem.

Plate 4.8 On North Eastern Railway 4-4-0 No. 1621 the drive from the valve-gear to the valves, as well as the centre-line of valves, is inclined to cylinders, with the front higher than the rear. This is a typical solution adopted when this type of gear is used for valves positioned above the cylinders.

Plate 4.9 Another alternative with inside Stephenson's valve-gear is for the valve-chests to be mounted below the cylinders, as on the preserved Great Eastern 0-6-0 No. 8217 at the National Railway Museum. Even then the installation is not straightforward, as forgings have to used on the drive to the valves to avoid the leading coupled-axle. To allow the wheel-set to be removed, the forgings are constructed to enable them to be detached quite easily.

designed with integral relief-valves, but these are difficult to inspect and keep clean, and can leak steam from the live to the exhaust side if carbonization prevents them closing fully.

Types of valve gears

Stephenson's valve-gear

Stephenson's valve-gear has the benefits of simplicity and compactness, and it can easily be installed between the frames of an inside-cylinder locomotive. It should not be forgotten that, in the UK, over half the locomotives built for the mainline railways were 0-6-0s, and the majority of them had two inside cylinders. As late as 1930 Collett introduced his '2251' class, and the last of them were constructed in BR days, while all 289 of Gresley's J39s, dating from 1926, passed into BR service in 1948. The first of these designs had Stephenson's valve-gear, as did the vast majority of other UK 0-6-0s. Similarly, just after nationalization, more small shunting locomotives were required for the Eastern and North Eastern Regions, so Darlington Works built nearly 30 Class J72s to Wilson Worsdell's 1898 design, which were also provided with Stephenson's valve-gear.

There is much to commend the inside-cylinder layout for twin-cylinder steam locomotives. The combined cylinder and valve-chest casting makes a useful 'spacer' for the front-end of the frames, but the maximum size of cylinders is limited by the distance between the running rails. In post-Brunel UK, the total width available is 4 ft $8\frac{1}{2}$ in (now mainly metricated at 1435 mm although there are slight differences in some parts of the country), and from this must be deducted the thickness of the wheel flanges, and the clearance from the frames, as well as the thickness of the frames themselves. When account is taken of the wall thicknesses of the cylinder castings, the maximum bore diameter that can be accommodated between the frames is approximately 20 in (510 mm). When more cylinder power than this is needed, it becomes necessary to accept the added complications of multi-cylinder design, with two outside cylinders, and one or two between the frames.

This width limitation was not the first cause of the decline of the popularity of the Stephenson gear, as the original layout had both slide-valves between the cylinders, with their faces vertical. The steam-chests thus took up some of the limited width between the frames, and to make room for larger cylinders the valves had to be mounted on top or underneath the cylinders. This made the drive to them less direct, sometimes requiring the use of rocking-levers of some sort. An alternative way of accommodating the drive when the valves are on top of the cylinders is to incline the valve-chests upwards towards the front, which means that the steam passages at that end of the cylinder are much longer. The layout problem became still more acute when it was desired to adopt piston-valves, because these occupy more width than the steam-chests for slide valves.

There have, nevertheless, been other benefits from the use of the twin inside-cylinder design. As well as the valve-gear, most of the motion can be accommodated inside the frames, which conformed to Victorian engineering tenets of hiding as many moving parts of a machine as possible, although coupling rods could not be put inside. The top half, at least, of the driving wheels was kept behind splashers, which, like the statutory mudguards on cars, stop drops of dirty water being flung into the air. Some railways went even further, and, by adopting outside frames, banished nearly the whole of each wheel from view. The strength of this aesthetic aim to hide most of the working parts was perhaps exemplified longest with the Great Western, which put the valve-gear on its locomotives between the frames, even those which had outside cylinders. It did, however, spring a final surprise, when its final batch of ten 0-6-0 pannier tanks, which did not appear until 1949, were discovered to have outside cylinders and outside Walschaerts' valve-gear.

There were two other factors which caused railways to switch from inside to outside locations for cylinders. At one period crank-axle breakages became a matter for concern on certain railways, but better materials and design stopped this being a long-term limitation. Rather more persistent was the increasing diameter of boilers, which made it more difficult to lubricate and inspect the motion from above, through the narrow gap between the bottom of the boiler cladding and the top of the frames. Even this access was further restricted on side-tank locomotives when greater water capacity was needed, although a few designs were provided with cut-outs in the tanks. This work was hard enough in depots, where pits were available to enable the driver to get underneath; the job was even more frustratingly difficult on the frequent occasions when it needed doing during a stop or layover in a station.

Once it has been decided to put the cylinders outside the frames, the advantages of Stephenson's valve-gear become less. Positioning a pair of eccentrics outside the coupling and connecting rods is more clumsy and takes up more lateral width. One of the few modern attempts to do this was with the LMS Class 5MT No.44767, which, after being preserved, was appropriately named *George Stephenson* during the 1975 Stockton & Darlington celebrations.

Joy's valve-gear

Joy's gear was used in the UK by several railways, but is best known for its widespread adoption by Webb on the London & North Western Railway from 1880. The advantages it gave him were that it enabled the steam-chests to be put above the cylinders, and still retain a fairly direct drive for the valves. It also avoided having to occupy some of the width of the driving axle with four eccentrics, making space available for him to increase the size of the axle- and big-end bearings on his new express goods locomotives.

As shown in Fig. 4.7, with Joy gear the motion of the valves is derived from the movement of the connecting-rod. This is modified by the inclined movement of a sliding block in the expansion link, which is turned backwards or forwards to reverse the direction of travel.

Joy's gear was classified as a 'radial', rather than a 'link' type, such as Stephenson's or Walschaerts'. It did, however, produce valve events which were very similar to the latter, with the relationship between the geometry of the gear and valve-lap being clear and direct. These terms will be discussed in the description of Walschaerts' gear in the next section.

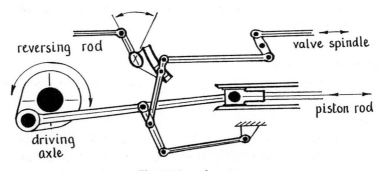

Fig. 4.7 Joy valve-gear.

The weakness of Joy's gear was due to two factors. The first was that the blocks were constantly moving up and down in the expansion link, which added to the loss of energy needed to drive the valve-gear. This, in turn, exacerbated the weakening problem posed by the hole required in the middle of the connecting-rod, which was already a highly-stressed component, so fractures were not infrequent. As a result, Joy's valve-gear fell out of favour, and it never became a widespread competitor to Stephenson's.

The valve-gear situation in 1913 was summed up by A. R. Bell, the Director of *The Locomotive Magazine*, who wrote in *Modern Railway Working* as follows:

> So far as Britain is concerned, the Stephenson link motion has reigned supreme, although Joy's radial gear had some vogue and the Allan straight-link motion has also been in use. With the advent of the large modern boiler, however, accompanied as it was by the practice of driving off axles other than the leading, came the much more extended use of the outside position for the cylinders, and this in turn has led to a growing disposition to employ the Walschaert (*sic*) gear. But here again the native conservatism of British locomotive engineers receives further illustration, and the advantages to be derived from its use are admitted with considerable hesitancy in the minds of many. However, the gear has obtained a firm footing on the Great Western, London and South-Western, Great Northern, London Brighton and South Coast, and in the north of Ireland, and it is easy to foresee a much extended employment in the near future. The Walschaert gear...was first brought prominently into notice by reason of its introduction by Egide Walschaert on the Belgian railways some sixty years ago. But although it made its appearance in this country in 1882, and in 1890 was utilized in the Worsdell–von Borries two-cylinder compounds for the Belfast and Northern Counties line, very little was heard of it until the purchase of the Great Western de Glehn compounds and the advent of the rail motor car. There is now every reason to believe that the gear will soon be adopted as standard practice with the larger types of engines quite irrespective of whether the cylinders are placed inside or outside the framing.

Walschaerts' valve-gear

Walschaerts' valve-gear differs fundamentally in operation from the Stephenson arrangement, as shown diametrically in Fig. 4.5, with an exploded view in Fig. 4.8. The link containing its die-block is similar in both cases, but, by giving it a central pivot on a bracket attached to the framing, only a single eccentric, or, more usually, a return crank, is needed to drive it. This is attached to the bottom of the link, so with the

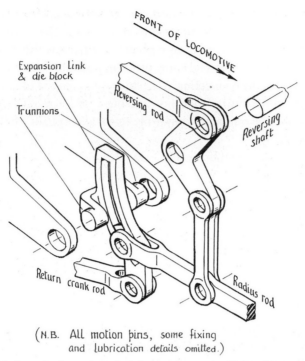

Fig. 4.8 Walschaerts' valve-gear: exploded view of expansion-link and its connections.

pivot half way up, the top is 180 degrees out-of-phase with the lower end, which provides the necessary reversing ability. If the die-block were to drive the valve-spindle direct, it would virtually be a variant of the old Trevithick gear, but the introduction of the combination lever between the link and the valves alters things fundamentally. As the bottom of this lever is driven in phase with the piston, the overall effect is to combine a small component of in-phase motion with the usual 90 degree drive from the eccentric or return-crank. This causes the valves to 'dwell', or pause, at each end of their stroke, enabling the vital times when they are open to inlet and exhaust to be extended. Vector diagrams, as shown in Fig. 4.9, demonstrate the fundamental difference in the way in which Stephenson's and Walschaerts' gears derive the motion for their valves.

It is less easy to fit Walschaerts' valve-gear between the frames, because it is more demanding on lateral space than Stephenson's, particularly with the need to accommodate the combination lever, and align it with the valve-chest. It is necessary to provide one eccentric, rather than a return-crank, to drive the link. Nevertheless the GWR, when it designed

Great Western Railway valve-gear for locomotives with two outside cylinders

For many locomotives with two outside cylinders, Churchward used Stephenson's valve-gear mounted between the cylinders.

Plate 4.10 This photograph gives an impression of the heavily-constructed valve-gear on the GWR heavy-freight 2-8-0 No. 2818, preserved at the National Railway Museum.

Plate 4.11 Each half of the valve-gear drives an inclined link which connects with a rocking-shaft mounted on top of the frames.

Plate 4.12 The outside arm of the rocking-shaft is connected to the valves by a horizontal rod close to the underside of the foot-framing.

In spite of all these complications the GWR gear gave good steam distribution to and from the cylinders, as evidenced by the very regular exhaust beat of their locomotives.

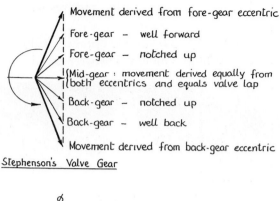

Movement derived from fore-gear eccentric

Fore-gear – well forward

Fore-gear – notched up

Mid-gear : movement derived equally from both eccentrics and equals valve lap

Back-gear – notched up

Back-gear – well back

Movement derived from back-gear eccentric

Stephenson's Valve Gear

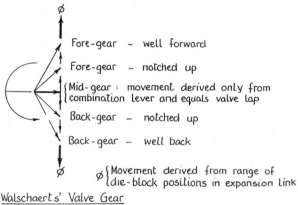

Fore-gear – well forward

Fore-gear – notched up

Mid-gear : movement derived only from combination lever and equals valve lap

Back-gear – notched up

Back-gear – well back

ø {Movement derived from range of die-block positions in expansion link

Walschaerts' Valve Gear

Fig. 4.9 Vector diagrams showing how valve-spindle movements are derived.

its four-cylinder express locomotives, adopted inside Walschaerts' gear, and continued to use this arrangement until its final days. (Rocking-levers were used to drive the valves for the outside cylinders, and we will be discussing the principles of derived-gears generally later in this section.)

As a result of the provision of the combination lever, the valve-events with Walschaerts' gear can be made very different from those with Stephenson's arrangement. Table 4.1 shows the differences in forward gear between a GWR 'Hall' with inside Stephenson's valve-gear, and a BR 'Britannia' with outside Walschaerts'. It will be seen that the GWR, by using the Stephenson gear's inherent characteristics, caused the lead to decrease as the cut-off was lengthened. At long cut-offs, used only

Table 4.1 Valve-gear events[1]

| GWR 'Hall' | | | | | | | | BR 'Britannia' | | | | | | |
| Internal Stephenson valve-gear[2] | | | | | | | | Outside Waelschaerts' valve-gear[2] | | | | | | |
Nominal cut-off (%)	Valve travel (ins)	Lead (ins)	Opening to steam (ins)	Steam cut-off (%)	Release (%)	Compression (%)		Nominal cut-off (%)	Valve travel (ins)	Lead (ins)	Opening to steam (ins)	Steam cut-off (%)	Release (%)	Compression (%)
Full	6.91	−0.17	1.65	77.2	94.2	94.2		78	7.75	0.25	2.03	79.2	93.8	92.2
75	6.75	−0.14	1.58	75.9	93.5	93.5		75	7.25	0.25	1.81	76.5	92.9	91.0
70	6.29	−0.09	1.36	72.2	91.9	91.9		70	6.63	0.25	1.53	72.0	91.3	89.1
60	5.58	−0.01	1.02	63.4	88.7	88.7		60	5.69	0.25	1.08	62.1	87.7	85.0
50	4.99	+0.06	0.71	51.6	83.9	83.9		50	5.03	0.25	0.78	51.2	83.6	80.6
40	4.57	+0.10	0.53	40.2	79.3	79.3		40	4.56	0.25	0.56	40.2	79.2	67.2
30	4.28	+0.13	0.39	29.4	73.6	73.6		30	4.51	0.25	0.22[3]	29.6	74.0	71.5
25	4.15	+0.14	0.33	24.7	71.0	71.0		25	4.16	0.25	0.38	24.2	70.8	67.8
20	4.05	+0.16	0.28	19.3	67.5	67.5		20	4.06	0.25	0.33	19.3	66.9	65.5
15	3.95	+0.16	0.24	15.5	64.1	64.1		15	3.54	0.25	0.28	14.2	62.2	61.8
Mid	3.83	+0.18	0.18	6.0	-	-		Mid	3.88	0.25	0.25	7.1	51.0	52.1

Source British Railways Test Bulletin No.1 (1951)

Source British Railways Test Bulletin No.5 (1953)

Notes:
1. The quoted figures are for the Forward Stroke, and there were some slight differences between these and those for the Backward Stroke.
2. The openings for the 'Hall' were quoted in inches and decimals, but those for the 'Britannia' were given in inches and fractions to the nearest sixteenth.
3. There was a large difference between the measured openings quoted for the Forward and Backward Strokes.

when a locomotive is travelling slowly, lead is not necessary as there is plenty of time for the steam to enter the cylinder, and there is no possibility of early entry of steam before the piston reaches the end of its travel, which could increase the back-pressure and so reduce the tractive effort. GWR two-cylinder locomotives were thus said to be well-equipped for slogging up the steep banks to be found in the West of England, and performed better than their four-cylinder sisters with Walschaerts' gear. They also had a tendency to over-compression at the end of the exhaust stroke, which explains some of the steam emissions from the locomotives' cylinders in the frontispiece.

Baker gear

In the latter days of steam traction Baker valve-gear was used on many north American locomotives, and is a variant of Walschaerts'. As shown in Fig. 4.8, the expansion link and its die-block, as used on an orthodox Walschaerts' installation, is complicated to make, and therefore expensive in first cost. In addition, wear between the link and the die-block affects its accuracy.

As an alternative, Baker used a number of simple swinging links to achieve the same result, connected at their ends with pin-joints, which were much easier and cheaper to construct, and the wear was a lot less. Although the pin-joints could easily be grease-lubricated, in later versions they were replaced by sealed needle-roller bearings which required even less servicing and maintenance attention.

The operation of the Baker valve-gear is not easy to follow without the aid of a working model, but the basic principles can be understood by means of a simplified diagram. As shown in Fig. 4.10.1, there are three links (A, B, and C), which in mid-gear and mid-stroke lie roughly parallel to each other. Link A is attached to the locomotive's frames at its bottom end, and at the other is connected, by means of a pin-joint (E), with the reversing rod and Link B. At the other end of Link B there is a similar pin-joint (F) connecting it with the Return-Crank rod and the bottom of Link C. At G there is a pin-joint between Link C and a bell-crank, pivotted on the frame, which drives the equivalent of the radius rod on Walschaerts' gear.

When the locomotive is in mid-gear, as shown in Fig. 4.10.2, the movements of the return-crank rod simply cause Links B and C to swing backwards and forwards without moving the radius rod. If the reversing rod is moved, pin-joint E is moved in the direction the driver wishes the

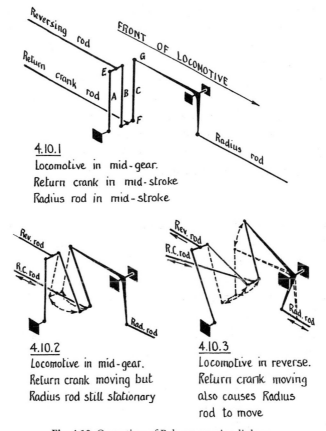

Fig. 4.10 Operation of Baker expansion linkage.

locomotive to travel. Fig. 4.10.3 shows it fully reversed, so, with the return crank moving backwards and forwards, pin-joint G now rises and falls, and the bell-crank causes the radius rod also to move back and forth, thus supplying steam to the correct end of the cylinder to make the locomotive move in the required direction. The amount of valve-travel can be varied as needed by 'linking-up' the reverser, in exactly the same way as with other valve-gears.

In practice, the link arrangements have to be somewhat more complex, as they are replicated on either side of a vertical plane, as shown in Fig. 4.11. This is to prevent any torsional forces on the pin-joints.

Derived gears

It is not always necessary to provide a set of valve-gear for each cylinder on a locomotive. In the case of most four-cylinder designs, the pairs of

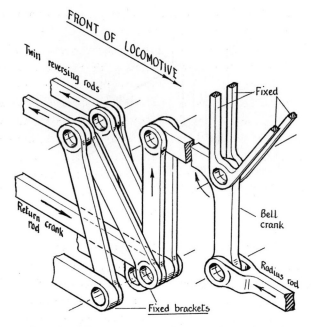

Shown in full reverse gear, return crank rod forward
and radius rod rearward.

(N.B. All motion pins & some fixing & lubrication
details omitted.

Fig. 4.11 Baker expansion linkage as applied to Walschaerts' valve-gear.

pistons on the same side of the locomotive are set at 180 degrees to each
other. The movements of their valves will also be out-of-phase by the
same angle, and one of them can therefore be connected to the other by
a rocking-lever instead of being provided with a separate valve-gear of
its own. The GWR used this arrangement extensively on its four-
cylinder designs, the two sets of gear being between the frames. To
divide the drive between the front and middle axles, the inside cylinders
are mounted further forward than the outside ones, and the rocking-
arm connects the spindle at the rear of the inside cylinder with the front
of the outside one. Because of the angularity of the connecting rod, the
required valve events at rear end of the cylinder have to be slightly
different from those at the front. This presents a problem with the GWR
rocking-arm arrangement, but Churchward compromised neatly by
putting the pivot slightly in front of the line connecting the pins at the
two ends of the lever. The photograph of the rocking-lever on the

preserved *Lode Star* shows this feature clearly, together with the fittings provided for making micro-adjustments to set the valves.

A similar system, the other way round, was applied in 1947 to one of the Stanier 'Princess Royal' Pacifics, No. 6205 *Princess Victoria*. In this case the outside Walschaerts' gear additionally drove the inside cylinders by means of rocking-levers in front of the outside valve-chests. This made it harder to adjust the valve events when the locomotive was cold, because the expansion of the outside valve spindles as they heated to working temperature altered the valve events of the outside cylinders. Another form of derived gear had been used on some other Crewe locomotives thirty or so years earlier. A few of Bowen-Cooke's 'Prince of Wales' 4-6-0s were fitted with outside valve-gear which drove the inside valves by means of rocking-levers. This prompted the locomotives to be nicknamed 'Tishies' after a race-horse of the time which had the unfortunate habit of crossing its legs during a race!

Probably the best-known derived or 'conjugated' gear is that for three-cylinder locomotives used by Gresley. It is usually known by his name, although the basic principle was worked out by Holcroft. In its most frequently-used form, Gresley provided a set of Walschaerts' gear for each of the two outside cylinders. The right-hand valve-spindle is also linked to a long lever, which is pivoted to the locomotive's frame at a point corresponding to two-thirds of its length, as shown in Fig. 4.12. This is known as the 2:1 ('two-to-one') lever, and at its shorter end carries a pivoted 1:1 lever. The free end of the latter is driven by the other outside valve-spindle, and the inner end drives the valves for the centre cylinder, its motion being at 120 degrees to both the outside cylinders. The vector diagram for this is also shown in Fig. 4.12.

In its more usual form, Gresley's conjugated gear is mounted in front of the cylinders, which presents the valve-setters with a similar expansion problem as that on *Princess Victoria*. There is a further snag with this arrangement, as the two levers are positioned just below where the char is shovelled out of the smokebox. Although protection is provided, if the small door required for lubrication-access to the end of the 2:1 lever gets left open, and the seals on the individual pin-joints are not fitted properly, some of the droppings will get into the bearings and cause abrasion. Initially there was also a tendency for the 2:1 lever to 'over-run' at the high speeds which were frequently achieved by the Pacifics and Class V2 2-6-2s in regular service. This distorted the valve events so that the middle cylinder was doing much

Cylinders and valve-gear on GWR 4-6-0 Lode Star (Built in 1907)

Inside and outside cylinders on the same side of a 4-cylinder locomotive could be driven by the simplest type of derived gear, one version being extensively used on the GWR four-cylinder locomotives.

Plate 4.13 The rocking-lever connecting the inside valve-gear to the outside cylinder (left). The piston-rod for the inside cylinder can be seen through the access hole in the main-frame. An 'syphon' oil reservoir is provided where the valve-spindle emerges from the outside steam-chest. The snifting-valve is mounted inboard, between the cylinder and valve-chest covers. This admits air to the cylinder and valve-chest when the locomotive is coasting to avoid any possibility of combustion gases or ash being drawn into them from the smokebox.

Plate 4.14 The fine-adjustment and locking arrangement on the intermediate link used when setting the outside valve. Note the disc-shaped copper bearings between the polished steel components.

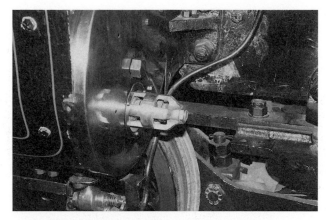

Plate 4.15 Relief valve on the front cylinder cover.

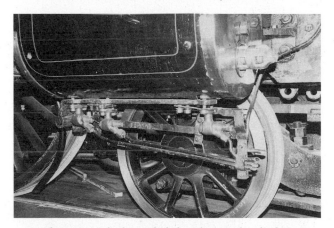

Plate 4.16 Cylinder-cocks below the outside cylinder.

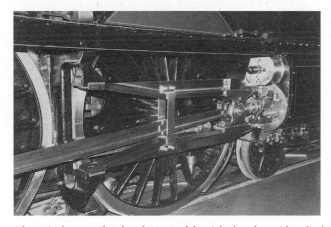

Plate 4.17 The twin-bar crosshead at the rear of the right-hand outside cylinder.

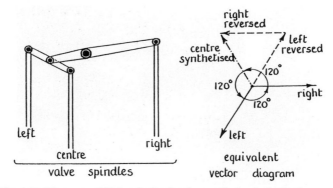

Fig. 4.12 Diagrams of Holcroft–Gresley three-cylinder derived valve-gear.

more than its fair share of the work, and was sometimes blamed for causing the overheating of the middle connecting-rod big-end. All these problems got worse during the rigours of World War II, and, after Gresley's death, Thompson modified examples from several of his predecessor's classes and removed the 2:1 gear, while he and his successor fitted three separate sets of valve-gear to their own Pacific designs. On one design of North American locomotive which also used the 2:1 gear, the equipment was far more massive, each of the levers having cross-sections approximately the size of those of connecting rods in this country!

A very different location for the 2:1 gear was used with the D49 4-4-0s in 1927. It was positioned *behind* the cylinders, as all three of these were in line and drove on the leading coupled axle. This was a much better arrangement, as it avoided the expansion problem, and all three sets of valve gear were parallel with their cylinders. In addition the conjugated motion was kept well away from any smokebox char.

When running, locomotives with Gresley's conjugated valve-gear frequently produced an exhaust beat with a very characteristic syncopated three-beat rhythm. As described later, this was not caused by the inclination of the centre cylinder on some of the classes.

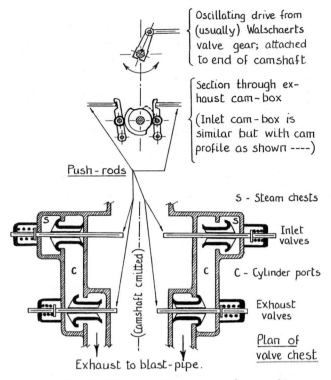

Oscillating drive from (usually) Walschaerts valve gear; attached to end of camshaft

Section through exhaust cam-box

(Inlet cam-box is similar but with cam profile as shown ----)

Push-rods

S - Steam chests

Inlet valves

(Camshaft omitted)

C - Cylinder ports

Exhaust valves

Plan of valve chest

Exhaust to blast-pipe.

Fig. 4.13 Oscillating-cam (OC) poppet-valve assembly.

Cam-driven valve-gears

In the 1920s considerable interest developed in the use of cam valve-gears, one of the main advantages being that they separated the inlet and exhaust events. If required they could drive individual inlet and exhaust valves, rather than having the one valve perform both functions from the opposite sides of the same valve-head. In their simplest form, 'oscillating cams' (OC) were used, usually being operated by Walschaerts' valve-gear. Figure 4.13 shows the way in which the separate exhaust and inlet valves at each end of the cylinder were operated. For a short period six of Gresley's D49s were fitted with this form of gear.

Designers moved on from the OC system to the 'rotary cam' (RC) arrangement, which did not rely on a conventional valve-gear for its primary actuation. Instead, a cam-shaft was provided which ran laterally across the locomotive above the cylinders. Gresley used this system on no less than 40 of the D49s, all of which were named after fox-hunts which operated in the area served by the LNER. A small gearbox

Plate 4.18 Oscillating-cam valve gear, driven by Walschaerts' motion, on Landeseisenbahn Lippe 2-8-2 tank No. 931410, seen on the Exertalbahn in 1993.

on the right-hand side of the locomotive was driven by a return crank mounted on the leading coupled axle, and the output from this was taken forward to the cylinders by a rotary shaft. Here it drove the cam-shaft through bevel gears, its rotation being synchronized with the rotation of the driving axles. Each cylinder was provided with a group of cams which drove the inlet valves, and a single cam for the exhaust ones. A group was made up from several separate cams, each with a different profile corresponding to a particular direction of travel and cut-off. The driver's reversing gear selected the profile to be brought into use, but, unlike locomotives with conventional valve-gears, the cut-off was not infinitely variable. Initially only five different settings were provided in forward gear, but on a later batch this was increased to seven. One of the class was subsequently fitted with a different gear which gave an infinitely-variable cut-off.

After World War II this work was to lead to a more versatile design of RC valve-gear, and some LMS Class 5s, followed by thirty similar BR Standard locomotives, were fitted with such gears, in addition to the sole BR-designed Pacific, *Duke of Gloucester*. In these designs, one or two cam-shafts were driven in a similar way to that on the 'Hunts', but the camboxes were very different in concept. Each cylinder has two inlet cams and a single exhaust one. The rotary position of the inlet cams

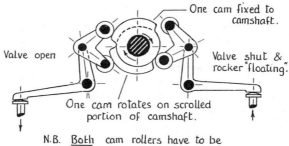

One cam fixed to
camshaft.

Valve open

Valve shut &
rocker "floating".

One cam rotates on scrolled
portion of camshaft.

N.B. <u>Both</u> cam rollers have to be
forced outwards to open their valve.

<u>Inlet cams and rocking cam-followers.</u>

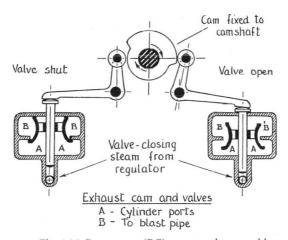

Cam fixed to
camshaft

Valve shut

Valve open

Valve-closing
steam from
regulator

B B
A A

B B
A A

<u>Exhaust cam and valves</u>
A - Cylinder ports
B - To blast pipe

Fig. 4.14 Rotary-cam (RC) poppet-valve assembly.

relative to the drive shaft is controlled by means of a scroll on the shaft,
along which two collars are moved when the driver operates his
reversing wheel, as shown in Fig. 4.14. The exhaust valve is opened by a
single cam and 'follower', while the inlet valve has a swing-beam with a
pair of followers, one running on each of the two inlet cams. In the
direction of rotation, the position of these two cams can be altered by
the movement of the sheaves. One of these is arranged to open the inlet
valve, and the other to close it, and by varying the amount of overlap
between the cams, the cut-off can be continuously varied over the full
range between full forward and full reverse gear.

Tests showed that the use of this gear improved the thermodynamic
performance of the Class 5 locomotives compared with those of the

same class fitted with Walshaerts' gear. As originally fitted to the LMS locomotives, the exhaust cams were incorrectly profiled, and opened their valves too early, which reduced the output and produced a fierce exhaust blast from the chimney. Many drivers tended to set the cut-off to give what they considered was the right degree of exhaust noise, and they would, as a result, link the motion up further than would have been the case with a comparable locomotive fitted with Walschaerts' gear. The scale on the reversing-gear had also been calculated incorrectly, so drivers who used this to set the cut-off, also linked it up too far. As a result, the locomotives got a reputation for being sluggish in their performance. Both faults were identified when indicator diagrams were taken during tests, and were duly corrected.

The Pacific's gear was similarly criticized for its sharp exhaust in service. When the locomotive was withdrawn, its cambox was placed on exhibition in the Science Museum, after being sectioned to show the working of this up-to-date steam locomotive fitment. Eventually the locomotive was rescued from the scrap-yard and restored, the successful manufacture of a new cambox being one of the most ambitious tasks undertaken by a preservation society. A slight alteration was made to the exhaust-valve cam profiles, and the locomotive has since behaved impressively on charter specials, having lost its previous epithet of 'The Fiery Duke'. In Autumn 1995 it made a record ascent of Shap, out-performing both the A4 and 'Duchess' Pacifics on comparative runs a few days apart, thanks to the detailed modifications made by its new owners.

Whenever the regulator is open, Caprotti-type valves are held closed by steam pressure until opened by the cams. This makes the locomotive very free running when steam is shut off, but, unfortunately, the valve stems can become coated with carbonized oil after some time in service, giving them a tendency to stick open. This has been known to result in the locomotive moving off in the wrong direction if the regulator was opened when the boiler pressure was low, to the detriment of the walls of more than one locomotive depot!

Cylinders

The locomotive's cylinders are where the energy in the steam from the boiler is converted into thrust to drive it and its train along the track. They consist of fairly complicated castings, and are usually made integral with their valve-chests. While inside cylinders used to be cast in two pieces and then joined through the centre of the steam-chest, later designs were cast in one piece. With some locomotives, as many as four cylinders and their steam-chests were all cast together, while the final North American practice was to cast the cylinders integrally with the frames when foundry technology had progressed to this stage. Most outside cylinders were cast separately, but nearly always they had integral steam-chests, although, again, US practice was to include half the smokebox saddle in each casting. The same arrangement was also adopted by Churchward for his two-cylinder GWR locomotives.

The casting process requires the prior production of wooden patterns which are used to make the moulds. These can be extremely complicated, and those for each of the cylinders cast in 1997 for the Great Western Society's 'Saint' had three main sections, several of them over six feet (1.8 m) long. As the patterns are removed from the mould before casting takes place, they can be reused, but each cylinder also needs a number of cores which are inserted into the mould to provide the various steam passages, etc., in the final casting. These stay in their correct places when the molten iron or steel is run in, but later have to be 'knocked-out' of the casting, so are expendable. The patterns have to be oversize to allow for the subsequent shrinkage of the casting in each direction by approximately one-eighth of an inch per foot (one per cent) as it cools.

In view of the complicated patterns needed, most railways adopted some degree of standardization to enable the same patterns to be used for both left- and right-hand cylinders, as well as interchanging them between classes. Some other countries tended to be more advanced with this practice than the UK, which had an unexpected result in World War II after British troops had liberated Iran. The retreating Germans thought they had immobilized their steam locomotives by blowing off one cylinder on each, but those on both sides were identical. So, by cannibalizing half the fleet, the rest were made operable.

Cylinders are heavy items. Each of the two cast-iron cylinders for the GWS 'Saint', with their steam-chests and half-saddles, weighed just over 2 tons 12 hundredweight (2670 kg). By latter-day North American standards these were lightweight, as each of those for a typical Lima 2-8-4 weighed over $11\frac{1}{2}$ tons.

After the cylinder has been cast, a considerable amount of machining is needed before it is mounted on its frames. Although during a major

Class A1 Pacific *Tornado* under construction at Darlington in 1997

Plate 4.19 A rear view of the locomotive's left-hand cylinder-block. The diameter of the valve-chest appears to be over-large, because the cylinder itself is hidden within the casting, and only the gland for the piston-rod is visible. The substantial bracket nearer the camera is required to support the slidebars from the main frame, enabling them to take the vertical thrusts produced by the angularity of the connecting rod.

Plate 4.20 Viewed at this angle, the duct for the exhaust steam from the valve-chest can be seen as it starts on its way through the main-frame to reach the blast-pipe in the smokebox. The integral bracket to attach the slide bars to the cylinder-block can also be seen.

Plate 4.21 A view of the locomotive's right-hand cylinder-block from the front, providing a true comparison between the diameters of the steam-chest and cylinder. It will be noted that far more studs are required to secure the cylinder-cover in place, compared with that on the valve-chest. This is because the cylinder can contain steam at full boiler pressure, whereas the outer ends of the valve-chest are connected to the blast-pipe. One of the entry-ports for steam to the end of the cylinder can also be seen at about '1 o'clock', while the hole for the rear cylinder-cock is visible at the bottom of the bore.

Plate 4.22 A view of the rear-end of the locomotive's inside cylinder mounted between the frames. The valve-chest is off-centre, because the driving-crank occupies the centre of the space between the frames, and so displaces the independent set of valve-gear to the left. An off-set position like this was also noticeable from the front of many classes of locomotive, because the chest cover was left exposed to permit the valve to be withdrawn in the forward direction for examination.

overhaul any of a locomotive's cylinders needing reboring would be dealt with *in situ*, with new castings it is easier to carry this work out before they are attached to the frames. The rough castings also require precision machining in many other places, to take the various attachments, such as steam-pipes and the end-covers. The latter require a considerable number of studs to hold them on, as every stroke they are subjected to the same forces as the piston. There are 20 such studs around the periphery of the front of the 19-in (483 mm) outside cylinders on the newly-built A1 Pacific *Tornado*, but only six are needed at the end of the steam-chest immediately above it. This is because the latter, although having a diameter two-thirds that of the cylinder, contains valves with inside admission, so its outer ends are connected to the blastpipe, and are not subjected to steam at full boiler-pressure.

The cylinder block is normally constructed so the pistons and valves can be withdrawn from its front end. At the rear the corresponding cylinder opening will be considerably smaller, as this is where the gland has to be provided to withstand full boiler pressure during the forward power strokes of the piston. At one time it was customary to fit pistons with 'tail-rods' at their front ends, which similarly passed through a gland in the cover. These were a throw-back to the early days when the position of the cylinders on stationary engines changed from vertical to horizontal, when there was considerable concern that their bores would wear oval. Care was thus taken to support the piston at both ends, but the irregular wearing of the bore never seems to have been a major problem. It is difficult, therefore, to understand why this feature continued to appear for so long on steam locomotives, particularly on the European continent, because piston heads usually incorporate a spring-loaded phosphor-bronze pad to take their weight. A tail-rod required the provision of a second gland, as well as the machined rod moving through it, and it was not always straightforward finding space for the lengthy protuberance at the front of the locomotive. Having a rod at each end of the piston did ensure that the area on which the steam acted, and hence the thrust, was identical for both strokes, but the cross-section of a two-inch diameter rod is only about one per cent of that of an 18-in diameter cylinder, which means that the correction is minimal.

Holes also have to be bored in the cylinder castings to enable them to be bolted to the frames, and these fastenings have to withstand the same traction thrusts as well as the weight of the casting. Other holes are

Plate 4.23 This 1912 Royal Bavarian State Railway S³/₆ᵉ Pacific is exhibited in the transport museum at Nuremberg. The housings for the tail-rods on the pistons of its four cylinders are very prominent. It is a compound, being designed for a boiler pressure of 230 lbf/in² (16 bar), and exhausted to the blast-pipe at 17 lbf/in² (1.2 bar).

required for fitments such as the cylinder-cocks, and the covers have holes for the relief-valves. Most of these are spring-operated, but some are kept closed by an auxiliary steam supply when the regulator is open, so will operate whenever the pressure in the cylinder rose above that in the boiler.

All this precision work makes the task of manufacturing cylinders lengthy and expensive, so it is clearly desirable to ensure that they have a long working life. This means it is necessary to provide adequate lubrication for all moving parts, which requires the provision of suitable holes in the casting to deliver the oil from the lubrication system which will be described in Chapter 5.

Proper lubrication can lengthen the time between successive rebores, but cannot completely eliminate the need for them, so the design of these castings should provide plenty of wall thickness for the cylinder and steam-chest. This enables several rebores to take place when needed. As a result, various members of the same class frequently had different cylinder diameters. When the GWR was building the 'Kings', its officers were anxious to be able to claim that the new locomotives had, not only a higher tractive effort than any other railway's express locomotives in this country, but one that exceeded the 'magic' figure of 40 000 lbf (178 kN). They started with the figure of 31 625 lbf for the 'Castles', and increased the boiler pressure from 225 to 250 lb/in², (15.5 to 17.3 bar), as well as reducing the driving-wheel diameter from 6 ft 8½ in to 6 ft 6 in (2045 to 1981 mm), but this still was not quite enough to top the 40 000 lb-mark. They accordingly bored the cylinder out by an extra ¼ in, which did the trick. However, when new, only the first of the class, *King George V*, actually had cylinders this size. The rest remained at 16 in (406 mm), like those for the 'Castles'. (The significance of tractive-effort figures will be discussed later.)

In later years, techniques have been developed to insert liners into the cylinder castings when successive rebores have increased their diameter as far as can be permitted. To do this, the liner is turned so that its outside diameter is a few thousandths of an inch larger than the bore into which it is to be inserted. The liner is then cooled by immersion in liquid nitrogen, which causes it to shrink sufficiently to be inserted. Once in place it warms up, and the expansion fixes it firmly. The fitter has every incentive to get it into exactly the right position because there is no way in which it can be freed again once it has warmed up. This is not an easy job when handling an item at −196 °C.

The pistons in the cylinders have to be as steam-tight as possible to minimize losses, and eventually this was ensured by the use of several split rings as used on automotive pistons. It took a remarkably long time for these to be generally adopted, the 'Royal Scots', for instance, being provided with a single broad ring when they first appeared in 1927. These wore quite quickly and allowed steam to leak past, increasing the coal consumption appreciably. Other, more complicated, ring assemblies were used by other railways, which were, in theory, self-sealing under steam pressure. The piston is usually a hollow disc, suitably fixed to the piston-rod.

Expansion

When the efficiency of steam locomotives is being discussed, their ability to benefit from the expansive properties of steam is always stressed. This is thus an important subject which we will now look at in some detail.

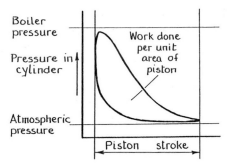

Fig. 4.15 Typical cylinder indicator-diagram.

We are unable to see what is happening inside many of the important parts of a working steam locomotive, which includes the main pressure-vessels—the boiler and the cylinders. Conditions in the latter are constantly changing during each revolution of the driving wheels, but, from an early stage in the development of steam technology, it was found possible to chart what was happening in the cylinders by obtaining 'indicator diagrams'. The equipment has a pen which is moved up and down by the pressure from a small tapping through the end-cover in the cylinder. This makes a trace on a chart which is oscillated horizontally by a link from the piston, giving diagrams like that shown in Fig. 4.15.

The area inside the figure traced out by the pen represents a force (pressure × piston area) multiplied by distance (stroke), so is proportional to the work done. By integrating the area in the experimentally-obtained diagrams, the useful mechanical energy being obtained from the steam can be measured for any set of operating conditions. If the duration of each cycle is also measured, the power (rate of doing work) being produced in the cylinder can be calculated. Although first developed for stationary engines, this system was adapted for use on locomotives, and continues to be employed by owners who are interested in how their machines are behaving. The conditions facing those who had the job of obtaining diagrams out on the road were somewhat daunting, as they had to work in a special shelter constructed around the smokebox to protect them and their equipment during the tests.

Figure 4.16 shows some idealized diagrams of this sort, to illustrate how the cylinder pressure, and the work performed, can vary under

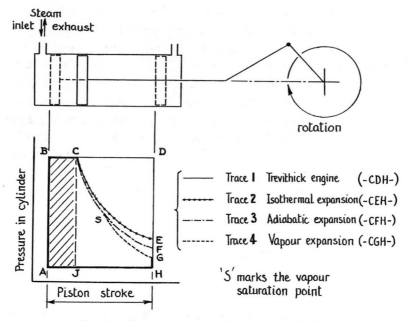

Fig. 4.16 Various steam expansion-modes in cylinder.

different operating conditions. With Trevithick's valve arrangements, the inlet valve is opened at the beginning of the stroke (A), when the crank is at dead-centre. This immediately raises the pressure in the cylinder to that of the boiler (B), neglecting any pressure-drop in the steam passages. As shown by Trace 1, this is maintained until the end of the power stroke (D), when the exhaust valve opens, immediately discharging all the steam to atmosphere. Pressure in the cylinder falls to a little over atmospheric (H), and remains there until the crank reaches dead-centre again (A). In this particular case, the average pressure on the piston throughout the power stroke—referred to as the Mean Effective Pressure (MEP)—is theoretically the same as the boiler-pressure related to atmospheric, as measured by an ordinary pressure gauge.

Operating in this way is wasteful as it makes no use of steam's expansive properties. It is still at full pressure when released to the blast-pipe, and thus contains much more energy than that needed to take it (and the flue gases) up the chimney. However, before going further it is vital to appreciate that steam is not unique in this respect—every gas and vapour exhibits the same basic property. Because steam is a vapour rather than a gas (i.e. is in a condition when it could be liquefied by pressure alone), it can at times not perform as well as air would if it were being used as the working fluid, and had entered the cylinders at the same pressure and temperature. The difficulty with a *gas* is that it has to be compressed as well as heated to reach the same starting conditions, which was a very inefficient process compared with turning water into steam inside a closed pressure-vessel by simply applying heat. Hot, high-pressure, air as a working fluid only became a serious rival to steam after the development of the technology which enabled it to be generated and utilised in gas-turbine engines.

The Gas Laws relate pressure, volume and temperatures for a perfect gas by the following equation:

$$\frac{\text{Pressure} \times \text{Volume}}{\text{Temperature}} = \text{Constant}$$

or

$$\frac{P \times V}{T} - R.$$

From this one can see that, for example, if the volume of a given quantity of gas is doubled at a constant temperature, the pressure will halve. Similarly, if the temperature were to go up by 10 per cent at constant pressure, the volume would increase by the same amount. When using this equation one has to make sure that the units employed are absolute ones. So, for pressure we must add the standard atmospheric pressure (14.7 lb/in^2 or approximately 1 bar) to whatever figure is shown on the pressure-gauge. The temperature also has to be on an absolute basis, usually referred to as the Kelvin scale, the zero of which is –273 °C (or –460 °F).

This equation can be used to calculate the fall in pressure in a cylinder when expansion takes place after the inlet valve has closed. Trace 2 shows what happens when the cut-off is takes place, for example, at 25 per cent of the stroke (C). Up to that point the pressure in the cylinder still equals that in the boiler, but, when the valve closes, it immediately starts to fall, as shown. When the piston has completed its stroke, the steam which was originally filling 25 per cent of the cylinder space has expanded to fill four times that volume. The equation shows that its pressure will have fallen to a quarter, as at E. Similar calculations can be carried out for the intermediate stages of the stroke, to give the series of points making up Trace 2. Exhaust takes place at point E, when the piston completes its stroke, and pressure falls to H. (For simplification in this example we have ignored any clearance volumes at the ends of the cylinders, and have assumed that the steam remains at a constant temperature.)

It will be seen that, although the total area and the MEP have both decreased, the area ABCEH is obviously much greater than 25 per cent of that of Trace 1, which would be represented by the shaded area ABCJ. Only 25 per cent of the quantity of steam has been used and the work represented by the area CEHJ has been obtained *gratis* from the expansion.

However, the ideal Gas Laws only apply with a perfect gas, and Trace 2 only applies when changes take place infinitely slowly, with the gas maintaining the same temperature. During any real-life expansion process the temperature actually drops. (The reverse effect is what causes a bicycle-pump to get hot when one is blowing up tyres.) Sudden expansion like this, without any external heat input, is said to take place 'adiabatically'. So instead of being able to use the formula to calculate the pressure drop in inverse ratio to the increase in volume, we must also take account of the decrease in temperature. This has been done to obtain Trace 3, which shows that the pressure falls somewhat more steeply after the cut-off point. Although this means that the improvement in efficiency is not quite as large as predicted by the Gas Laws, it is still worthwhile.

Using steam, which is a vapour rather than a gas, to drive the pistons produces a further complication. It is possible that the combined decreases in pressure and temperature can take the steam below its saturation point, and condensation will begin. As liquid water occupies a lot less volume than the same mass of steam, this will cause the pressure to fall further than calculated from the previous equation. Trace 4 indicates what would happen if saturation conditions are reached at some intermediate point, (S). Consequently, if the condensation point is reached during the expansion stage, the MEP will be somewhat lower still, but there is nevertheless still a considerable efficiency advantage over the original 'Trevithick' arrangement.

Steam below saturation point is referred to as being 'wet', and in these conditions heat losses through the walls of the cylinder can increase rapidly. When dry steam is in contact with a cool surface, heat transfer is limited by the conduction rate through the vapour, which is not very high. Once the temperature has fallen below saturation point, the steam close to the relatively-cool walls is immediately turned to water as soon as it touches the surface. The resulting local drop in pressure will quickly cause the vapour to expand, and more will come into contact with the cylinder walls. In another context, Watt's stationary engines very effectively removed a considerable quantity of saturated steam during each stroke of their large cylinders using quite small condensers.

The same effect can be seen in reverse in many industrial processes which involve the evaporation of water from solutions by the use of steam in some form of heat-exchanger. Unless arrangements are made for this steam to remain saturated under all operating conditions, the

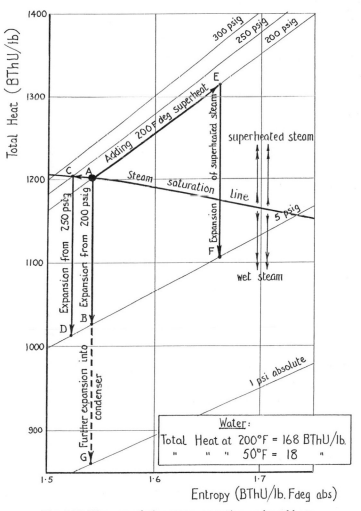

Fig. 4.17 Diagram relating steam expansion and total heat.

overall evaporation rate will drop significantly whenever it becomes superheated. Without the aid of condensation, the heat-transfer rate drops in spite of the actual steam temperature increasing.

The importance of steam to produce motion of one sort or another has resulted in a lot of experimental measurements to quantify how it behaves under different conditions. The resulting tables and graphs can be used, at the design stage, to predict how a proposed system will work. One such steam diagram is given in Fig. 4.17, which is so arranged that the likely operating changes are all shown by straight lines, making them easy to plot. This, and the calculations which follow, are in Imperial units, because these were used by most English-speaking engineers during the heyday of the steam locomotive. For those more familiar with metric units, Table 4.2 gives both sets of figures for all the quantities concerned, including the temperatures.

We have chosen a hypothetical locomotive which uses feed water at 50 °F to produce saturated steam (Point A) at a pressure of 200 lbf/in² gauge (psig), which means it is 200 psi above normal atmospheric pressure. In the cylinders this steam is expanded adiabatically to 5 psig (Point B), this being the pressure needed to enable the exhaust to force its way through the blastpipe and out of the chimney. The total heat, in British Thermal Units (BThU), added to a pound of water to make the same mass of saturated steam is:

$$1201 - 18 = 1183 \text{ BThU/lb.}$$

During expansion, the heat turned into useful work is:

$$1201 - 1026 = 175 \text{ BThU/lb.}$$

Table 4.2

Point	Pressure*		Temperature		Total heat		Entropy	
	(psi)	(kN/m2)	(°F)	(°C)	(BThU/lb)	(kJ/kg)	(BThU/lbF°)	(kJ/kgK°)
A	200(g)	1379(g)	388	198	1201	2792	1.541	6.451
B	5(g)	34.5(g)	227	108	1026	2385	1.541	6.451
C	250(g)	1724(g)	406	208	1203	2798	1.522	6.372
D	5(g)	34.5(g)	227	108	1012	2354	1.522	6.372
E	200(g)	1379(g)	588	309	1314	3056	1.661	6.954
F	5(g)	34.5(g)	227	108	1107	2575	1.661	6.954
G	1(a)	6.9(a)	102	39	861	2001	1.541	6.451

* (g) = gauge, (a) = absolute

as shown by the length of the line A–B in the steam diagram. The best possible efficiency of a cylinder operating under these conditions is

$$175 \div 1183 = 14.8 \text{ per cent.}$$

If we were to increase the boiler pressure to 250 psig, still without superheating, the heat content of steam in the boiler rises, as shown by the line A–C, but the increase is only 2 BThU/lb. However, we can now expand the steam appreciably more, from C to D on the diagram, which yields a useful work output of 191 BThU/lb. The maximum cylinder efficiency thus rises to

$$191 \div 1185 = 16.1 \text{ per cent.}$$

This is a modest, but useful gain, but it has to be off-set against the additional costs involved in constructing and maintaining the higher-pressure boiler. In practice, for locomotives there is an optimum in the range 200–300 psig. The curve is fairly 'flat', which explains why other factors, rather than scientific rigour, have traditionally influenced the actual pressures adopted by designers.

The second variation we can test is to superheat the steam by 200 °F while retaining the 200 psig boiler-pressure. This moves the starting point from A to E, and requires an additional heat input of

$$1314 - 1201 = 113 \text{ BThU/lb.}$$

The maximum useful work obtained from this starting point is given by the line E–F, which is

$$1314 - 1107 = 207 \text{ BThU/lb.}$$

This makes the cylinder efficiency

$$207 \div (1183 + 113) = 16.0 \text{ per cent.}$$

Once again a modest gain over the base conditions has been achieved, albeit at the expense of providing a set of superheater tubes in the boiler, and giving lubrication specialists the challenge of developing oils which can withstand higher temperatures. On balance, superheating is a major advantage without introducing too much complication or new technology. It thus became the choice for locomotives other than those intended for intermittent work like shunting duties, which does not require long spells of effort. (Superheaters require some time to reach their effective working temperature.)

A third variation we can explore from the diagram is to preheat the boiler feed water, using the heat which would otherwise be wasted in the hot exhaust gases. If we were able to raise the feed water temperature to 200 °F, this saves 150 BThU/lb, so the total heat required to produce saturated steam at 200 psig becomes

$$1201 - 150 = 1051 \text{ BThU/lb.}$$

Recalculating the maximum cylinder efficiency we get

$$175 \div 1051 = 16.7 \text{ per cent.}$$

This is again a worthwhile improvement over the base conditions, but the question that then arises is, 'Can the feedwater be preheated without burdening the locomotive with new problems?' There are various possibilities, the obvious first one being to fit a 'feedwater preheater', which was tried by Gresley on several classes. A considerable number of the Great Eastern 4-6-0s which had been built by Holden were provided with the French AFCI system, which involved fitting a tandem steam pump on the running plate, together with two heat-exchangers on top of the boiler. The latter fitments were said to have prompted the locomotives' nickname, 'Hikers', although others maintain this came from the long distance the firemen had to carry each shovelful of coal from the tender to the fire-hole! Feedwater heaters of this sort were widely used on the continent of Europe and in North America, but were not extensively adopted in the UK, partly because of the smaller loading-gauge.

The steam injector itself, described in Chapter 3, provides a certain amount of preheating, compared with the use of a mechanical feed-pump. However, the live-steam type takes steam straight from the boiler, so does not improve the thermal efficiency. On the other hand an exhaust-steam injector reuses much of the heat in the waste steam, which means that it does provide an overall benefit, but again there are added complications which resulted in this form of injector only being fitted to locomotives likely to work hard for relatively long periods.

Another method for preheating the feedwater, tried in the UK at the end of the steam era, was the Franco-Crosti system. As fitted to a number of the Class 9F 2-10-0s, the smokebox gases were diverted through a multi-tubular heat-exchanger, positioned below the main boiler drum. Unfortunately, under some operating conditions the exhaust gases from the grate were cooled to well below their dew-point and condensation occurred. The droplets then dissolved acid-forming gases from the exhaust, which badly corroded parts of the structure, and led to maintenance costs out of all proportion to the saving in fuel. The chimney, situated just in front of the cab on the right-hand side, was not in a popular location for the footplate crews either.

A fourth system we can look at is to expand the steam to a much lower pressure, as for example shown by the line A–G on the steam diagram, but this requires a condensing system to get it below atmospheric pressure. While such systems are universally applied at electrical generating stations, it is much harder to accommodate an adequate condenser on a locomotive which has to be mobile and whose size is constrained by the loading-gauge. The only locomotive condensing systems which became, at best, partially successful, were not primarily intended to improve the thermal efficiency. Apart from the use of condensers to improve environmental conditions in tunnels, such as those on London's Inner Circle, they were fitted either to enable water to be conserved in arid areas, or to prevent a tell-tale exhaust plume which could seen by enemy aircraft.

Ideal indicator diagrams would be somewhat different from that shown in Fig. 4.16, and would resemble that shown by the full lines in Fig. 4.18. At IC the inlet valve closes, and expansion continues to EO, when the exhaust valve starts to open. This takes place slightly before the end of the stroke, as time is needed for the steam, being at a relatively low pressure, to flow out of the cylinder and force its way through the blast pipe and chimney, into the atmosphere. For this reason the pressure never falls to atmospheric, and useful work is lost at the bottom of the diagram throughout the return stroke, which prompts designers

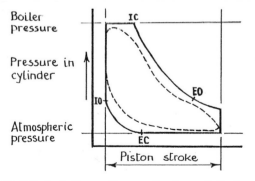

Fig. 4.18 Cylinder indicator-diagram, showing typical valve events.

to aim at reducing the back-pressure to the lowest possible level without jeopardizing steam production. At EC, appreciably before the return stroke is completed, the exhaust valve closes, and the remaining steam in the cylinder is then compressed to the point IO, at which the inlet valve reopens and the cycle begins all over again.

A diagram like this would only be obtained at low speeds, and, when a locomotive is running faster, the corners get rounded off, as shown by the inner dotted lines, because the time available for each of the steam flows decreases. The shape is also affected by the design of the valve-gear, which cannot provide exactly the right valve events at all speeds and cut-offs. To give an idea of what is actually achieved, Fig. 4.19 shows indicator diagrams for an 'Austerity' 2-8-0 running at 30 and 40 mph (48 and 64 km/h), with 23 per cent cut-off in each case. The diagrams at the higher speed look 'thinner' because the greater losses of steam

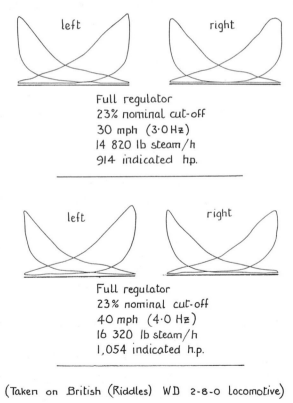

left   right

Full regulator
23% nominal cut-off
30 mph (3·0 Hz)
14 820 lb steam/h
914 indicated hp.

left   right

Full regulator
23% nominal cut-off
40 mph (4·0 Hz)
16 320 lb steam/h
1,054 indicated h.p.

(Taken on British (Riddles) WD 2-8-0 locomotive)

Fig. 4.19 Examples of locomotive indicator cards.

pressure entering and leaving the cylinders reduce the amount of work produced per cycle. The locomotive was nevertheless generating 1054 hp (786 kW) compared with only 914 hp (683 kW) at 30 mph because it was making 33 per cent more power strokes in a given time. Scaling from the published indicator diagram at 40 mph, one can calculate that the locomotive was achieving a pressure ratio of approximately 8.0, much greater than the expansion ratio of about 4, because of the rapid drop in pressure after the exhaust valve opened.

When the valve-gear is 'linked-up', reference is made to the driver using 'such and such a percentage cut-off'. In Fig. 4.18 this is represented by the point IC, and the cut-off is the ratio of its distance from the pressure axis, expressed as a percentage of the full stroke.

The relationship between the cut-off and the expansion ratio is affected by the 'clearance volume' in the cylinder. This is the totality of the free internal space between the piston at the beginning of its stroke and the valve-head. It is also affected by the point at which the exhaust valve opens. We will consider a cylinder having a clearance volume of 5 per cent of the swept volume, with a valve-gear which is cutting-off at 25 per cent and opening to exhaust at 85 per cent of the stroke. This means that there are 30 volume units (25 + 5) of steam in the cylinder at the moment the inlet valve closes, and they will have expanded to 90 units (85 + 5), when released to exhaust. The expansion ratio is thus

$$90 \div 30 = 3.00,$$

rather than 4.00 as one would at first imagine. If the clearance volume of the cylinder is 10 per cent, then, under the same conditions, the expansion ratio would be:

$$95 \div 35 = 2.71.$$

This represents a reduction of just under 10 per cent in the ratio, which is still further removed from the figure of 4.00 which one would have expected.

As implied above, the outer trace in Fig. 4.18 cannot be achieved in practice for several reasons. The first is due to the imperfections of the valve-gear, and another is the time taken for the steam to flow through the small ports as they are uncovered by the valves, while the possible partial condensation of the steam has already been mentioned. The four critical points in the cycle are as follows.

Inlet valve opening (IO)

Admission of steam should begin just before the piston reaches the end of its stroke, the point referred to as front or back dead-centre with locomotives, which is equivalent to 'top dead-centre' in automotive parlance. This is done to ensure that the pressure in the cylinder has built up well before the piston has moved significantly along the bore. It is likely, however, that full boiler pressure is not reached inside the cylinder, and the actual trace takes the form of the inner dotted curve.

Inlet valve closing (IC)

Similarly, the inlet valve does not close instantaneously, and starts to throttle the flow of steam before the nominal cut-off point is reached, the effect being known as 'wire-drawing'. This is a function of the valve design, being worse with short-stroke valve movements and small steam ports—poor design of these parts can seriously reduce a locomotive's power output. An example of this was provided by the GWR's 'Achilles' class single-drivers, some of which were converted from Broad Gauge 2-2-2s. Figure 4.20, from the third impression of J. W. Heyward's 1906 book, *First Stage Steam*, shows three different indicator diagrams taken with No.3013 *Great Britain* at about the turn of the century. Trace A was 'at full gear, B at $\frac{1}{2}$ full gear and C at $\frac{1}{6}$ full gear', the latter two corresponding to approximately 40 and 15 per cent cut-offs respectively. It will be seen that while plenty of steam got into the cylinder with the two longer cut-offs, there was very bad wire-drawing at 15 per cent, which, as with the 'Austerity' locomotive diagrams shown in Fig. 4.19, would have seriously reduced the power output.

These GWR locomotives were nevertheless noted for their fine performances, the most outstanding being the 1904 run of *Duke of*

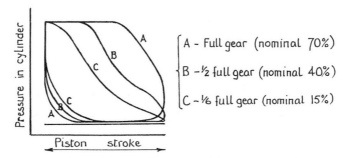

Fig. 4.20 Effect on indicator card of shortening cut-off.

Connaught, after it had taken over the Ocean Mail special at Bristol from *City of Truro*. The single-wheeler averaged no less than 71.2 mph to Paddington, with a maximum of 87 mph at Maidenhead. The locomotives were not fitted with superheaters, so the *Duke* would probably have been worked with a partially-open regulator, which gave a degree of superheating. (The pressure-drop that occurs as steam flows past a partly-open regulator reduces its pressure energy, but, as no external work has been performed, no energy has actually been lost from the system. The lost pressure-energy is thus converted into superheat.) A correspondingly late cut-off would be needed to compensate for the lower steam-chest pressure, so, in all probability it would have been working at a cut-off longer than that at which the wire-drawing became significant.

Superheated locomotives should normally be driven using full regulator, with the driver adjusting the required power output by varying the cut-off. Most well-designed modern locomotives with Walschaerts' valve-gear, including Gresley's A4s, traditionally did their best running on the level with a nominal cut-off of about 15 per cent. With all valve-gears there is a characteristic minimum figure which should be used practically, for reasons which will be mentioned when we discuss the closing of the exhaust valve. When power requirements are low, the driver has to close the regulator partially to avoid the use of cut-offs shorter than this minimum.

French work on the thermodynamics of steam locomotives in the twentieth century showed that, not only was it was necessary to avoid wire-drawing at the inlet valve, but generously-sized pipework was needed throughout the steam circuit. When Chapelon increased the power output of one of the French 1912 Pacifics by 85 per cent, the changes of this sort made twice the contribution to the improved drawbar efficiency compared with that provided by higher superheat.

Exhaust valve opening (EO)

The steam from the cylinder should be exhausted as late as possible to prolong the expansion, but it must begin sufficiently early to allow it to be flowing out freely by the time dead-centre is reached. As a result, the pressure starts to fall at EO, as shown by the dotted line, and it has still not dropped to the back-pressure level until after the return stroke has commenced.

Exhaust valve closing (EC)

The piston will continue to push steam out of the cylinder against the back-pressure from the blastpipe during the return stroke, but the exhaust valve should close early enough to trap sufficient steam in the cylinder to ensure that the resulting compression has increased the pressure well towards that in the boiler by the time the inlet valve opens at IO. This reduces the amount of steam needed to fill the clearance volume, as well as decreasing the shock when a charge of high-pressure steam enters a low-pressure space. The trapped steam also acts as a cushion to slow the movement of the piston as it approaches dead-centre.

This is the point where difficulties can arise from the interdependency of the inlet/exhaust events which is inevitable with ordinary valve-gears. At short cut-offs, Stephenson's gear is inclined to close the valve to exhaust somewhat early, which can lead to over-compression, sometimes to well over boiler pressure. In extreme cases the cylinder relief-valves could be operating every stroke. For this reason it was not customary to link-up locomotives with Stephenson's gear below a setting of about 25 per cent nominal. On the other hand, as just described, Walschaerts' valve-gear on the A4s and other equally well-proportioned locomotives worked satisfactorily at a nominal cut-off of 15 per cent.

We have seen that the efficiencies of reciprocating steam locomotives are relatively low, and for this reason they are sometimes adversely compared with other steam-powered prime-movers. The reason is that the constraints on locomotives means they can only employ a relatively-limited pressure range, whereas larger static power plants are able to utilize more extreme conditions.

The data in Table 4.3, extracted from Fig. 4.17, demonstrate how much more significant expansion ratios are than actual pressure drops.

The first stage of this expansion makes available only 6 per cent more heat than the second, even though the actual drop in pressure is more than 10 times as large. The second stage, however, has twice the expansion ratio, so, although the expansion ratio does not exactly equate with the heat given up as mechanical work, it has a closer relationship with the power output. The lack of proportionality is due to the effects of condensation, as the whole of the line A–G lies in the wet-steam zone.

With static steam-powered turbines, far higher expansion ratios can be obtained, and the generous space available in a modern steam

Table 4.3

Point on Fig. 4.17	Absolute pressure psi (bar)	Heat content BThU/lb (kJ/kg)	Pressure drop psi (bar)	Heat change BThU/lb (kJ/kg)	Expansion ratio
A	215(14.82)	1201 (2792)			
			195 (13.44)	175 (407)	10.75
B	20 (1.38)	1026 (2385)			
			19 (1.31)	165 (384)	20
G	1 (0.07)	861 (2001)			

power station permits the use of multi-flow steam circuits, with larger cross-sections, and steam is returned to the boiler for reheating between several of the expansion stages. The size of the turbine wheels has to increase as the pressure falls, and the limiting design factor can sometimes be the need to avoid the blade-tips of rotors reaching supersonic speeds. Turbines have another important advantage compared with reciprocating engines. Steam flows through them in one direction only, so steady-state temperature profiles are established. With reciprocating pistons, the flows of inlet and exhaust steam, at different temperatures, are alternately in contact with the cylinder walls and steam passages. This inevitably leads to heat transfer from the high-temperature inlet steam to the low-temperature exhaust, and can even result in alternate condensation and re-evaporation.

In a multi-stage steam turbine, the pressure at the steam stop-valve can be as high as 2400 lb/in^2 (163 bar), and some very advanced installations operate above the critical pressure and temperature, where water becomes indistinguishable from steam, at 3206 lb/in^2 (218 bar). Even with these installations, it is surprising how few stages it has to pass through before its pressure falls below atmospheric. Some five-stage turbines driving compressors at a chemical factory in the north-east used to take steam at 250 lb/in^2 (17 bar), and discharge it to condenser vacuum. They achieved an expansion ratio of approximately 4 at each stage, so, after the second stage turbine, the pressure was below atmospheric. From that point onwards it was necessary to prevent the ingress of air, rather than the escape of steam. Because air cannot be condensed, the inevitable small quantities that did get in had to be removed by other means. If allowed to accumulate they put up the 'sink' pressure, which reduced efficiency. Overall the expansion ratio of these five-stage turbines was about 1000.

A twin-stage compound steam locomotive with a 250 lb/in^2 (17 bar) boiler discharging to the blastpipe at 5 lb/in^2 (0.34 bar), would apparently achieve an overall ratio of 50, but, when one uses absolute pressures, the ratio drops to just over 13, as given by

$$(250 + 15) \div (5 + 15) = 13.25.$$

It is the low-pressure end which provides so much of the expansion and really low pressures are only feasible with a condenser. Dropping the condenser temperature by a few degrees is more useful than a corresponding increase in the steam inlet temperature. A modern steam generating station achieves an overall thermal efficiency approaching 50 per cent—a lot more than the 12 per cent or so which is the best efficiency which has been achieved with a steam locomotive. This is one of the reasons why so much modern railway traction is provided electrically.

Compounding

To reduce the temperature drop (and the corresponding heat losses) across a locomotive's cylinders, it is possible to share the overall expansion required from a simple reciprocating engine by using the steam sequentially in a pair of cylinders. This is known as 'compounding', and the process can, in theory, be carried out using a number of cylinders in series, although, on locomotives, space considerations normally restricted compounding to two stages. Figure 4.21 shows the pressure/stroke diagrams for a two-stage compound, but, with a locomotive, the increased amount of work obtained in this way from a given quantity of steam is not all that great, because of two particular constraints. The first is finding space for a sufficiently large cylinder, or cylinders, at the low-pressure stage. Secondly, there is the problem of the locomotive being able to start its train. To obtain the required tractive effort, some means usually has to be provided to admit high-pressure steam to the low-pressure cylinder(s), as well as bypassing any exhaust from the high-pressure one(s) straight to the blastpipe. These arrangements are needed until the train has reached about 15–20 mph, at which point compound working can commence. Such an arrangement is complicated to

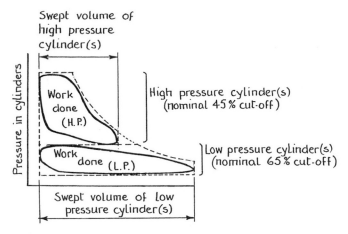

Fig. 4.21 Indicator diagrams showing expansion of steam in two stages on a compound locomotive.

provide, and, when working compound, the valves may leak and let a significant amount of steam short-circuit the compounding system.

Various different compounding arrangements have been used on locomotives at one time or another. Two-cylinder compounds have the disadvantage that they are asymmetrical, and have not been all that popular. With the three-cylinder designs, some have had two low-pressure cylinders and one high-pressure one, while others have been provided with the opposite arrangement. A single low-pressure cylinder of considerable diameter can often be accommodated between the frames, the most notable examples being those of Webb for the London & North Western Railway. Probably the most popular arrangements have been the four-cylinder designs, with two inside and two outside, although, as mentioned later, the 'true' Mallet articulated locomotives had all their cylinders outside their frames. A more unusual arrangement with four-cylinder compounds was that invented by S. Vauclain, who later became the president and chairman of the Baldwin Locomotive Works. His cylinders were in pairs, cast one above the other in the same cylinder block and sharing a common crosshead and connecting rod. Narrow-gauge versions were used on some of the 'Elevated' city railways in the United States.

In Britain, Webb went in for compounding in a big way on the London & North Western Railway from 1878. However, on his three-cylinder designs, he only provided a slip-eccentric to operate the valves for the single central low-pressure cylinder. This drove a single axle, and the twin outside high-pressure cylinders were connected to a separate, non-coupled, axle. So, although the usual Joy valve-gear enabled the outside valves to be reversed, the locomotive had to run for about ten feet in the new direction before the low-pressure valve-gear similarly reversed itself. This presented a problem at Euston whenever one of the compounds set back on to its train to start its journey to the north. With only a single driving axle taking the thrust of the twin high-pressure cylinders, the wheels very easily lost adhesion, and often slipped badly. Considerable quantities of steam were exhausted into the intermediate receiver, and, as the pressure built up, the centre piston also started to move, and turned the other driving wheels—in reverse! The result was that the train remained stationary while the locomotive's driving wheels spun round uselessly in opposite directions. Eventually gangs of men with pinch-bars had to be provided to get trains away. When Whale took over as CME in 1903, his predecessor's compounds disappeared extremely quickly, 110 new, simple, locomotives being built at Crewe in 26 months, while a similar number of 'Ladies' and compounds was scrapped.

The Midland Railway was much more successful with compounding, and used the Smith system, with two outside low-pressure cylinders, and a single high-pressure one between the frames. All had the same stroke, but the low-pressure pair were 21 in (533 mm) in diameter, whereas the high-pressure one was only 19 in (483 mm). The ratio of the cylinder volumes in the two stages was thus 1:2.4. Superheating improved their performance considerably, and the LMS built a further batch after 1923.

Although, at first sight, Fig. 4.21 appears to show that the LP cylinder's stroke is longer than the HP one, the diagram uses the swept volume as the horizontal axis, and the ratio between the stages is 1:2.0, which is slightly smaller than provided on the Midland Compounds.

Compounding was never extensively used in the UK, where suitable coal was, on the whole, readily available and comparatively cheap. The British verdict was that, on a good day, a compound used about 10 per cent less coal than a comparable simple locomotive. At the time when compounding was being closely considered, similar, if not greater, improvements in economy and power output were being achieved by the use of superheating, better-designed valve-gear, and improved steam-flow.

Abroad, however, particularly in France where there was not a lot of native coal, the compound had a long innings, reaching its zenith under Chapelon. It was also customary for French drivers to be trained mechanically, and they were thus able to get the best out of the compounding by varying the settings of the separate high- and low-pressure valve-gears. They were also paid bonuses for fuel economy and time recovery, which provided an incentive for them to learn how to utilize the controls in the optimum way to meet either requirement.

Nevertheless, in spite of the widespread use of compounding between the two world wars, the SNCF was happy to accept no less than 1340 two-cylinder simple 2-8-2 locomotives from North American builders after the 'Liberation' in 1944, to get their railways working again. In 1945 Chapelon was also considering several twin-cylinder *simple* designs for secondary routes, where long spells of high power output, on which the compounds thrived, were not required.

In North America articulated locomotives were used widely during the first half of the twentieth century. Many of them were of the Mallet design, which had one set of driving wheels under the rear-half of the boiler, and another set on a separate articulated frame further forward. There were usually carrying wheels under the firebox and ahead of the front driving axles. The original design used compound expansion, with the low-pressure cylinders at the front where their exhaust could more easily be directed up the chimney. The world's largest steam locomotives, the Union Pacific's 'Big Boy' 4-8+8-4s, were of the non-compound variety. On the Virginian Railroad, its 800-class 2-10+10-2 Mallets had low-pressure cylinders no less than 48 in (1219 mm) in diameter. The Erie Rail Road even built a triple-expansion locomotive, with a 2-8+8+8-2 wheel arrangement, the third set of driving wheels being under the tender.

Triple-expansion engines were common on ocean liners in the days before steam turbines had been developed, and their use in freighters continued much longer. In such installations it was usual to re-heat the steam between two of the stages, by passing it through what amounted to another superheater in the boiler. In this way internal condensation was reduced, but the third-stage cylinders always discharged to condensers, which increased the overall expansion ratio even further, as well as recovering the high-purity water used. The very large final-stage cylinders and condensers could relatively easily be accommodated in a ship, unlike on a locomotive. Ocean-going ships benefit from the fact

Plate 4.24 Triple-expansion arrangements were rarely used on steam locomotives because of the difficulty of accommodating the huge low-pressure cylinders. Ships had space to house large engines of this type, and could easily exhaust to condenser vacuum. The resulting higher efficiency made considerable economies on long voyages with the engine running at a constant speed. This 2800hp (2110 kW) engine is fitted to the preserved Baltic ice-breaker, *Sankt Erik*. Its cylinders, the access covers for which are visible in the photograph, are 590, 960, and 1550mm (23, 38, and 61in.) in diameter, the volume ratios being 1:2.6:6.9. Nothing comparable could be attained within a railway loading-gauge, although the Virginian Railway's 2–10+10–2 Mallets of 1918 managed to accommodate twin 48 in. (1219 mm) low-pressure cylinders on the front unit, mounted ahead of the smokebox.

that their engines operate under constant conditions for long periods, often for days on end, which enables them to be designed for an optimum rotational speed. By contrast, the speed and power output of railway locomotives are constantly altering with every change in gradient, a factor which also reduces the benefits of compounding.

Turbine-driven locomotives

Although most steam locomotives were propelled by reciprocating pistons, over the years a number of significant designs were tried which used turbines to convert the steam produced in their boilers into tractive effort. This form of power production, with simple rotating parts, has a number of advantages over the more usual design. The most obvious is the smoothness and quietness of the drive, which was most apparent when turbines were adopted for ocean-going steamers, a benefit which has now been lost with the subsequent switch to diesel prime-movers.

A turbine provides a constant torque, whereas that produced by a piston driving a crank varies cyclically, and is only partially smoothed out by the use of multiple cylinders, as we will see in the next chapter. The advantage of this was well demonstrated by the best-known of the British turbine-powered locomotives, LMS Pacific No. 6202, built in 1935 and often referred to as the 'Turbomotive'. This factor permitted the provision of 11 per cent more tractive effort without increasing the tendency to slip, but there was a further advantage. The absence of the heavy reciprocating masses of the pistons and connecting-rods fitted to an orthodox steam locomotive meant that the balance weights on the driving wheels could be much lighter. This was because they only had to balance the coupling-rods, which, in turn, eliminated hammer-blow on the track, as will be described in more detail in a later section. As a result, the axle loading of No. 6202 was raised to 24 tons compared with the $22\frac{1}{2}$ allowed for its sister 'Princess' Pacifics with their reciprocating drives.

Although a 'one-off', the 'Turbomotive' accumulated a mileage of over 450 000 during the 15 years for which it operated in its original form. This period included World War II, when its unique design saw it out of action at times for over a year because of national workshop priorities. It had a multi-stage forward turbine on the left-hand side, mounted between the smokebox and the bogie. This was permanently connected to the leading driving axle by a 34.4:1 triple-reduction gear with a flexible final drive, this last item generally following the arrangements used for contemporary electric locomotives with body-mounted traction motors. Turbines can only drive in one direction, so a second, smaller, one was used for reversing, and was provided with an inching-gear to line up the teeth of its clutch, if needed, when it was being engaged.

The forward turbine had six steam nozzles, and the driver could select as many of these as was required for each part of the journey. All were used when working a train up Camden, Shap or Beattock Banks, with four or five on other climbs, and three on the level. During tests the locomotive's overall thermal efficiency was 8 per cent better than one of the ordinary Pacifics, and the turbine efficiency worked out at 81 per cent. The estimated maximum indicated horsepower achieved was 2350, compared with 2200 measured on one of the class with a conventional drive.

R. C. Bond gave a paper about the locomotive in 1946, and considered that a small fleet of similarly-powered locomotives, with higher-pressure boilers and more superheating, made sense, but the diesel revolution prevented any such developments. Across the Channel the SNCF also seriously considered fitting a turbine drive to the last of the de Caso 4-6-4s which had not been completed at the time of the German invasion. This was based on experience with the turbine-powered 232Q1 from 1940, but eventually the locomotive appeared in conventional compound form as 232U1.

The designers of most of the other turbine-powered steam locomotives attempted to combine turbine-drive with a condenser, but the latter has always proved extremely difficult to adapt to the 'rough and tumble' of railway operation. The last two turbine-powered steam

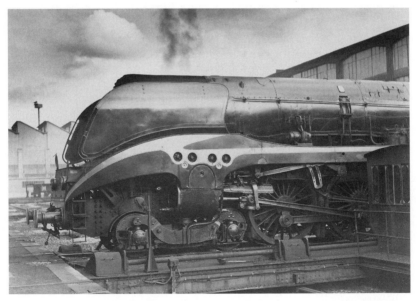

Plate 4.25 The unique SNCF compound 4-6-4 No. 232U1, designed by de Caso, represented the pinnacle of French steam locomotive development. Its aerodynamic front-end is apparent as it stands on the traverser at La Chapelle depot in Paris in 1959. Fitted with a mechanical stoker it was capable of producing 4200 indicated horse-power. With tender, it weighed 213 tons. It is now exhibited at the French Railway Museum in Mulhouse. (Photo: Dr J. A. Coiley.)

locomotives did not have condensers, and were built in 1945 and 1954 for the Chesapeake & Ohio and Norfolk & Western Railroads. They were of the steam-electric type, with the turbines producing electric power which was then used in traction motors similar to those currently becoming common with diesel-electrics. This system was a partial throw-back to one used on a number of locomotives early in the twentieth century, where the electrical power was produced by a reciprocating steam engine connected to a dynamo. None of these was sufficiently successful to make any significant change to the mainstream development of steam locomotives worldwide, so this branch of the evolutionary chain just petered out.

CHAPTER 5

Transmitting the power

Frames

In the same way as a heavy lorry has a chassis on which are mounted its motor, transmission, wheels, cab and load, a steam locomotive is constructed around its frames, which, in effect, carry its personal identity. When a locomotive was overhauled, particularly in a major railway's Main Works, the boiler and many other smaller components became dispersed for repair, and could subsequently appear on various other locomotives of the same type, but the frames retained the machine's original running number. Only in the largest repair establishments was any spare set of frames kept, and then only for numerically-large classes. These could be substituted, say, when a locomotive which had been particularly badly damaged in an accident arrived for overhaul.

In the very early days of locomotives, the boiler also acted as part or all of the frame structure, but, as they grew in size, it quickly became clear that the boiler was best left to its primary function of generating steam. It was a much better idea to provide a separate structure to take all the mechanical forces that bear on a locomotive.

Primarily the frames distribute the locomotive's weight. As shown in Fig. 5.1, which represents an 'Atlantic' 4-4-2, they support the smokebox, boiler, and firebox near each end, and other heavy components, such as the cylinders, are mounted on them. The weight of these items, as well as that of the frames themselves, is distributed to the wheels in varying ways. Axles suspended from the frames, whether driving or carrying, are linked to it by spring hangers, which are usually secured to the bottom edge of the cut-outs ('horn spaces') that take the axleboxes, and are shown as 'support points'. Bogies and pony-trucks take their share of the weight via bearing pads. The details of how they do this will be discussed in a later section, but they are shown

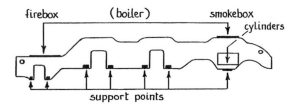

I. - Weights of main components

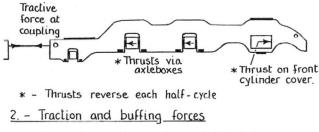

2. - Traction and buffing forces

Fig. 5.1 Forces acting on a locomotive's main-frames.

diagrammatically in the figure. The overall effect is that the frames act as a large beam.

Secondly, the frames keep the locomotive 'all of a piece' as it traverses curves in the track. When the leading wheels enter a curve, they are forced sideways, and, in turn, drag the front of the locomotive after them. Similarly, when the wheels regain straight ('tangent') track, the frames hold the whole machine in line.

Thirdly, in the course of hauling or propelling vehicles, the locomotive produces a whole set of fore-and-aft forces, again as shown in Fig. 5.1. We have already seen that steam works by pressing on the piston faces, but it also acts on the end-covers of the cylinders, which are themselves fixed to the frames. The driving-wheel axleboxes, located in the horn spaces, are subject to the forces transmitted to them through the connecting and coupling rods, as well as from the wheels themselves. The net sum of all these is the locomotive's tractive effort, which is applied to the train through the couplings (when hauling) or the buffers (if propelling). The buffers can also inflict very substantial loads on the

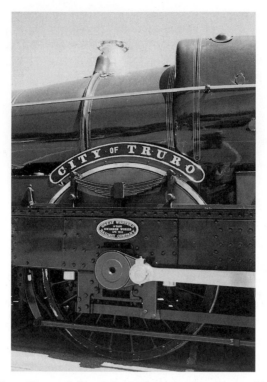

Plate 5.1 The Great Western Railway's 4-4-0 No. 3440, *City of Truro* achieved a speed of about 100 mph between Exeter and Taunton in 1904. In spite of the use of double frames on each side, patches later had to be riveted around the axleboxes to provide extra strength. The top-feed arrangement used on GWR locomotives will be noted, as described in Chapter 3.

frames when a locomotive comes into contact rather too quickly with other vehicles or fixed stops.

Numerous apertures are made in the frames for various purposes. Some are to provide access for servicing or maintenance to parts of the locomotive located between the frames. Others are purely to reduce the weight at points where stresses are low, but probably the most critical from a structural point of view are those in the bottom of the frames to take the axleboxes for the driving wheels. Stresses produced by irregularities in the track and the thrusts of the pistons are concentrated in the top corners of these horn-gaps or horn-spaces, so these areas are often reinforced by extending the horn-blocks, on which the axleboxes bear, in an inverted U around the top of the gaps. Stays are also clamped across the bottom of the gaps to take some of the stresses away from the

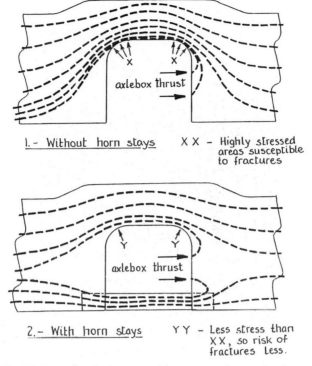

1. - Without horn stays   X X - Highly stressed
                                    areas susceptible
                                    to fractures

2. - With horn stays   Y Y - Less stress than
                               X X , so risk of
                               fractures less.

Fig. 5.2 Stress distribution around horn-gaps in locomotive frames.

top corners (see Fig. 5.2). Even so fractures do sometimes occur at these points, so it is important to make careful and regular checks to identify and deal with any fatigue cracking before it becomes dangerous. We will discuss the way in which the axleboxes themselves are accommodated later in this chapter.

A locomotive's frames also provide the attachment points for many other important items. In addition to those already mentioned, there are the spring-hangers, brakes, the valve-gear and its associated reversing mechanism.

Plate frames

For use on its own railways, Britain favoured the use of plate frames, although the bar type was used on many locomotives built for export, such as the 4-8-4 for China now in the National Collection. Plate frames consist of a pair of vertical steel plates, up to $1\frac{1}{2}$ in (380 mm) thick and a much as $3\frac{1}{4}$ ft deep (1000 mm). Cross-stays of various sorts are used to

Plate 5.2 By the end of the steam era in the United Kingdom, much more massive frames were being used, as demonstrated by those for the 1948-designed Peppercorn Class A1 Pacifics, one of which has been built at Darlington in the 1990s. The locomotive has a wide firebox, so the frames are swept down behind the rear driving axle to pass under the grate and ashpans.

keep them generally parallel to each other. In some applications the plates may be joggled along vertical axes to provide the necessary clearances for individual items of equipment. At the front and rear they are bridged by the buffer-beam and drag-box, carrying the buffers and couplings. On a locomotive having a tender, buffers are not always provided at the rear, a rigid drawbar between the two being used instead.

At the front end of the locomotive, the cylinders are bolted or riveted to the frames, and carefully aligned so their centre-lines are parallel to the fore-and-aft axis of the locomotive. These also usually pass through the centre-line of the corresponding driving axle(s), but there were cases where a vertical off-set was necessary for clearance purposes. In the case of locomotives with inside cylinders, the castings for these form a useful means of linking and supporting the frames at the front of the locomotive. In latter-day British practice, the two outside cylinders were quite separate castings, but some railways, particularly the GWR in this country, as well as many builders in North America, designed each such casting to include half the smokebox-saddle. When the two were bolted together, they formed a substantial cross-member. In some cases the double assembly was cast as a single item.

With this combined cylinder and half-saddle arrangement, the line of the plate-frames could only be carried forward to the front buffer-beam by providing a particularly large cut-out, which weakened the whole assembly. To make up for this, the GWR adopted the North American practice of providing bar stays between the smokebox saddle and the buffer-beam for those locomotives which frequently needed to use this end of their frames to haul or propel trains.

When Hawksworth produced his 'Modified Halls' during World War I, he adopted separate castings for each cylinder, which allowed him to extend the plate-frames to the buffer-beam. Their sloping top-edges provided instant recognition of the subclass, even at a distance before the differences in the cylinder casting could be seen. He was therefore coming into line with the 'through-frame' arrangement which had been the standard on the other three 'Grouping' companies for many years. Through frames are sufficiently strong to have holes through each of

Plate 5.3 As mentioned in the text, the Great Western railway adopted the North American practice of strengthening the front buffer-beam by means of twin struts from the smokebox saddle on many of its locomotives, such as this Class 45xx 2-6-2 tank, seen at work in Cornwall in 1956.

them at the front-end, which provided a lifting-attachment for the overhead cranes during works overhauls.

During the long working-life of a steam locomotive, its plate-frames require repairs from time to time. Holes for bolts and rivets become oversize, but the most serious problem is fractures. Originally the latter would be dealt with by riveting patches on to the affected part, but the development of welding techniques permitted the cutting out of a whole section of frame and its replacement with a new section of plate.

The design of a locomotive's frames has always been dependent on the availability of suitable materials. Steel plate of the required strength and thickness was not always being manufactured, and, as a result, double frames were sometimes needed to give the required strength, one half of them being situated outside, and the other inside, the wheels. In early days, frames were manufactured from two sheets of metal bolted or rivetted together with stout timber beam as strengthening between them. Outside frames themselves were popular at one time, and were used for new top-link locomotives, such as the GWR 'Cities', into the twentieth century. In the course of their working life many such locomotives required to have their frames reinforced over a considerable proportion of their area. Some nineteenth-century frames used to flex in service, and it was said that this could be seen happening on some 2-2-2 designs as they took a turn-out in the track.

Bar frames

Bar frames basically consist of a two-dimensional grid of steel bars with cross-sections of about 3 in × 3 in (76 × 76 mm). Some are riveted together, while others are bolted or welded. In the vertical plane the depth of the framing varies from point-to-point along the length of the locomotive, but, overall, the frames are considerably shallower than the plate variety. As a result there is always a lot more 'daylight' behind the wheels and cylinders, and access to internal fittings is a lot easier. Bar frames are thicker laterally, and because it is possible to put more metal where it is wanted, they tend to suffer less from the unwelcome tendency to fracture, which is often a feature of some plate frames.

Cast frames

As foundry practice developed it became possible to cast bar-type frames for locomotives, either in two halves or as a single item weighing up to 20 tons. In a few cases the casting also included the cylinders. Such frames were carefully annealed after casting to avoid adding to the service stresses which could cause the development of cracks. The task of carrying out any subsequent repairs which might become necessary, particularly those involving welding, had to be done carefully to avoid the production of any further local stresses, as the locomotive would have to be virtually dismantled if any full-scale annealing were needed.

Motion design

Each piston of a steam locomotive transmits its thrust to a crank-pin on the driving wheels or crank-axle by means of the piston rod and a connecting rod. The former consists of an accurately-machined cylindrical rod, which passes through a steam-tight gland in the rear cover of the cylinder, and, as a result, is constrained to move linearly. On the other hand, in a vertical plane, the crank-pin follows a circular path with every revolution of the driving wheel, and the big-end of the connecting rod has, perforce, to do the same. It clearly follows that, for most of the time, the axes of the piston rod and connecting rod are not in the same horizontal plane. This lack of linearity produces an off-axis force on the piston rod, which can reach the order of 5 tonf for a typical steam locomotive, so some means of countering this is needed to prevent wear or damage to the gland and perhaps even the piston rod.

This problem exercised the designers of the early stationary steam engines, and the first solution was to fix radial formers to the ends of the overhead beam, which ensured that the final free links of the flat chains that connected it with the steam and pump pistons were maintained vertically above the centres of their cylinders. The engines had to be designed so that these chains were always in tension, avoiding any compressive forces which would cause them to buckle, which constricted the use to which they could be put. To overcome the constraint at the steam end, Watt invented his 'parallel motion', which he said provided more personal satisfaction than his idea of the separate condenser. Although used extensively on stationary engines, such an arrangement was not easily applied to a steam locomotive, although the 'knitting' on top of the boilers of *Locomotion* and its sisters was another version of this system.

The final solution was to fit slide-bars to the end-cover of the cylinder which constrain a crosshead fixed to the outer end of the piston-rod. This carries the pin to which the little-end of the connecting rod is

Plate 5.4 When *Locomotion* was built for the opening of the Stockton & Darlington Railway in 1825, it was considered desirable to keep the cylinders warm by mounting them partly inside the boiler. Extremely complicated linkages were then needed to constrain the angular thrusts of the vertical connecting rods as the wheels rotated. When the 1975 reproduction started operating, this assembly got known by its drivers as 'the knitting'!

attached. The end-cover of the cylinder is provided with cast lugs to attach the bar(s), and it is also necessary for the bar(s) to be supported adequately by brackets attached to the main-frames.

Over the years many different designs were employed, with varying numbers of individual bars from one to four. The two-bar design is perhaps the most common, with one vertically above the piston-rod and the other below, and a fairly-substantial crosshead spanning the gap between them. Often the ends of the bars away from the cylinder are splayed vertically outwards to be fixed to their attachments, prompting the 'alligator' nickname. In their most usual form the bars are rectangular in cross-section. There were instances where circular ones

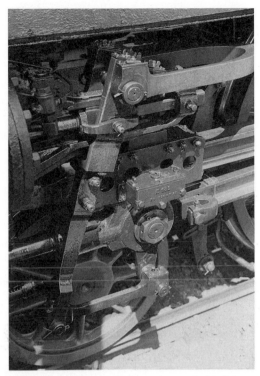

Plate 5.5 The single slide-bar, part of which can be seen behind the crosshead on this Deutsche Bundesbahn Pacific No. 03.1010, forms the simplest means of constraining the little-end of a locomotive's connecting-rod. As described in the text, designs using one to four bars were adopted by different engineers, the two-bar crosshead probably being the most common, as shown in Plate 4.17.

were used, but with such an arrangement it was difficult and labour-intensive to provide white-metal bearing surfaces, which complicated long-term maintenance of the locomotive, as described later.

Single slide-bars are usually mounted above the piston-rod, and the crosshead consists of a box-shaped component, with bearing surfaces on all four internal faces. This arrangement has the disadvantage that either the rear attachment to the frames has to be dismantled to remove the crosshead, or the upper and lower bearing surfaces on the latter have to be capable of being unbolted from each other. This presents problems with alignment and the security of attachment at a highly-stressed point which undergoes rapid motion.

The three-bar system, as used on the 'Britannia' Pacifics and some other BR standard locomotives, has an assembly of one wide bar on the top and two narrower ones below, but all situated above the crosshead itself. These are mounted so the gap between the upper and lower bars is accurately parallel throughout its length. The top of the crosshead is machined with a T-shaped profile which fits into these two slots to provide the necessary guidance, its vertical and horizontal bearing surfaces being white-metalled. The four-bar type of slide-bar is generally similar to the three-bar version, the difference being that the single top bar is replaced by a pair of parallel ones, mirroring the lower pair.

The reason for the larger bar being on top in the three-bar design is because, when a locomotive is steaming smokebox first, the vertical forces produced by the crosshead on the slide-bars are *always* in the upwards direction. On the other hand, when steaming in reverse or coasting forwards, the vertical forces on the slide-bars are all downwards. This was demonstrated somewhat catastrophically near Settle in 1960, when the fastenings for the lower bars of one cylinder on a 'Britannia'-class locomotive worked loose during a journey on a dark snowy night. The driver heard some knocking and stopped the train to look for the cause, but in the difficult conditions could not find anything amiss. He continued

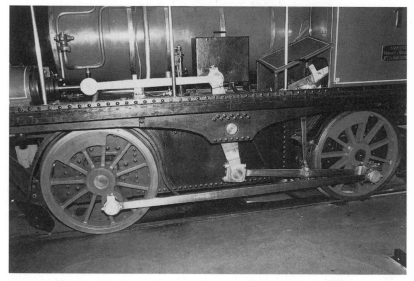

Plate 5.6 This unusual Charles Brown motion was adopted for the small 0-4-0T locomotives used to haul mail through the Gotthard Tunnel before it opened to normal traffic. This arrangement was originally developed for steam-powered trams to keep the cylinders well clear of the ground. The rear of the locomotive's left-hand cylinder can be seen above and ahead of the left-hand driving wheel.

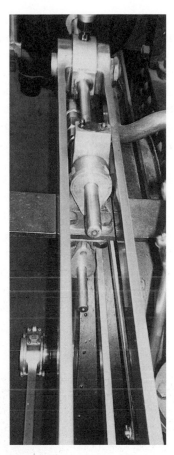

Plate 5.7 Although at first sight the Brown motion dispenses with a crosshead, there is an equivalent constraining arrangement mounted between the pair of rods connecting the piston with the top of the rocking-lever. The gland on the rear cover of the cylinder can be seen ahead and to the left of the oil reservoir mounted on the equivalent of the 'little end' bearing.

on his way, and all went well until steam was shut-off, whereupon the vertical forces on the slide-bars reversed, and the sudden stresses on the bottom ones completed their detachment. The piston-rod then fractured, and the unsupported front of the connecting rod assembly dropped on to the track, where it dug into the ballast and 'pole-jumped', becoming badly bent in the process. This caused it foul the other track, where it derailed a passing freight, which, in turn, tore the side out of some of the coaches of the train behind the damaged locomotive.

The connecting rod clearly has to be strong enough to take the full thrust of its piston when the cylinder is filled with steam direct from the boiler, and rigid enough to resist buckling. In practice its strength is much greater than this, because of the possibility of water being trapped in the cylinder which could make the pressure rise higher still before the relief-valve on the cylinder cover opens. As the same time it must not be too massive, so it is manufactured from high-quality steel. To obtain maximum strength from a given weight of metal, it is machined all over to provide a cross-section that matches the stress profile, and to eliminate any rough places which might otherwise initiate fatigue cracks.

Bearings are needed at each end of the connecting-rod, and take the form of bushes pressed into a machined hole. At the small end, a suitable pin is passed through this and the similar bushes in the crosshead, before being secured with a nut and cotter. The method of attaching the big-end to the crank-pin depends mainly on whether the cylinder concerned is inside or outside the frames and driving wheels. In the latter case a single, circular, bearing can be used, as the rod can

Plate 5.8 Means has to be provided to keep coupling rods on their crank-pins. Typically this was done by a steel washer, secured with a split-pin, as seen on the Beyer-Peacock 2-4-0 No. 326, built for use in The Netherlands, and now preserved at the Utrecht Railway Museum.

be placed in position over the end of a crank-pin which has been pressed into the driving-wheel boss, and then held in place with a collar secured by a nut and cotter. With an inside cylinder, the big-end bearing has to be in two halves to enable it to be placed around the cranked bearing in the centre portion of the driving axle, and the two halves are then held together by bolts. Several different designs have been used for this type of big-end, which is consequently a large and heavy item. This adds to the forces exerted on the crank-axle, especially the centrifugal ones, which are proportional to the square of the locomotive's speed.

In spite of this drawback many designers also used the split-bearing arrangement on outside-cylinder locomotives. It does provide a means of taking-up any wear of the bearing or crank-pin without the need to dismantle the bearing completely, which is a particularly difficult task to carry out in the confined space available between the frames.

Plate 5.9 During the twentieth century, most British locomotives were fitted with one-piece bearings for their outside big-ends. However, Ivatt used the two-piece design on his large 'Atlantics' for the Great Northern, dating from 1902, which required a much larger (and heavier) big-end. The main retaining bolt is on the right-hand side, with a tapered wedge inboard, which can be moved vertically to adjust the clearances. It is secured in the correct position by the two bolts at the right-hand corners of the bearing. Such arrangements were much more common on locomotives built for railways in continental Europe. In the final years of steam in North America many locomotives there were fitted with massive roller-bearings on their big-ends and connecting-rods, but none was ever used in Britain.

Plate 5.10 The middle big-end from the fastest steam locomotive in the world—
Mallard. The split brass bearing will be noted (inevitable with a crank-axle) the two
halves being held together by the nuts above and below the connecting rod. The oil
reservoir with its filling hole can be seen at the top. For many years the big-end bearings
on this class were a source of trouble, so much so that a 'stink bomb' was fitted to each
of them, to warn the driver if it overheated. The final solution was found in the late
1950s, by incorporating a continuous white-metal shell in the bearing, and using a
harder metal for the spacers between the two halves of the big-end.

All these bearing surfaces have to be provided with suitable means of
lubrication, and this aspect of steam locomotive design will dealt with in
general terms later in this chapter.

Most steam locomotives were provided with more than one driving
axle, and coupling rods were thus needed between the wheels on different
axles, except in the rare 'double-singles' design which had a vogue in the
late nineteenth century. One well-known locomotive engineer said that a
locomotive with coupled wheels looked like two small boys fighting inside
a sack! He did have a point, as providing a *pair* of connections between
two moving parts of a machine always causes difficulties, because, unless
the drive-lines are all *exactly* identical in size, cyclical stresses will be set
up, as every locomotive-modeller knows only too well.

The coupling rods on the driving axle are normally mounted on the
same crank-pin as the connecting rod. In most cases a convenient layout
is obtained if the connecting rods drive the second coupled axle, or
sometimes the third in the case of eight- or ten-coupled locomotives. In

such cases clearance considerations with the other crank-pins make it necessary for the connecting rod to be on the outside of the coupling-rod, unless the cylinder is very steeply inclined, but such an arrangement does have an important disadvantage. As the vertical centre-line of the cylinder must coincide with that of the connecting-rod big-end bearing, larger diameter cylinders can only be accommodated within the loading gauge by placing the coupling-rods outside the connecting ones, which means that the connecting rods have to drive the leading pair of driving wheels.

Many locomotives have to be designed so that the same space is occupied by two separate rotating or oscillating components at different parts of each cycle. For this reason, whenever a locomotive is towed with its connecting rods removed, the crossheads must be carefully *secured* in positions where nothing will hit them.

On locomotives with more than two coupled axles, joints have to be provided in the coupling-rods to permit vertical movements of individual axles as their wheels traverse irregularities in the track, which include changes in overall gradient. Such joints are provided close to one of the crank-pins. A few long-wheelbase designs had to be provided with a degree of lateral flexibility for some of the driving axles, when the use of thin flanges, or even flangeless driving wheels, was not sufficient to prevent the locomotive 'spreading the track' on sharp curves. As well as providing the usual joints in the coupling-rods to permit vertical movement, additional ones were necessary with such designs to accommodate in-built lateral freedom of the leading and/or trailing wheelsets in their axleboxes.

All connecting- and coupling-rods produce out-of-balance forces on the axles, for which a considerable amount of compensation has to be provided, as will be discussed in a later section. It has clearly always been desirable to reduce the weight of these components, and throughout the steam era steels with successively better strength:weight ratios were developed. A major step forward was when Gresley adopted high-tensile steel for the motion of his later designs, which gave them a characteristic 'ring' when coasting.

Tractive effort

The force available at the rim of a wheel driven from a cylinder via a connecting rod can easily be calculated by trigonometry at any part of

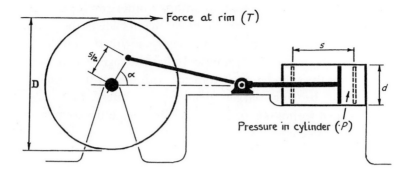

$$\text{Force on piston} \quad = \quad P \times \tfrac{\pi}{4} d^2$$

$$\text{Force at rim (T)} \quad = \quad \left(P \times \tfrac{\pi}{4} d^2\right) \times \left(\frac{s/2}{D/2} \times \sin \alpha\right)$$

$$= \quad \frac{\pi}{4} \frac{d^2 \, s \, P}{D} \sin \alpha$$

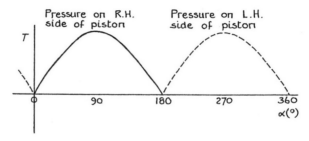

N.B.   This curve assumes that P is constant throughout each piston stroke.

Fig. 5.3 Forces produced by single-cylinder stationary engine.

its cycle. Figure 5.3 is a diagram of a single-cylinder stationary engine. The piston has a diameter of d (inches/millimetres), which means its area, A, is $\pi d^2/4$ (inches²/millimetres²). The piston stroke is s (inches/millimetres), which is twice the radial distance of the crank-pin from the centre of the axle for the driven wheel. The diameter of this driven wheel is D (inches/millimetres), and the steam pressure in the cylinder is assumed for the moment to be constant at P (pounds per square inch/bar indicated), with no back-pressure on the opposite side. At any angle of the crank with the centre-line of the cylinder α, the force (in lbf, the metric equivalent being in Newtons) exerted on the rim of the driven wheel is:

$$\frac{\pi}{4} \times \frac{d^2 \times s \times P}{D} \times \sin \alpha.$$

As the crank-angle varies during the rotation of the wheel, the force available on the wheel-rim varies from nil (when the crank and piston-rod are in line) to a maximum when the crank is at right-angles to the connecting rod. Neglecting the effect of the angularity of this rod, the plot of the force will form a sinusoidal curve, as shown in Fig. 5.3. The maximum force will actually be registered just before the crank has rotated 90 degrees from when the piston is at the far end of the cylinder ('front dead-centre' in automotive parlance), but for our purposes this effect can be ignored.

In practice, the pressure on the piston is not constant, but varies as described in Chapter 4. Combining this with the sinusoidal effect, means that there is a very considerable variation in the force available during every revolution of the wheel. As a result, the power delivered to any machinery being driven by our imaginary single-cylinder engine will be extremely irregular. One way over this is to provide a heavy flywheel, which stores a considerable quantity of kinetic energy while it is rotating. Once such a machine has reached operating speed, the fluctuations caused by the piston forces during each cycle are proportionately reduced, which is one reason why single-cylinder steam traction-engines and steamrollers are provided with flywheels. (These are also situated within the reach of the driver, which enables them to be rotated by hand to move the piston off dead-centre should it stop in that position.)

Having seen how the piston forces are transmitted to the circumference of a wheel by means of a crank, we must now consider how these are transferred to the drawbar of a steam locomotive. Figure 5.4 is a diagrammatic transformation of our single-cylinder stationary engine on to wheels, and we will consider the successive situations when the piston is in mid-stroke moving forwards and then backwards. In diagram A the piston is being pushed forwards by steam in the rear half of the cylinder, which, neglecting the diameter of the piston-rod, exerts equal forces (F) on the piston and the rear cylinder-cover. With the crank assumed to be at right-angles to the connecting rod, and neglecting friction, the same forward force will be exerted on

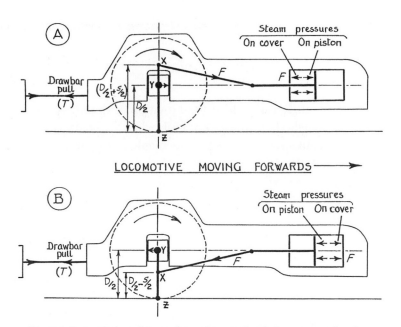

Fig. 5.4 Transmission of forces from piston and cylinder-cover to drawbar.

the crank-pin (X), which can be considered as one end of the lever XYZ. This will therefore exert leverage about the point of contact (Z) of the driving wheel with the rail, which produces a force

$$\frac{(D/2 + s/2)}{D/2} \times F(1 + s/D)F$$

on the axlebox and the frame at Y. At the same time the steam pressure on the rear cylinder cover is transmitting the same force (F) to the locomotive frames, but in the opposite direction. The net force is the difference between these two. This simplifies to ($s/D \times F$), which becomes the tractive effort at the drawbar.

In diagram B, the driving-wheel is assumed to have taken half a turn, and the crank is now at the bottom, being pushed backwards relative to the axle by the steam in the front half of the cylinder. Under these conditions the directions of both forces are reversed. That on the axlebox becomes

$$\frac{(D/2 - s/2)}{D/2} \times F = (1 + s/D)F.$$

Because the force F on the cylinder block is also acting in the opposite direction, the difference between these two opposing forces is still

($s/D \times F$), as in diagram A, so the tractive effort has the same value, and still acts in the same direction.

Our rudimentary locomotive thus gets pulled and pushed along by a combination of two fluctuating forces, but, for a given crank-angle, the result is the same whether the piston is moving forwards or backwards. However, there is a lot of difference in the way they are actually applied, because, when the piston is moving forward the axlebox is exerting a forward force on the frame. On the other stroke the axlebox is hard up against the rear of its guide, on which it is exerting a backward force.

Each cylinder in a locomotive behaves individually in the same way, so, with a twin-cylinder design, both cranks are in the top half of their wheels, or crank-axles, for a quarter of each cycle, and in the bottom for another 90 degrees. As a result, if there is any significant play between the axleboxes and their guides, the axle as a whole is continually being pushed backwards and forwards once every revolution of the wheels. With a locomotive nearing the time for a works overhaul the effect can be very marked, and correspondingly uncomfortable for the crew.

The vast majority of steam locomotives built have had two cylinders, with their cranks at 90 degrees to each other. The top diagram in Fig. 5.5 shows the tractive forces contributed by the two individual cylinders, as well as the combined effect. It will be seen that the overall force now varies in the ratio 1.11:0.79 (a difference of 29 per cent between the maximum and the minimum) and there are four peaks per revolution. The driving wheels of a steam locomotive act as flywheels, and their inertia helps smooth out the tractive forces on the train when it is moving reasonably fast. At low speeds, particularly just after starting, when there is little rotative energy in the wheels, passengers in the leading coach can sometimes detect some 'fore-and-aft' motion, particularly from a locomotive with a long piston-stroke. This is in spite of the fact that its mass, together with that of its tender, also helps to dampen the overall effect. When the double-headed steam special was operated up Lickey Bank in 1997, this effect was quite discernible in the second coach up to speeds of about 20 mph.

A normal four-cylinder locomotive, with the cranks all at 90 degrees, will give a similar overall curve to a two-cylinder one, but in the case of the Southern Railway's 'Lord Nelsons', with one exception, their cranks were 135 degrees apart, which made the variation within a cycle only 7 per cent. You never get something for nothing, so the maximum force available with such valve-gear is 92 per cent of that from a conventional

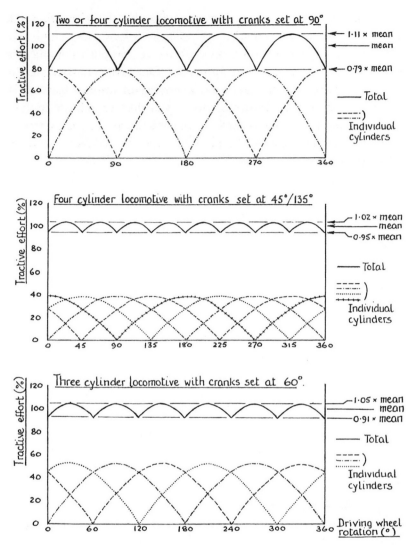

Fig. 5.5 Variations of tractive effort with different numbers of cylinders and crank-settings at constant steam pressures.

layout, although there are now eight peaks per revolution, rather than four. Three-cylinder locomotives produce six peaks per revolution, and the variability is only 13 per cent, appreciably less than with a conventional two- or four-cylinder locomotive.

We saw earlier that the driving-axles on two-cylinder locomotives were subjected to fore-and-aft forces during each revolution. For balancing purposes, a normal four-cylinder locomotive has the inside and outside cranks on each side at 180 degrees to each other. This means that, when one is moving forward, the other is going backwards, which also balances the piston forces throughout the wheel's revolution. The situation is more complex with the 'Lord Nelson' arrangement, but it can more easily be shown that a three-cylinder locomotive always has one piston in its most favourable position and the other two moving in the opposite direction, thus again making the cyclic forces on the driven axles even.

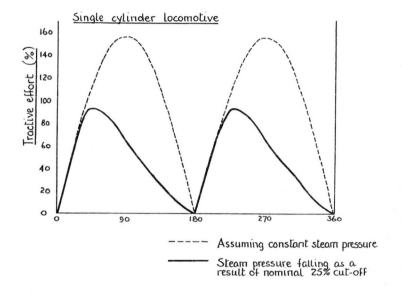

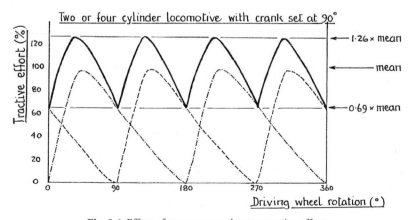

Fig. 5.6 Effect of steam expansion on tractive effort.

Figure 5.5 compares the forces produced in normal two-, three- and four-cylinder locomotives, assuming that the steam pressure in the cylinder remains constant throughout the cycle. However, as described in Chapter 4, this does not happen, because of the advantage being taken of expansion to increase the thermal efficiency. As a result the force available from the piston falls after the cut-off point. Figure 5.6 compares the constant-pressure curve for a single cylinder with what would be obtained if the pressure was following that actually produced by Stephenson's gear cutting off at 25 per cent on a locomotive travelling at 25 mph. It will be seen that the variability has decreased, as has the size of the 'peak', and when both cylinders are combined, the minimum becomes 45 per cent less than the maximum. As this only applies when the locomotive is moving at a reasonable speed, the cyclic variations are damped by the considerable amount of kinetic and rotative energy the whole locomotive has acquired. Even so, riding on a run-down example can be trying for the footplate crew at any speed!

There are two different possible layouts for the cranks on every steam locomotive. In the two-cylinder design the leading crank in forward motion can be either the right- or left-hand one. Reversing the axle in the frames will not alter whichever arrangement has been chosen by the designer. The easiest way to convince oneself of this is to get a pair of corks and some pins. It is then a simple task to stick two of them at right angles to each other in one cork, and then make a mirror-image arrangement with the other. However much they are twisted about, they cannot be made identical, as shown in Fig. 5.7. The same applies with the three- and four-cylinder layouts, which can again be proved with the aid of the requisite number of pins.

When a locomotive is being designed, it is important to have a simple means of comparing the different tractive efforts available at starting from various proposed cylinder, wheel and boiler combinations. This prompted the concept of Nominal Tractive Effort (NTE), which is given by the formula

$$\text{NTE} = \frac{d^2 \times n \times s \times (0.85 \times P)}{2 \times D}$$

where d is the piston diameter (inches/millimetres), s the stroke (inches/millimetres), P the boiler pressure (lbf/in^2 or kgf/millimetres^2), n is the number of cylinders provided, and D the diameter of the driving-wheels (inches/millimetres).

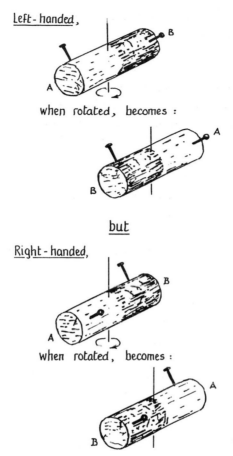

Fig. 5.7 Diagram showing that twin-cranks at 90 degrees are intrinsically left-handed or right-handed.

The factor 0.85 is used to allow for the difference between the nominal maximum pressure in the boiler and the mean achieved in the cylinders, allowing for pressure-drop and the fact that all valve gears give a significant amount of expansion, even when in the nominal 'full-travel' position. The Nominal Tractive Effort is thus often stated as being calculated at 85 per cent boiler pressure. At times a factor of 0.75 has alternatively been used in the calculation of the NTE.

This formula was developed in the days of Imperial units, and the result is expressed in lbf. For a main-line locomotive the Nominal Tractive Effort would be upwards of 20 000 lbf (89 kNewtons), and the inevitable slight variations in the actual dimensions used in the calculation make it wise to quote the result to the nearest 100 lbf only.

The Nominal Tractive Effort is a force, and its use in publicity material to claim that a particular class was more *powerful* than those on other railways was misleading. Power is the rate of doing work, rather than a force. For a given set of cylinders and motion, one gets the same NTE regardless of the size of the locomotive's boiler and grate, and hence its steam-raising capacity. Indeed, it would be possible, on paper, to 'out-power' another design using the right cylinder and wheel dimensions with a domestic kettle adapted to produce steam at the specified pressure! The Nominal Tractive Effort is, however, a useful indication of the starting (and low-speed) capabilities of a particular design, as it gives a reasonable representation of the maximum tractive effort available at the drawbar, but this does not necessarily apply under all conditions. In practice it can sometimes even be exceeded. One reason is that a higher average steam pressure than the 85 per cent assumed in the formula can be attained in the cylinders at slow speeds. Also, as can be seen from Figs 5.5 and 5.6, the combined tractive forces of several cylinders fluctuate above and below the nominal value, and, depending on the exact angularity of the cranks, the combined effect can be larger and smaller than that calculated by the formula.

Balancing

As the size of the early locomotives increased, and their speed rose, it became necessary to balance some of the asymmetrical moving parts. The disturbing effects of any out-of-balance parts on the wheels increases in proportion to the square of their rotational speed, which, for a given locomotive, is directly proportional to its speed along the track.

A locomotive's carrying wheels are almost always free of any attachments, so present no balancing problems, as long as they can be cast or fabricated with a uniform circumferential weight distribution. However, with the introduction of high-speed trains in recent years, it has been necessary to correct even minor manufacturing imperfections by adding balance weights to carrying wheels, or, in the case of the Mark IV coaches used on the east coast route in Britain, by drilling balancing holes in them. On steam locomotives, the main out-of-balance effects arise with the driving wheels, as the crank-pins and inside cranks have

Plate 5.11 The centre driving-wheel of a Deutsche Reichsbahn Class 42 2-10-0 'Krieglok' ('War Locomotive'). Nearly half the area of the wheel is used for the balance weight to compensate for the massive big-end and heavy connecting-rod. Some 7600 of this class, together with the slightly smaller Class 52s, were built between 1942 and 1952, in no less than 17 locomotive works across much of continental Europe.

to be positioned off-centre, and then have heavy motion-rods attached to them.

We will initially consider the balancing of the cranks, crank-pins, and coupling-rods. All these parts are only subjected to simple rotary movement, so can be balanced completely by attaching mass to the diametrically-opposite side of the corresponding wheel. As it is desirable to minimize the total amount of added material, it is usual to place the balancing mass as near the rim of the wheel as possible. Sometimes it is possible to cast the wheels with integral crescent-shaped sections, but more usually they are built up by bolting plates across both sides of several adjacent spokes. Molten lead is then poured into the pockets so created to achieve the necessary balance. Main Works, where locomotives might receive newly-assembled wheel-sets, would have a 'balancing rig' on which a wheel-set could be rotated at speed to check the balance, and more lead added if necessary. Extra weights, intended to simulate the mass of the coupling-rods, were attached temporarily to the crank-pins during the process.

Wheel-sets which have to accommodate four cranks usually require less balancing, as it is customary to position each inside crank on the driving axle 180 degrees out-of-phase from the crank-pin on the adjacent wheel. This provides some counterbalance, and further adjustments can be achieved by the appropriate shaping of the crank webs. If the inside cylinders drive the same axle as the outside ones, the inherent balancing is concentrated on a single axle. On designs where the drive is split there can be out-of-balance forces on each driven axle, even if the locomotive is fully balanced overall.. As with the traction forces, the out-of-balance loading produced by the cranks on a three-cylinder locomotive is less than on two- or four-cylinder designs, so smaller balance weights are required.

Rotational balancing of the wheel-sets and coupling-rods is not the whole story, as there is also the disturbing effect of the reciprocating parts to be considered. In the course of every stroke of a piston, its own mass, plus that of its crosshead and part of the connecting-rod, moves backwards or forwards. At the start of each stroke these items are stationary relative to the frames, but then have to be accelerated to full speed by the time the crank-angle has reached 90 degrees, at about half-stroke. They then decelerate to zero speed by the time the piston completes its stroke. The inertia effects involved in these processes are shared with the locomotive as a whole, which means that, as each assembly accelerates forwards, the locomotive decelerates slightly below average speed. As a piston assembly accelerates backwards, the reverse happens, and the locomotive accelerates to slightly above average speed. All this is quite independent of the traction forces being transmitted to the driving wheels, and does not alter when the locomotive is coasting.

With a two-cylinder design having cranks set at 90 degrees to each other, the accelerations and decelerations of the two sets of motion do not cancel each other out, but combine in an analogous way to the traction-force curves discussed earlier in this chapter. Some of the steam-powered paddle-steamers on the Swiss lakes provide an example of what happens at relatively low rotational speeds. Passengers experience a noticeable 'for'ard and aft' surge of the whole vessel during each revolution of the directly-driven paddle-wheels, which can be quite disconcerting until one gets used to it!

With locomotives it is possible to compensate for these reciprocating 'out-of-balance' forces by adding further mass to the driving wheels to compensate, but this upsets the rotational balance previously achieved. Any additional mass on each wheel produces a radial 'centrifugal' force throughout its revolution. When that part of the wheel carrying this mass is adjacent to the rail, the centrifugal force is added to the locomotive's weight, subjecting that bit of track to 'hammer-blow', the magnitude of which increases with the square of the locomotive's speed. As will be readily appreciated, this is not popular with the permanent-way engineers.

Conversely, as the extra mass passes the high-point during each revolution, the centrifugal force removes some of the locomotive's static weight from the rail. In cases of severe over-speeding it is not impossible for the wheel to be lifted right off the rail once every revolution! It was thus customary to compromise by balancing only a third to a half of the reciprocating mass on two-cylinder locomotives. The 'Austerity' locomotives built primarily for military-support purposes during World War II had no reciprocating balance at all, to enable them to operate on extremely light track. The comfort of the enginemen was a secondary consideration!

With multi-cylinder locomotives the problem becomes easier to deal with. The Stephensons considered one solution, and applied it to two unusual three-cylinder locomotives in the 1840s. Each had a pair of half-sized outside cylinders, driving cranks in-phase, and a full-size inside cylinder was phased at 90 degrees to them, but such a layout was too complicated and restrictive for general use. Locomotives with three or four cylinders of similar size phased at equally-spaced angles are not far from being fully balanced throughout, particularly if all the connecting-rods are the same length and drive on the same axle. The magnitude of the reciprocating out-of-balance forces can be reduced by limiting the length, and thus the mass, of the connecting rods. This will be at the expense of angularity, which increases the forces on the crossheads and slide-bars.

If a locomotive's cylinders are steeply inclined relative to the track, the vertical forces between the wheels and cylinders vary as the crank rotates, making the locomotive roll from side to side on its springs. In the extreme case of some early locomotives with vertical cylinders, it became almost impossible to provide adequate springing. *Locomotion* in its original form had no springs at all, although Mike Satow managed to include a minimal one in each of the axleboxes of the 1975 working reproduction. The LMS Class 5F 2-6-0s, built from 1926 onwards, were one of the few British designs with outside cylinders which were inclined sufficiently to be visually obvious, their ungainly appearance getting them the nickname 'Horwich Crabs'. 'Big Bertha', the 0-10-0 banker built by the Midland Railway for the Lickey Bank, also had inclined cylinders, but it only operated at low speed. However, it should not be overlooked that most of Gresley's three-cylinder designs had their inside cylinders is inclined at 1 in 8 (about 7 degrees), although this is largely hidden from the ordinary observer. In their case the resulting vertical forces act along the centre-line of the locomotive, and are shared equally by the springs on both sides of the leading driving axle, so there would be none of the rolling forces associated with steeply-inclined outside cylinders.

So far we have combined all the various forces and considered their effect of the locomotive as a whole. In practice these forces act in different vertical planes across its width, and consequently tend to produce a yawing motion. As this results from inertial effects, its magnitude is related to the square of the locomotive's speed. The magnitude of this phenomenon also depends on the distance between the planes in which the forces operate. This is thus most noticeable on designs with two outside cylinders, but it is not entirely absent on three- and four-cylinder designs.

A somewhat similar yawing effect is produced by the steam thrusts on the pistons and cylinder covers as described in the 'Tractive effort' section of this chapter, but the latter are related to the steam pressures in the cylinders rather than speed, so tend to be more obvious when the locomotive is pulling hard at low speeds.

If there are other driving wheels in addition to those being driven directly by the cylinders, the balancing masses provided to compensate for the reciprocating forces can be confined to these particular axles, which avoids having to transmit any of these forces through the coupling rods from one axle to another. On the other hand, this concentrates the hammer-blow, which may not be acceptable to the railway's permanent-way engineer who likes to have it distributed over as many wheel-sets as possible.

Lubrication

A steam locomotive contains many parts which have to move against one another, which means that some suitable means of lubricating them is required if they are not to overheat or suffer unduly rapid wear. Many different lubricants have been used during the reign of steam, depending on the availability of materials. Animal fats were already in use for wagon axles when the first steam locomotives were built, and vegetable oils were also used. After man started to exploit the world's mineral-oil resources, many of the heavier fractions from the distillation columns were also used for lubricating metal surfaces, and now form the basis of most lubricants used on steam locomotives.

In recent years chemical and metallurgical research has provided a lot of information on the causes of friction and how lubricants work, but, by and large, the traditional materials available performed satisfactorily during the steam era. Perhaps the biggest challenge was to develop oils which retain their lubricating effectiveness at the temperatures attained by highly superheated steam, which could reach levels of 750 °F or 400 °C. A number of different techniques are, however, required to get each different lubricant to the right place in the right quantity all the time it is required.

The simplest way of providing oil to moving surfaces on steam locomotives is from the driver's oil-can. Almost all the motion on a simple shunting tank that operated in a works could be dealt with in this way, the crew 'oiling-round' during the frequent pauses in activity. It is a very different matter on the main line, where locomotives have to run for considerable distances between stops. Even so, a century ago it was not unknown for the driver to walk along the foot-framing while the train was moving, and apply oil to parts of the inside motion. As speeds and the diameter of boilers increased, this became much too dangerous, and other means had to be adopted to carry out the necessary lubrication.

The next simplest way of applying oil is from a pad. This is used on rotating parts like axles, where an oil-soaked pad in an underkeep is constantly pressed against the bottom of the rotating axle, enabling a film of the lubricant to be carried round 180 degrees to the bearing on the top. Piston-rods are sometimes similarly dealt with, although in their case the motion is reciprocating rather than rotary, but the pad can be wrapped around its full circumference. There are, however, relatively few places where this method can be used.

There are various means of applying oil at regular intervals to parts of a locomotive from a some sort of reservoir with the aid of gravity. The simplest is to have a restriction on the delivery pipe which provides drips at the right rate. An adjustable cock or a restriction in the pipe would do this, but neither is satisfactory on a steam locomotive in the long term. Vibration can alter the position of the cock, and small-bore holes in the pipe are easily clogged up with dirt. Enclosing the reservoir completely to keep out dirt is not a practical solution, as air has to get in to balance the outward flow of oil.

For many years the most common way of applying a drip-feed was to use a siphon, made from a few strands of twisted worsted. One of its ends would dip into the reservoir, and the oil would drip off the end of the other, slightly longer, end into the delivery-pipe leading to where it was needed. Although grease lubrication, which will be described later, has become much more widely used, the siphon system is used extensively on motion pins and bearings where it is virtually impossible to provide a piped grease-supply system. One of the first jobs given to trainee enginemen was the preparation of the vital trimmings. The BR *Handbook for Railway Steam Locomotive Enginemen*, published in 1957, has a diagram showing how the different types are made.

In most cases it was desirable to be able to interrupt the siphon when the locomotive was standing for any length of time between duties. The trimming incorporates a loop of wire, enabling the end in the reservoir to be pulled out to stop it working, as shown in Fig. 5.8. At the start of the next shift, as well as topping up the level, the driver pokes the end back into the operating position. The reservoir is normally closed with a small cork to avoid the ingress of too much dirt, but it has to be provided with a small groove or cane-insert to admit air.

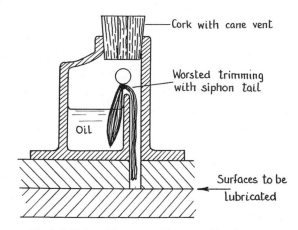

Fig. 5.8 Siphon lubricator with removable trimming.

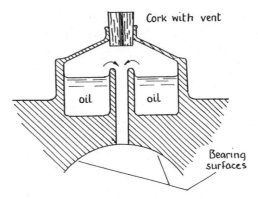

Fig. 5.9 Splash lubricator.

Corks are also needed to close the oil reservoirs built into the bearings on various parts of the motion. Where there is considerable vertical movement, as with the big-ends and the coupling-rods, this is enough to splash oil over a central collar, from where it will flow down a narrow tube to the bearing. A screw cap is sometimes used as a closure instead of a cork. A typical example is shown in Fig. 5.9.

The most critical lubrication requirements are in the cylinders and valve chests, where the metal surfaces move against one another in a very hostile atmosphere. For part of the time they are in contact with superheated steam at temperatures as high as 400 °C (750 °F), and half a cycle later with cool, wet steam. These conditions require a specialized grade of oil and appropriate continuous feeding arrangements, which have to be capable of delivering the oil against full boiler pressure. The viscosity of most oils decreases with rising temperature, and the high temperatures that have to be withstood in these conditions results in 'cylinder oil' not being very fluid in ordinary atmospheric conditions.

The first way of delivering a continuous supply of oil to the cylinders was with a displacement lubricator. There have been several different designs used in this country, but the basic method of operation is the same with each. A supply of saturated steam from the auxiliary take-off is led through some small-bore tubing to condense it. This is traditionally done in a spiral fixed to the side or roof of the cab, where the enginemen would not accidentally come into contact with the hot surfaces. The boiler pressure pushes the condensate into the bottom of the oil reservoir, where it displaces the oil upwards. Figure 5.10 shows the principle of the way such a lubricator operates. Depending on the

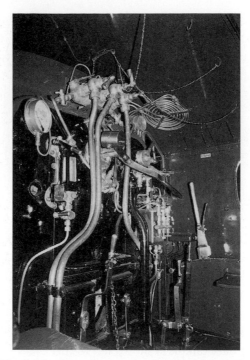

Plate 5.12 The driver's side of the cab on GWR 2-8-0 No. 2818. On the inside of the roof can be seen the copper coils which condense steam for the displacement lubricator, which, with its sight-glasses and controls, can be seen below the handle of the regulator.

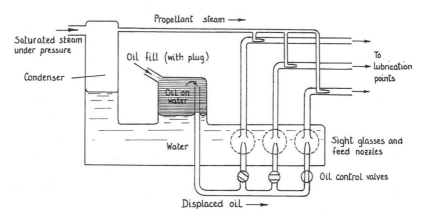

Fig. 5.10 Diagrammatic representation of a displacement lubricator.

design of the locomotive, there would be different numbers of take-offs from the top of the pressurized oil reservoir, each with its own valve to control the flow. Some designs have a sight-feed arrangement on each, enabling the enginemen to see the oil passing on its way to the cylinders,

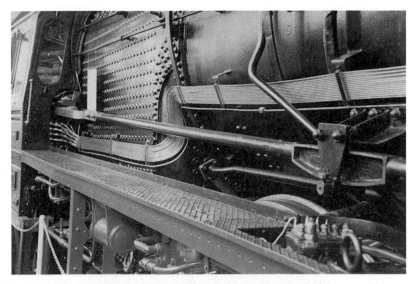

Plate 5.13 The Deutsche Reichsbahn high-speed Class 05 4-6-4s had two extensive displacement lubricators in the cab, to enable the crew to adjust the flows as required during long periods of high-speed running. The array of individual copper pipes taking oil from these to various parts of the motion was normally hidden by the streamlined casing. The stays on the firebox are provided with tell-tale holes, as described in Chapter 2.

a vertical wire guiding the drops upwards. A displacement lubricator contains a finite quantity of oil, so, at intervals, it has to be shut down, the water drained out and the oil replenished. This is not a job to be done on the road.

The development of small metering pumps enabled mechanical lubricators to take the place of the displacement variety. They are usually driven via a ratchet-wheel by a drive from any suitable reciprocating part of the motion. The required bank of pumps is immersed in an oil bath, which can be topped up at any time, and each is individually adjustable to give the required rate of delivery. The oil is then piped under pressure to the parts of the locomotive requiring it. Narrow-bore pipes are vulnerable to cracking and being damaged, so it is desirable to limit their length as much as possible. Mechanical lubricators have the advantage that they can be installed much nearer the cylinders than the displacement variety, which have to be located in the cab.

Lubricant for the valves and cylinders has to be spread over quite an area of the internal surfaces in the cylinders and valve-chests, particularly those for piston valves. To do this it is usually atomized by steam, using a separate supply from the auxiliary take-off. It is not a

Plate 5.14 A mechanical lubricator on the foot-framing of the preserved LMS 3-cylinder 2-6-4 tank, built in 1934 for the London, Tilbury & Southend line. A lever from the valve-gear oscillates the lever extending downwards from the circular wheel on the side of the lubricator, which contains a ratchet. Regardless of the direction of travel, the internal shaft makes the submerged pumps feed oil under pressure to the required parts of the motion through the narrow pipes branching out of both sides of the lubricator. For less-demanding requirements a four-feed siphon lubricator is fitted to the front of the side-tank.

good idea to spray steam into the cylinders of a stationary locomotive for too long, for two reasons. It could remove the oil film, so causing corrosion, and the pressure could build up in the cylinders at any time it is turned on, potentially causing the locomotive to move unexpectedly if the brake leaked off. The second of these reasons makes it vital to keep the cylinder cocks open when the locomotive is standing with the atomizing steam turned on, however unpopular the resulting plumes of steam from the front-end might be with any waiting photographers! The Great Western used a valve which was operated by a cam on the regulator, arranged to activate the oil system before the steam supply was admitted to the cylinders. A notice instructed drivers not to move the regulator handle right back to its stop until the locomotive had come to a stand.

By the time the BR standard designs were being built, many of the lubrication points which had traditionally been provided with oil

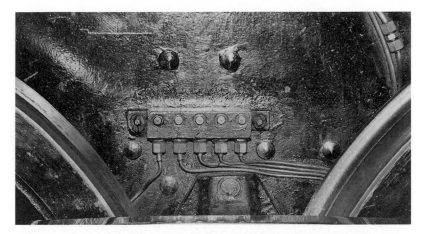

Plate 5.15 Some of the grease nipples on the BR 2-10-0 *Evening Star*, with their feeder pipes.

reservoirs were changed over to grease lubrication. Narrow-bore pipes are led to the various points from an easily-accessible group of feed nipples to make it quicker for them all to be recharged. The application of a grease-gun to each, followed by a few strokes of the delivery lever, fills each system with sufficient grease to keep it oozing out into the bearing as needed. The injection end seals itself automatically as the gun is removed, so such systems maintain the pressure that has been created for a limited length of time, which delivers the grease steadily where it is required,

Wheels and axles

Every steam locomotive has to be provided with at least four wheels, of which two must be driving wheels. In practice, British main-line locomotives had up to 10 driving wheels and usually at least two carrying ones. The latter will normally be smaller in diameter, although some minor railways were not above removing the rods from one driving axle on a locomotive to cope with their own peculiar operating problems, such as extreme track curvature.

Broadly-speaking, the majority of wheels used in Britain were of the spoked variety, although Bulleid joined forces with Firth-Brown to produce the disc-centred design which was used on his Pacifics and the Class Q1 0-6-0s. These had a resemblance to the 'Boxpok' type in North America, a version of which was used on the WD 'Austerity'

Plate 5.16 The huge diameter of the single pair of driving wheels on GNR No. 1, dating from 1870, is very apparent on this lineside shot of a 'convoy' of locomotives returning to the National Railway Museum after exhibition at Doncaster. The wheels have a diameter of 8 ft. (2440 mm).

locomotives. These designs were claimed to provide a more uniform support for the tyres around their periphery.

Although certain of Stirling's celebrated 'Singles', as well as some of the GWR Broad Gauge locomotives, had driving wheels 8 ft in diameter, latterly the maximum size adopted for express passenger locomotive in this country was around 6 ft. 9 in (ca. 2060 mm). Those for freight locomotives were smaller, some no larger than 4 ft 6 in (1370 mm) in diameter, reflecting the lower speeds at which they operated. Each of the four 'Grouping' companies adopted its own range of standard sizes for wheels with new tyres.

A pair of large driving wheels with an ordinary axle would weigh about 3 tons/tonnes, but if they were mounted on a crank axle, the weight would increase by about another ton. On the other hand, a carrying axle would typically have wheels only about 3 ft (1370 mm.) in diameter, and such a wheel-set would weigh up to 1.5 tons. The wheels and axles for a Pacific and its tender would thus form a total mass of getting on for 20 tons. This is an appreciable unsprung weight for the track to withstand, even before hammer-blow from the driving wheels is taken into account.

Plate 5.17   **Plate 5.18**

A pair of Broad Gauge driving wheels from a 1877 locomotive built for the Bristol & Exeter Railway. With a diameter of 8 ft 10 in (2690 mm) they are believed to be the largest locomotive wheels in existence, and are flangeless to help the locomotive negotiate curves.

Although some locomotives have had monobloc wheels, the vast majority used a fabricated design, with steel tyres shrunk on to the wheel-centre, which is normally, but not always, made of cast steel. Those on modern coaches and wagons are often of the monobloc type, which have to be scrapped when they have been reprofiled a number of times and the rim has become too thin. A simple, small-diameter, cast disc is not too expensive to replace, but there is an economic argument for being able to retyre large locomotive wheels, which are also inclined to wear at faster rates than those on passenger and freight vehicles. The World War II 'Austerity' locomotives, however, were provided with disc wheels on their pony axles.

A steel tyre is manufactured from a single billet of steel, and hot-rolled to the diameter required. It is then turned to the required external profile, while its internal diameter is made slightly less than that of the wheel-centre. To fit the tyre, it is heated uniformly around its circumference, placed on the wheel-centre, and then allowed to cool. Various forms of supplementary fixing are subsequently available to ensure it is held securely (see Fig. 5.11), although the Bulleid and BR locomotives used an alternative arrangement of a second lip on the inner circumference of the tyre, which avoided the need for any other fixing arrangement.

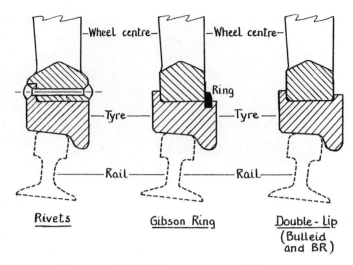

Fig. 5.11 Methods of fastening tyres to wheel-centres.

Typically a new tyre would be 3 in (75 mm) in thickness, but it becomes worn both on the tread and the sides of the flange, as shown in Fig. 5.12. Successive machining is then necessary to restore the original profile, and this is permitted down to about half the original thickness. On many railways the minimum allowed thickness is marked by a small circumferential groove on the outside rim of the tyre.

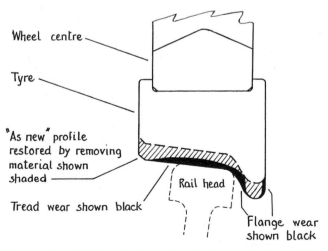

Fig. 5.12 Cross-section of rail-head and tyre showing how profile is altered by wear and can be restored by turning.

Wheel centres are pressed on to an axle which may be either straight or cranked. The wheels on a carrying axle are not called on to withstand any significant torsional stresses, but all the joints between driving wheels and axles are subject to such forces. On a locomotive with inside cylinders only, all the tractive effort generated in the cylinders has to be transmitted from the crank axle to its driving wheels. Only then can a share of the forces be transferred to any other driving wheels by the outside coupling rods. Even with a locomotive having two outside cylinders driving direct to the crank-pins on a pair of wheels, the piston thrusts on the two sides vary throughout each revolution, and the axle has to transmit a proportion of the effort from one wheel to the other. Accordingly it is normal practice for driving wheels to be keyed to their axles, instead of relying solely on the interference fit when the wheel is forced on to the axle by a hydraulic press. These keys are rectangular in cross-section, and are driven into matching slots machined into the axle and the centre of the wheel, as shown in Fig. 5.13.

Most British locomotive designs introduced in the twentieth century have had inside frames, which meant that their outside cylinders drive on crank-pins forced into the driving wheels with a hydraulic press. If the locomotive has coupled wheels, the coupling rods also operate on the same crank-pins. All such axles have to be provided with inside axleboxes, but the same restriction does not apply to carrying axles.

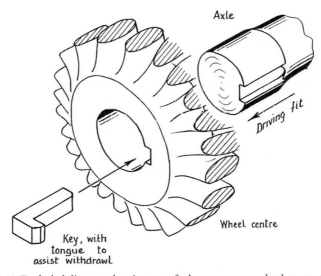

Fig. 5.13 Exploded diagram showing use of a key to secure a wheel-centre to axle.

Most engineers also use inside bearings on leading bogies and pony trucks, thus making the frames of the bogies and trucks lighter and more compact. On the Great Western 'Kings', Collett was forced to adopt outside bearings on the rear axle of their bogies to provide sufficient clearance from the inside cylinders. As a result the bogie frame had to be cranked. Trailing axles for wide-firebox designs are usually given outside bearings, including virtually all British Pacifics. This arrangement provides increased lateral clearances between the axleboxes and the lower parts of the firebox structure, as well as positioning the boxes away from the heat and ash.

Locomotive axles are subject to bending forces. The wheels support each of them at two points, while the weight of the locomotive is applied to them by the bearings in the axleboxes. With the normal inside-frame arrangement, this produces compressive stresses in the upper part of the axle and tensile ones in the lower side. Every time the wheel-set rotates through 180 degrees, these forces reverse direction. With a six-foot driving wheel, such a reversal takes place every time the locomotive moves ten feet. In the course of a modest day's duty of, say, 200 miles, there would thus be upwards of 100 000 such stress reversals. Over relatively few years of such duties, this could easily take an axle into the regime where fatigue-cracking can occur. It is thus vital to select the right grades of steel, proportion the axle's diameter generously, and avoid any sudden changes in cross-section. One must additionally remove any stress-raisers, and also check the axles carefully for flaws during overhauls. As a supplement to ultrasonic testing, a component needing to be checked would be wiped clean, and the suspect area whitewashed. Any cracks would still contain small quantities of oil, and, within minutes of the whitewash drying, this would weep out to show as a tell-tail dark line.

The first major railway accident occurred on the Paris–Versailles line in 1842, when a fatigue crack in an axle caused 70 fatalities. This focused attention on such components, and by the 1880s there were only 2.0 axle failures per 10^6 train-kilometres in Britain. Since then improved materials and inspection systems brought the failure-rate for 1992–94 down to a corresponding figure of 0.04.

The crank-axle might well be thought of as the 'Achilles heel' of the steam locomotive, because of the constant source of trouble it caused in early days. While it is not too difficult to produce a robust straight axle, the design and manufacture of one with a crank or cranks in it were

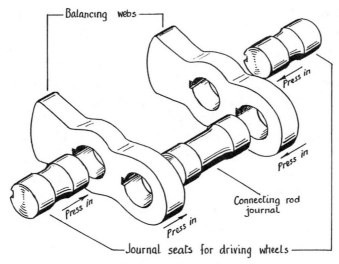

Fig. 5.14 Exploded diagram of a balanced, built-up crank axle.

much more difficult problems. In early days a crank axle was forged in one piece, a complicated operation, even with the aid of a steam-hammer. As shown by the slag laminations still visible on the surface of the metal, some had the two cranks formed 'in-line', and the axle between them was then twisted through a right-angle to give the required geometry!

Webb at Crewe developed the built-up crank-axle, which had the various components shrunk and keyed to each other. This was such an improvement that it became standard British practice. Not only did it result in fewer inbuilt manufacturing stresses and flaws, but it had the advantage that the webs could be extended on the other side of the axle to balance the crank and big-end (see Fig. 5.14). On mainland Europe the forged type was preferred, and some very fine examples were produced, as shown in the illustration (Plate 5.19).

A steam locomotive's axleboxes perform a number of vital functions. They have to transfer the weight of the locomotive to the rotating axles, and also transmit the traction forces to the frames. In addition they have to be able to move vertically to allow for irregularities in the track, but still keep the axles aligned across the frames to ensure the locomotive remains on the rails and within the loading gauge. All these movements involve appreciable loads, and the necessary lubrication must be provided to ensure free movement and prevent undue wear of moving parts.

Plate 5.19 The leading driving axle of the Swiss four-cylinder compound A3/5 No. 779, dating from 1908, showing the cranks for the two low-pressure cylinders. The two outside high-pressure cylinders drove crank-pins on the 5 ft 10 in (1780 mm) diameter wheels of the centre driving axle. The whole wheel-set weighs 3.3 tons.

Latter-day British main-line axleboxes are steel castings, into which shell-bearings of brass or gun-metal are pressed. These are bored to a slightly larger diameter than the journal on the axle which passes through them. This is to enable the lubricant to be dragged by the rotating axle into the area above it where the weight and tractive forces are transferred. The alternative of introducing oil vertically down through the bearing at its uppermost point from an external lubricator is not a good idea, as the inevitable break in the smooth bearing-metal liner disrupts the continuity of the oil-film just where loads are greatest.

The leading and trailing faces of an axlebox are provided with flanges which fit around the two horn-blocks, to locate the axle laterally. The faces which bear against the horn-blocks are lined with white-metal, bronze or sometimes a steel alloy containing 13 per cent manganese. In the last instance the horn-blocks, in which they move, are often lined with separable manganese-steel plates which can be packed to give an accurate control over the clearances between the pairs of working faces. Adequate lubrication is important to permit free vertical movement of the axle in the frames. If an axle were to jam in the horn-blocks when it was forced upwards by a track irregularity, its wheels could leave the rails. In 1951 a serious accident occurred at Weedon in Britain after a pair of axles had been incorrectly exchanged on a locomotive's bogie, one of them having an interference fit in its new position.

Axleboxes also have to transfer any sideways thrusts of the axle to the frames. Accordingly a collar is turned on the axle, which has to be restrained from moving sideways by the shape of the main bearing. In addition, the outside face of the axlebox is usually lined with white-metal, which bears against the inner boss of the wheel-centre

In the later years of steam power, many locomotives had axleboxes which were fitted with roller-bearings. To cope with the sideways thrusts, the axes of the rollers have to be inclined to that of the axle centre-line. If individual axleboxes are used on each end of the axle, the sets of rollers have to be used in pairs, mounted back-to-back and inclined in opposite directions. This ensures that sideways thrusts on the axle in either direction are transferred to the axlebox. The 'cannon' type provide an alternative arrangement for axles which do not have cranks in them. With these a rigid tube encloses the axle, its outer ends being provided with the necessary lips to fit the horn guides. Only a single bearing is needed at each end, as the outer tube rigidly links the two together.

Roller bearings can readily be enclosed to keep them clean, and lubricated with grease which is much easier to apply. They also have an appreciably lower rotating resistance compared with the plain type, although this can be a disadvantage if the wheels lose adhesion. A wheel slipping on a rail has a relatively low coefficient of friction, and, in the absence of any significant resistance from the axleboxes, this can allow the whole of the motion to accelerate rapidly to high rotational speeds. In extreme cases this will cause major damage to some of the components, so the driver has to take immediate action to stop it by closing the regulator quickly. If the slip is allowed to become too fierce, the rapid flow of steam out from the boiler can 'lift the water', the mixed flow making it much harder to force the regulator-valve closed.

In some of the promotional material for roller bearings, a shapely young woman was shown hauling a steam locomotive along with a rope casually flung over her shoulder. While such bearings undoubtedly reduce friction wherever they are used, they do not reduce it to zero, and all the sliding resistance in the pistons and motion remains to be overcome. If the advertisement had used a locomotive tender for the illustration, it might just have been credible!

Adhesion

The basic requirement for every type of railway motive power is its ability to exert sufficient tractive effort to haul the loads required to be moved. A highly-polished steel wheel on an equally shiny steel rail would not, at first sight, provide a good grip for such a purpose. At the time steam locomotives were first being developed, horses were the main form of motive power, and their iron-shod hooves relied on digging into the soft surface of unmade roads to get sufficient grip. The problem for locomotives, which depend on friction at the wheel/rail interface, exercised the minds of several inventors, and there was even one design which was driven by what amounted to a pair of mechanical legs! In the outskirts of Leeds, Blenkinsop used a pinion drive on an outside rack as early as 1811, and this arrangement was provided on several successful locomotives built by Matthew Murray for the Middleton Railway.

Two years later, William Hedley built his *Wylam Dilly* on Tyneside, and also carried out some important experiments to confirm the feasibility of adhesion drive. He constructed a special carriage, the wheels of which were driven by gearing from crank-handles operated by men standing on platforms attached to the vehicle. It was very quickly determined that, with adequate weight on the vehicle, sufficient tractive effort could be transmitted via the metal wheels to the cast-iron rails of the Wylam Colliery railway which ran past the cottage where George Stephenson lived. Although a decade or so later, 'Wor Geordie' still needed to use rope-worked inclines on the steeper sections of his early railways, the feasibility of relying on adhesion for locomotive haulage had been established.

With a steam locomotive, however, there was a problem which did not bother the motive power on Hedley's test vehicle. As we have seen, the thrust transmitted by the piston(s) to the wheels varies considerably during each half-revolution, and this variability cannot be directly controlled by the driver. Coupled with the irregularity of the early track and the rudimentary springing on contemporary locomotives, this must have made all too easy for their driving wheels to slip, which contributed to the early doubts about the suitability of adhesion drives.

With the benefit of hindsight and engineering tests, we know that the coefficient of friction between two polished and dry steel surfaces is normally about 0.25 (although in particularly favourable circumstances it can reach 0.5). This means that, in the first instance, the force required

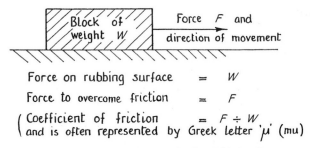

Force on rubbing surface   =   W

Force to overcome friction   =   F

(Coefficient of friction   =   F ÷ W
and is often represented by Greek letter 'μ' (mu))

Fig. 5.15 Relationship between load and friction force.

to make one such flat surface slide across another is 0.25 times the weight applied to it, as shown in Fig. 5.15. The area of the surfaces in contact does not affect the result. At first sight this seems strange, but looking at the interface with the aid of ultra-high-magnification it can be seen that only the minute irregularities in them actually come into contact. The forces on these are so high that some degree of plastic flow takes place to relieve them, with microscopic welds being formed between the two faces. Severing these produces the friction. The actual area of contact between the two surfaces is thus determined solely by the forces pressing them together, which, in our case, is the weight on the driving wheels of the locomotive. An important indicator of a locomotive's tractive abilities is thus the 'adhesion weight' on its driving wheels.

The friction of the locomotive's internal moving parts is deliberately reduced by the application of suitable lubricants, but the presence of many materials between wheel and rail will similarly reduce the adhesion factor for a steam locomotive at the very place where maximum friction is desired. Spilt lubricant is an obvious problem, but there are curved sections of track where the civil engineers need to lubricate the inner faces of the rail-heads to reduce wear from flanges. Unless the delivery-point of all such applicators is carefully located, lubricant can drift on to railheads, and cause locomotives to lose adhesion.

There have been many other causes of low adhesion between wheel and rail. One of the more unusual has been mass migrations of caterpillars across the track! From an everyday point of view, adhesion in some colliery sidings can be bad, as small particles of coal and waste form a slurry with water which has significant lubricating properties.

With lightweight modern trains, which have low adhesion weights but relatively high tractive forces to give the demanding levels of performance now required, another 'natural' cause of poor adhesion becomes apparent—fallen leaves. When these get wet and are mushed on to the rail surface by passing trains, a chemical reaction takes place between the decay products in the leaves and the iron. This forms a thin coating on the rail which has a low coefficient of friction, and is extremely difficult to remove. Every autumn Railtrack undertakes a major campaign to minimize the effects of leaf-fall, which is now more disruptive than it was in the days of 'heavy-footed' steam locomotives. As much of the deposit as possible is removed from the rail heads, and 'Sandite', a gel containing abrasive particles, is applied to increase the coefficient of friction.

It was nevertheless necessary to provide steam locomotives with sanding equipment to increase the coefficient of friction in difficult

Plate 5.20 Gravity sanding equipment on the GWR 4-4-0 *City of Truro*. The sandbox is immediately in front of the driving-wheel splasher, and the sand is released by moving the lever on its side from the cab.

Plate 5.21 A steam sander. The narrow pipe carries the supply of steam which, when turned on from the cab, ejects the sand from the larger pipe coming from the sand-box.

conditions. In early days the fireman sometimes had to trickle sand, fine ballast, or even coal-dust, on the rails in front of a slowly-moving locomotive, but it soon became usual to provide equipment which enabled the driver to apply sand from a reservoir to the rails ahead of the driving wheels, as described in Chapter 3. Initially this was done by gravity alone, but this had the disadvantage that in windy weather the sand could be blown off the rails in the time between when it fell on them and the first driving wheel reached it.

In the late nineteenth Century there was a major break-through with the development of the steam-sander, which blasted a stream of sand right into the narrow gap between the leading driving wheels and rails. It allowed the reappearance of the 'Single Wheeler' for express duties in this country, including such notable designs as the Midland 'Spinners'. If a locomotive is expected to haul heavy loads in either direction, sanding equipment is required behind, as well as in front of, the outer set of driving wheels.

For sand to flow out of the sandbox, it is vital for it to be dry, to prevent clogging in the delivery pipe. This applies equally with steam sanders, as the grains have to move by gravity and air-flow to the point at which they are picked up by the steam jet. (See Fig. 3.12.) Sand-drying equipment has thus been provided at most sites where steam locomotives are stabled, the warmth of the fire providing a welcome gathering point for depot staff during meal-breaks! To keep sand dry in locomotives' sandboxes, internal steam coils were provided at one time.

Unfortunately the abrasive nature of the sand tended to wear holes in the coils, allowing steam to escape, which made things worse rather than better.

Another important effect of adhesion with steam locomotives is the fact that it is not usual to provide brakes on their own carrying axles, although those on tenders are normally braked. When braking this means that a locomotive can only provide as much retardation as it can tractive effort, whereas today's motive power has brakes on every wheelset, regardless of whether they are powered or not. A steam locomotive running light, or hauling only a small load, thus requires more distance to stop in an emergency than if vehicles are being hauled which have continuous brakes, thus utilizing the total adhesive weight of the train. This often results in more restrictive speed limits being applied when steam locomotives are running light.

In recent years, and with the development of heavy-haul operations with modern diesels heading trains of several thousand tons, the principle of 'controlled slip' has been developed to maximize the loads. It has been found that, at speeds below about 20 mph (12 km/h), the maximum adhesive effect is attained when the locomotive's driving wheels are rotating slightly faster than the train is moving. Rapid-response control systems are needed because the speed of the slip will otherwise 'run-away', and effective tractive effort lost. This is only feasible with electric drives to the axles, the power to the traction motors being controlled within close limits and adjusted virtually instantaneously if the rate of slip changes. As will be apparent from an earlier section in this chapter, the tractive effort generated by a steam locomotive inevitably varies quite considerably in the course of every revolution of the driving wheels. There is thus no way in which a similar limited-slip regime could be used with steam and controlled by the driver using the regulator and reversing-gear.

Stresses, strains, and wear

As we have seen, there are many parts of a steam locomotive where metal surfaces move across to each other, often with quite heavy forces pressing them together. As a result, even with good lubrication, wear is inevitable in the medium to long term. Railway economics require an expensive asset like a locomotive to have an indefinite operating life, and this can be achieved provided the moving parts are periodically overhauled to counter the wear occurring during normal operation. These parts therefore have to be designed so they can readily be restored to 'as new' condition, by 'shopping' at intervals of, say, 3–5 years, although the actual time is dependent more on mileage run, rather than lapsed time.

The philosophy usually followed when designing surfaces that impact on one another in this way is to make one as hard as possible and the other distinctly softer. The former will need nothing more than a modest regrind at each overhaul, while the other will be easier to replace or build-up during the same visit to works. In the motion, most of the pins at the various working joints form the 'hard' component, and are made from case-hardened steel, which often only needs light grinding to remove score marks caused by trapped grit. On the other hand, the end-bores in the coupling and connecting rods and the valve-gear are bushed, usually in brass, which is soft enough to suffer most of the wear, but not too soft to have an unacceptably-short life. Although not used extensively in latter-day British practice, the design of big-ends in many countries incorporated bearings which could be adjusted to take up any wear, as shown in the illustrations.

With axleboxes the sacrificial material is usually a pad of white metal which has been cast into a suitably-recessed 'pocket' machined into the bearing brass, which bears on the axle journal—a parallel section of the hard steel axle. The white-metal pad can easily be removed at an overhaul by the application of heat, because it melts at a temperature which is well below that at which the brass housing will suffer distortion. A new pad is then cast in its place and machined to the required size and thickness. The brasses often have serrations cast or machined in them to ensure that these white-metal pads are securely fixed. When rubbing on a steel surface, white metal also has a low coefficient of friction, which provides an additional advantage, particularly on the inner curved surfaces of the axleboxes which surround the journals on the axles as each of these can be required to take a load of up to $11\frac{1}{2}$ tons in British practice.

White metal is generic name for various alloys of tin to which has been added varying proportions of lead, antimony, and copper, and is applied to many of the bearing surfaces in the motion. Different alloys are used, depending on the severity of the physical loading the particular bearing has to withstand, one of the other criteria being the cost of the alloying metals involved. For example, a higher proportion of relatively cheap lead saves money, but reduces the strength of the product. All types of white metal have good friction and wear properties, and consist of hard particles embedded in a softer matrix, which forms as the material cools. The hard constituent consists of crystals of tin and antimony in the ratio of 96.5:3.5, which are the first to crystalize out as the metal cools. White metal melts at a relatively low temperature of about 230 °C, but this varies slightly depending on the composition. If a bearing gets too hot, the white metal can even 'run' after being melted by the friction, thus delaying a more catastrophic seizure.

The reciprocating action of an orthodox steam engine has its main impact (quite literally) on the bearings at each end of the connecting and coupling rods. There are similar effects on the links which make up the valve gear, the die-blocks in the reversing links, the crosshead guide faces and the driving-wheel axleboxes. The thrusts from a single cylinder can reach 100 000 lbf (445 kN)—upwards of 40 tonsf—and the bolts or rivets holding the cylinder to the frames have to withstand similar forces transmitted from the end-covers. As we have seen, there are also racking forces between the two sides of the frames which stress the rivets holding the stretchers holding them in position. To these must be added the forces in the vertical plane produced as the wheels negotiate irregularities in the track, although the springing moderates the impact of these.

The forces between these various components can be sufficiently high to strain the bolts or rivets holding them in place, and it is then possible for the joint to 'work'. Once movement of this sort starts, its magnitude is liable to increase quickly with time as the holes become oval, elongating in the direction of the stresses. As soon as anything of this nature is detected it is desirable to take action to prevent the trouble escalating. The cure is to ream out the holes and refasten the components using oversize bolts or rivets. Ideally this is done at the locomotive's depot, but in serious cases it may be necessary to send it to a Works for attention.

The axleboxes, however, cannot be mounted rigidly in the frames, as they have to be able to move vertically in the horn-blocks, which means there is a finite (small) clearance between their faces. As a result the relative movement between them inevitably has a tendency to increase after being set-up at each overhaul. With some locomotives provision is made to insert packing or include adjusting wedges behind the horn-blocks to take up wear and so reduce the rate at which 'slogger' develops.

Modern locomotives also make use of the properties of 13 per cent manganese steel. As soon as this is subjected to wear an extremely hard skin develops on the stressed surface(s), which resists further deterioration. This material is used very widely on the rubbing faces of horn-blocks and axleboxes, which typically enables the distances locomotives can run between overhauls to be doubled.

Wear also occurs in the cylinders and valve-chests. It may be possible to take up some of this by fitting oversize rings to the pistons and piston-valves, but in the longer term it becomes necessary to rebore the castings to true cylindrical shape and then fit larger pistons. (Major railway companies stocked pistons in a range of 'stepped' diameters.) Eventually it may be necessary to fit a completely new liner and then start the wear/repair cycle all over again. Wear on the cylinders is more a function of maximum piston speed rather than sheer tractive effort. As the pistons move more slowly at the ends of their stroke, and fastest in the middle, wear along the length of the bore is not uniform. Designers could reduce the maximum speeds attained by providing larger diameter driving wheels and reducing the length of the stroke, but both these changes reduce the tractive effort. As with so much engineering work, a successful design is the right compromise between many different conflicting factors.

CHAPTER 6

The locomotive as a vehicle

Stability

To understand the problems of stability with steam locomotives, we must go back nearly 150 years before the construction of *Rocket,* to when Isaac Newton formulated his three 'Laws of Motion'. Some of their implications have already been touched on earlier in this book, but it is now worth stating them formally, as follows:

Law 1   Every body continues in its state of rest or uniform motion in a straight line, unless impressed forces act upon it.

Law 2   The change in momentum per unit time is proportional to the impressed force, and takes place in the direction of the straight line along which the force acts.

Law 3   Action and reaction are always equal and opposite.

The first of these tells us that any rail vehicle, including a steam locomotive, moving along a straight and level length of track would apparently continue to run at a constant speed, even without any power being applied. However, every such vehicle is actually retarded externally by the resistance of the air, and the rolling resistance of its wheels on the rail, as well as by the internal friction of its bearings, plus, in the case of a locomotive, its pistons, coupling-rods, etc.

As soon as the track begins to curve, some form of external force is required to make the vehicle follow the line of the rails, rather than continue in a straight line. This is provided by the wheel-flanges, which exert a sideways force on the locomotive and make it take the curve. However, the 'coning' of the top surface of the rails and the similar cross-section of the tyres also provide guidance, especially for today's high-speed trains. As shown in Fig. 6.1, the webs of the rails are not vertical, but are inclined inwards. The profiles of the tyres where they run on the rail-heads are also conical, and the interaction of these two linear surfaces provides a centering action for each wheel-set.

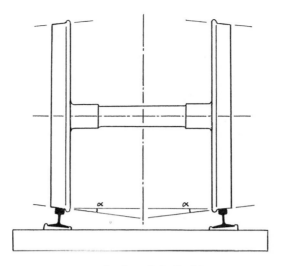

α = Angle of inclination

Fig. 6.1 Cross-section of wheel with coned tyres on rails with inclined heads.

This is derived in two ways. Statically, if the wheel-set is moved from a central position on the twin rails, the interaction of the two sets of cones lifts its centre of gravity slightly. As each axle also carries a proportion of the weight of the vehicle, there is a very small restoring force to 'encourage' the wheel-set to remain in a symmetrical position relative to the pair of rails. Dynamically, when an axle is displaced sideways, the conical shape of the tyres also alters the diameters of the lines of contact between them and the railhead. The wheel moving away from the centre of the track starts to run on part of the tyre that has a larger circumference than the one on the inner rail. As the fixed axle makes the wheels rotate in synchronism, this means that for every revolution the one displaced outwards travels slightly further forward compared with the other. The combination thus brings the wheel-set back towards the symmetrical position on the rails.

The controlling effect of a pair of flangeless cones is well demonstrated in one of the 'hands-on' exhibits at *Magician's Corner* in the National Railway Museum at York. Wheel-sets with different-sectioned wheels can be made to descend a steeply-inclined section of track of about 18-in gauge (half a metre), which turns through an angle of some 90 degrees. 'Wheels' with parallel treads are available as well as ones with conical surfaces which face inwards, as well as in the normal outwards direction. All of them are flangeless, but it is still possible to get the correctly-shaped wheel-set to traverse the track without derailing.

Under certain conditions in full-scale practice, it is possible for this built-in control system to over-correct and cause one or more axles to oscillate in a horizontal plane ('hunt') as the vehicle moves forward. This caused a lot of difficulties with the Mk. I carriage bogies in the early days of the Modernisation Plan. As InterCity speeds increased, very bad hunting occurred, making travel extremely uncomfortable for passengers as the bogies on their coach thrashed sideways between their stops for miles on end. Totally new bogie designs were needed to solve the problem, and the presence of large hydraulic dampers, plus changes to the tread profiles, on to-day high-speed bogies provide an indication of the way in which the problem was cured.

The fact that steam locomotives rely far more on flange-guidance is evidenced by the need to re-profile their wheels after what would be a relatively low mileage for modern traction. Over half the steam locomotives ever to run in this country were 0-6-0s, with rigid wheelbases, and a high proportion of the others also had a relatively lengthy group of six or more coupled wheels. With such an arrangement the conical effect is insufficient to provide guidance, and steam locomotive operators resigned themselves to accepting relatively high rates of wear on driving-wheel flanges, although there were ways of reducing the amount that took place, as will be described later.

The flanges are also required to compensate for various asymmetrical forces generated by the locomotive itself. As we have seen in the previous chapters, a locomotive with a short coupled wheelbase and twin outside cylinders experiences a considerable 'nosing' effect at slow speeds from the alternate cylinder thrusts. While these only produce significant movements up to about 20 mph, unbalanced reciprocating forces make themselves felt at high speeds as their magnitude increases with the square of the speed. These effects are less obvious in the case of long-wheelbase locomotives, but this is because of the restraining effect of the flanges.

The designer must take all these factors into account when producing a new class of locomotive, but the process has mainly been an evolutionary one, based on experiences with previous designs. During the twentieth-century history of the steam locomotive there were relatively few Oliver Bulleids!

As we saw in the last chapter, the flanges, as well as the tyre treads, on steam locomotives need reprofiling at intervals, which is a costly process with large-diameter driving-wheels. By providing smaller-diameter guiding wheels ahead of and/or behind the driving wheels, in the form of bogies or pony-trucks, it is possible to reduce the wear on the coupled wheels, as well as spreading the locomotive's weight over more axles. We will consider these matters in more detail later in this chapter.

Modern traction can be designed with relatively low centres of gravity, but a powerful steam locomotive requires a large-diameter boiler, which has to be mounted so it clears the large driving-wheels needed for high-speed operations. The danger of such a steam locomotive overturning on a sharp curve or because of cross-track level irregularities is consequently much greater than was the case with earlier designs, many of which had smaller boilers, mounted lower on their frames.

To make a locomotive pass round a curve in the track, Newton's second law indicates that a sideways force has to be applied. With a steam locomotive this is primarily provided by the rail pressing on the wheel-flanges on the outside of the curve, and thus acts at rail level, well below the locomotive's centre of gravity. There is therefore a tendency for the locomotive as a whole to continue straight ahead while the wheels are forced sideways. If this imbalance becomes large enough, it could make the locomotive roll over towards the outside of the curve.

There have, unfortunately, been many examples of such derailments, the most devastating being those when drivers failed to slow sufficiently to take the turn-out from the main-line on to a parallel loop or slow line, as at Bourne End in 1945, and Goswick in 1907 and 1947. In each case, as the locomotive took the turn-out at an excessive speed, it started to overturn to the right, sufficiently for its left-hand wheels to lift off the rails. The flanges on those were not then able to exert any guidance to bring the locomotive back over the reverse-curve on to its new track, parallel to the original. Instead it headed off into the lineside field, with the coaches piling up behind it. When Gresley was designing the A4 Pacifics for the 1930s streamline trains, he carried out some tilting tests to check that the locomotives' centre-of-gravity was actually where the calculations indicated it would be.

The danger of overturning can be reduced by canting the track on curves. It is easiest to think of the forces involved from the point of view of someone on the locomotive or train. We do not, however, need to confine ourselves to railways, as every cyclist relies on tilt to turn

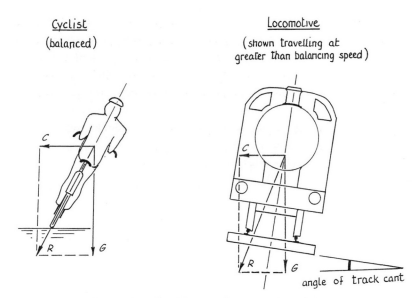

Fig. 6.2 Centrifugal forces acting on moving vehicles.

corners. In Fig. 6.2 the forces on a cyclist and locomotive are compared, as the two forms of transport negotiate a corner or curve. When riding a bicycle in a straight line, the cyclist's weight passes vertically from his centre of gravity down through the line between the points of contact of the tyres with the road. As soon as a turn is made, centrifugal force affects him, acting horizontally away from the direction of the turn. If he did nothing to counter this, there would immediately be a nasty accident. However, by tilting his body and the cycle into the turn, he can combine the two forces, and, using a 'Triangle of Forces', it is easy to show how the resultant force R can be made to pass down through the tyre-line as before, as shown in the figure. The arrows marked G and C indicate the direction and magnitude of the gravitational and centrifugal forces respectively.

It should be noted that the lateral friction between tyre and the road must be sufficient to resist the centripedal force necessary for the cyclist to make the turn. The point can be reached where the frictional effect is insufficient to control this force, and the bicycle will then slide out from under the rider.

A locomotive has wheels on each of the rails, and the only way it can tilt for a curve is for the track to be canted or super-elevated, as shown in the right-hand diagram of Fig. 6.2. It is not clear when this feature first appeared on the railways, but there is some evidence that the 'Races to the North' in 1888 may well have prompted its more widespread use in the UK. It was about this time that larger-boilered steam locomotives started to appear, and their higher centres of gravity significantly reduced the speed at which they would overturn on a ordinary curve of given radius.

There is a limit to the amount of cant that can be provided on a railway track, one of the requirements being that it must not be too difficult for passengers to move about inside the train if it comes to a halt on the curve. A cant of 6 degrees is the normal maximum in the UK, and corresponds to a cross-gradient of 1 in 10, which is quite a steep slope if one has to walk up it. In the late 1940s the track through the down platform at Penrith used to have one of the largest cants in the country, and it was quite an effort climbing across a compartment when getting in or out.

When we were discussing the cyclist, we saw that the rider would fall off if the curve was too sharp for the frictional forces between the tyre and road to resist. There is a somewhat different limitation with railway vehicles. The cant is fixed by the geometry of the track, and is therefore only correct at one speed. If this is speed is exceeded there will be a sideways force exerted by the flanges. Up to a point this is acceptable, but if it becomes greater than the rail fastenings can stand, it will 'burst the track', with disastrous results. A steam locomotive is usually much heavier than coaches, and would thus exert a greater sideways force on curves, making it the vehicle most likely to damage the track in this way by overspeeding, causing its own derailment, together with that of the train behind. As we saw above, designers also have to remember that, even if the track does not itself fail, an excessive sideways force can make the locomotive roll over, so there is another limitation on the safe speed, which depends on the height of the locomotive's centre of gravity above the rail. With the current worldwide interest in tilting trains, it is worth remembering that tilt only improves the comfort for the passengers, and it is the lateral strength of the track which forms the limit on how fast a train can negotiate a curve of given radius.

There is another way in which certain steam locomotives suffered from lateral instability. Every design has a characteristic frequency at which it is most inclined to roll. This depends on the height of the centre of gravity, the stiffness and type of the springing. (Coil springs are less 'stiff' than leaf springs which are inherently more heavily damped, as described later in this chapter.) It is possible for resonance to be set up between the rate of roll and sharp changes of cant through reverse curves or over stretches where the track-bed is not up to standard. The derailment of one of the South Eastern Railway's 'River' class 2-6-4 tanks at Sevenoaks in 1927 prompted considerable doubts about that design's lateral stability. It was possible that the tendency to roll could have been aggravated by the water 'sloshing' about inside the side tanks, in spite of the provision of internal baffles, when the locomotive was negotiating reverse curves at speed. Although the outcome of many tests indicated that the derailment was primarily due to the condition of the track, the whole class of 21 locomotives was rebuilt with tenders, as were several large tank locomotives from the London, Brighton & South Coast Railway which had also become part of the Southern's fleet at Grouping.

Flexibility

At an early stage in the development of steam locomotives it became necessary to provide additional axles to spread their weight over an extended length of track. From the point of view of maximizing the tractive capabilities of a locomotive, there would clearly be advantages in providing these in the form of extra driving-wheels, so increasing the weight available for adhesion. However, as more powerful and faster locomotives were required, this line of development reached two physical constraints. Big cylinders cause dimensional conflicts if they are mounted alongside large-diameter coupled wheels, and, if they are located forward of the wheels, their weight is likely to overload the leading axle. The solution was to provide one or two carrying-axles ahead of the coupled wheels.

An example of the early weight limitations was the failure of the leading axle of Gooch's 2-2-2 *Great Western*, built in 1846. Although the locomotive successfully averaged just over 60 mph between Paddington and Swindon with a train weighing 100 tons, its leading axle later fractured while it was hauling a train under less demanding conditions. It was subsequently rebuilt as a 4-2-2, setting the style for the extremely successful 'Iron Duke' class that followed. (The massive size of these machines could be appreciated when the Science and National Railway Museums constructed the reproduction *Iron Duke* in 1985.)

With certain types of locomotive there were other reasons for introducing carrying-axles. Tank locomotives were used extensively for commuter services and on branch lines where it was either too time-consuming to turn them between inbound and outward journeys, or there were no turntables. These locomotives needed bunkers, mounted on the main frames behind the cab, to carry adequate fuel supplies, as well as additional water, and their capacity for both would have been seriously constrained if there were large-diameter driving wheels below them. (The lateral space for the crew in the cabs would also have been reduced, but that already happened with some tender designs, the 'box' constructed around the rear driving wheels often forming a convenient, if somewhat uncomfortable, seat for the driver!) As this type of locomotive had to run equally fast in either direction, a rear-end pony-truck or bogie also provided useful guidance on curves when travelling bunker-first.

As locomotives became longer, some form of flexibility had to be introduced to enable them to negotiate sharp curves without spreading the track and becoming derailed. *Great Western* and its sisters had very little, if any, sideways movement provided on either of the front carrying axles. This was not too serious, because the fixed wheelbase of these locomotives was about 18 ft (5500 mm), which is comparable to just the coupled wheel-base of many later designs. Many twentieth-century locomotives in Britain had overall wheelbases of more than 35 ft (10 500 mm), including carrying axles, so lateral flexibility became the norm.

In latter-day practice a pair of carrying axles was often used in front or behind the locomotive's driving wheels, constructed as a self-contained unit, known as a bogie, which can pivot as well as move sideways. This not only enables the locomotive to negotiate curves more easily, but also provides guidance for the driving axles, which in the vast majority of cases, are rigidly kept in line by the frames. Where the weight to be carried, or the lateral steering forces needed, can be handled by a single pair of leading wheels, locomotives are provided with just one guiding/carrying axle at the front or rear of the coupled wheels, and in Europe this is known as a pony-truck. Like all good engineers, the designers of steam locomotives were past-masters at 'avoiding the need for' unnecessary equipment.

The lateral movements of many pony-trucks are controlled by a radial link, the other end of which is pivoted from a cross-member, located some distance towards the centre of locomotive's frames, which prompted certain classes using this arrangement to be known as 'Radials'. A means of transferring some of the locomotive's weight to the truck is also needed, and various different systems are used for this. Simple bearing plates provide one solution, but these are not self-centring, unlike the Cartazzi design, used under the fireboxes of the LNER Pacifics, where the slides are inclined. These lift the side of locomotive towards which the truck has moved, and the main frames then try to slide down again, the small restoring force keeping the locomotive aligned with the track. The aims of the designer are both to smooth the locomotive's transitions as it runs from straight (tangent) track into curves, and vice versa, as well as minimizing the amount of flange wear to the tyres fitted to the driving wheels. Not only are new tyres for large-diameter wheels disproportionally more expensive, but, if those on one driving axle need re-turning, all the others need to have their diameters reduced by the same amount, markedly increasing the maintenance costs. Putting the relatively small pony wheels on a lathe is a much less expensive price to pay.

For express locomotives the suspension arrangements for their leading carrying wheels are thus particularly important, and two different systems have been employed. One of these uses swing-links, which, as shown in Fig. 6.3, connect the truck with the main frames by means of a pair of struts. These are fastened at both ends with pivoted joints, with the points of suspension on the bogie being above those attached to the main-frame, which puts the struts in tension. This arrangement makes the front of the locomotive rise progressively as the bogie is moved sideways, providing a centring force which ensures the locomotive's alignment with the track as far as the curvature allows.

The swing-link arrangement, however, has disadvantages, the first being that the restoring force is zero as the truck starts to move away from its central position. This throws the task of controlling the initial nosing of the locomotive on to the flanges of the first driving-axle, which is situated much closer to the locomotive's centre of gravity, thus increasing the control forces needed, and therefore tyre wear. This absence of any initial force can also lead to the bogie oscillating ('hunting') on straight track. Another disadvantage of the swing-link arrangement is that the weight on the leading driving wheels is reduced as the locomotive's frame is forced upwards, and, in some circumstances, this has been known to cause a derailment, particularly if the track is not perfect. The LNER V2s suffered a number of such

Locomotive lifts on swing links
before following truck to side.

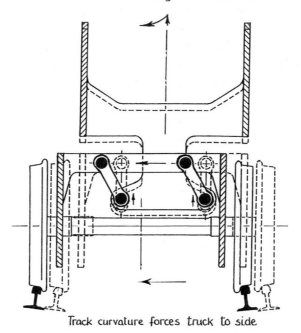

Track curvature forces truck to side

Fig. 6.3 Side-control swing links for a pony-truck.

derailments, as a result of which they had their leading pony-trucks modified to the spring-centred type. There was also a major investigation in 1936 into 11 derailments that occurred with Pacific locomotives in India, which was important enough for a high-powered team from Britain to visit the sub-continent. They concluded that at least some of the blame lay with inadequate side-control forces.

The alternative arrangement uses pairs of springs arranged horizontally, each providing lateral control in one direction only, and pre-loaded to the required force when the truck is central to the frames. If the adjacent ends of these springs are free to exert pressure on the bogie all the time, one will negate part of the loading of the other, so a stop is required to prevent their inner ends remaining in contact with the bogie as this moves away from its central position.

A leading pony-truck or bogie, if provided with adequate lateral control as described, considerably facilitates a speeding locomotive to enter a curve without excessive lurching. Equally, a similar truck or

Plate 6.1 The side-control springs on the leading pony-truck of the BR standard Class 9F 2-10-0, *Evening Star*.

bogie at the rear of the locomotive helps to stabilize it while running through the curve, and also produces a smoother exit. The fact that various Pacific designs have been the best-riding British locomotives is testimony to such an arrangement. Providing carrying wheels at both ends of the locomotive is expensive, and leaves less room for driving wheels, which form the active part of the machine's purpose. The popularity of the 4-6-0 wheel arrangement in the UK represents a compromise between good riding and plenty of adhesion, bearing in mind that when a locomotive is pulling there is a significant weight-transfer on to the axle(s) under the cab. This is why, other things being equal, Pacifics have always had more of a tendency to slip when starting.

Some locomotives have been designed with bogies which include coupled-wheels, and these are generally referred to as 'articulated' designs. Even worldwide their numbers were never all that large, but the intricacies of their design have always attracted considerable interest, particularly as they included the Union Pacific 'Big Boy', one of the largest types of steam locomotive to be built anywhere in the world.

Articulation goes back a long time, to the construction of the first Fairlie for the Neath & Brecon Railway in 1865, although that design is now better known from its association with the narrow-gauge Festiniog

Bogie suspensions

Plate 6.2 A view of the top of a BR standard bogie which has been removed for maintenance. The assembly holding the central pivot can move sideways on the slides when the locomotive is traversing a curve. The hemispherical cups either side engage with matching hemispheres mounted on the main frames, and transmit some of the dead-weight of the locomotive to the bogie.

Plate 6.3 The corresponding view of a Bulleid bogie, showing the differences in the detail design. The cross-slides for the central pivot are fairly similar, but the lateral hemispherical cups have been replaced with flat bearing plates. (Two extraneous brackets have been temporarily dropped into the holes in the foreground!)

Plate 6.4 The individual axles on a bogie are sometimes provided with overhung springing, as in this example from the GWR 4-4-0 *City of Truro*.

Railway, where *Little Wonder* entered service five years later. The type is still in service on that preserved railway today, although not all of these 'Double Engines' are restored veterans. These locomotives have a central firebox, serving a boiler and smokebox at each end. The whole assembly is mounted on a single frame, which is supported by twin 0-4-0 power bogies, one at each end, from which steam is exhausted through a separate chimney. The double-bogie arrangement now used on the majority of modern diesel and electric locomotives is directly descended from this 'double-engine' layout of Fairlie.

Worldwide, the vast majority of articulated locomotives had a single, more-or-less conventional boiler, and were of two different types: those with two separate engines between which the boiler was suspended, and those with one on the rigid frames at the rear, with a second engine mounted on a pivotted extension, which often had its own bogie in front of it.

Beyer-Garratts made up the majority of the former type, the first of which was built in 1909 for a narrow-gauge line in Tasmania. The prime purpose of this layout is to permit the use of more powerful locomotives, with larger boilers, particularly on lines where there is considerable curvature, or where light track construction limits axleloads. The engine units are positioned on separate frames at each end, between which the boiler unit and cab are carried. It is usual to fit the water-tank over the driving unit at the smokebox end, while the other supports the fuel supply, where it is accessible to the fireman. Another advantage of the design is that a much deeper and/or wider firebox can be provided, as there are no wheels or axles to be accommodated below it. Normally the cylinders are situated at the outer ends of each power unit, although on the Tasmanian design, which is a compound, they are at the inner ends to reduce the length of piping needed to carry the exhaust steam from the high-pressure to the low-pressure cylinders. On a simple expansion Garratt the exhaust steam from the 'rear' engine still has to be piped to the blast-pipe in the smokebox close to what is still usually described as the 'front' of the locomotive.

Although many Garratts were built in Britain for service overseas, only two such designs were used on our domestic main lines, and one of those consisted of a single locomotive, albeit the one with by far the highest nominal tractive effort of any locomotive to run in the UK. This was the LNER 2-8-0+0-8-2T Class U1, built in 1925 to bank freight trains up the 1 in 40 Worsborough Incline near Barnsley, in the West Riding of Yorkshire. (With the Whyte notation for wheel-arrangements, the use of a '+' sign instead of a hyphen is indicative of articulation). Each of its engines was based on that of the company's three-cylinder Class O2 2-8-0s, which gave it a nominal tractive effort of 72 900 lbf (324 kNewtons).

The other class of Garratts in the UK was 33-strong, and introduced by the LMS, primarily to haul heavy coal trains from the northern coalfields to London via the former Midland main line. They had the 2-6-0+0-6-2T wheel arrangement, and were significantly smaller, weighing only 155 tons/tonnes, compared with the figure of 178 for the LNER design. They were also expected to operate over long distances, rather than just the two miles of nominal 1 in 40 in West Yorkshire. All but a few of the class were modified with conical coal bunkers which could be made to rotate and thus feed the coal towards the cab to ease the task of the fireman.

The other main design of articulated locomotives is the Mallet, named after an engineer who was highly thought of in France (the 't' in his name is not pronounced). His design, with one pivoting and one fixed engine unit, was particularly well adapted for compounding, a principle for which he was a major exponent. The front, low-pressure unit, stretching out forward of the smokebox, could be fitted with large-diameter cylinders to give high expansion ratios. The Norfolk & Western Class Y6a 2-8+8-2s, for example, had 39-in (990 mm) diameter low-pressure ones compared with 25 in (635 mm) for those on the rear engine. Not all locomotives of this type were, however, compounds, and, with the widespread use of 'simple', or single-expansion, ones in North America, it has become usual to refer to the compound variety as 'True Mallets'. In the final years of steam, the Union Pacific Railroad had a large fleet of 'Challenger' 4-6+6-4s in addition to their 'Big Boys', all of them simples. The latter had the 4-8+8-4 wheel arrangement, and turned the scales at 340 tons/tonnes, with a full tender weighing in at another 153. Both these classes were primarily built for freight duties, but in World War II some were pressed into service for military passenger traffic.

Some single-expansion double-locomotives exhibited an interesting phenomenon—when steaming the exhaust beats of both engines became synchronized. In the case of the LNER Class U1 Worsborough Banker, this even included the usual Gresley three-cylinder syncopation caused by the derived valve-gear for the central cylinders, while André Chapelon was mystified by the four beats per revolution exhibited by the Baltimore & Ohio 4-4-4-4, which did not have the Garratt layout. A trial was carried out with one of the LMS Garratts at Wellingborough depot in 1931, when one of them was set-up with the cranks at each end out of phase. When it was steamed gently it duly produced eight 'beats to the bar', but as soon as some harder work was attempted within the confines of the depot, the cranks started to move into synchronization. One of the authors had an opportunity to ride on the LNER Garratt on the Worsborough Bank, when the combined exhaust beats were obvious, as described above, until one of the engines slipped. After the driver had regained full adhesion, the two ends were very much out of synchronization, with a jumble of twelve beats per revolution. However, the two exhausts immediately began to converge, and within a very few yards the two engines were synchronized again, which was maintained to the top of the bank.

The most convincing explanation for this lies with the phenomenon of resonance, which can be observed if two equal-length pendula are suspended from the same slightly flexible support. They will only swing in a stable fashion if they are exactly in phase, or 180 degrees out of phase. In any other condition energy feeds from one to the other until the first is stationary, after which the flow reverses until all the energy has been transferred to the second one. Presumably forces of this type on an articulated locomotive with two sets of driving wheels of the same diameter are sufficient to cause sufficient micro-slipping until both engines are in phase. It is worth mentioning that, if the connecting rods are removed from an ordinary locomotive and it is moved a short distance, the cranks quickly get out of line, even though the coupled wheels are all nominally the same diameter. If this happens the locomotive has to be jacked up so the wheels can be rotated the required amount to replace the rods.

Springing

Apart from a few very early designs with vertical cylinders, all steam locomotives have been fitted with springs on every axle. At the time of these pioneers, rail lengths were as short as 3 ft/1 m, and opposite rails were often supported on separate lines of stone sleeper-blocks, one under each end of every rail. Vertical alignment was thus extremely difficult to maintain, but that became easier as manufacturing improvements enabled rails of heavier section and longer length to be produced. However, speeds also rose, and this largely off-set any benefit from better vertical alignment of the track as far as springing was concerned.

Until the introduction of continuous-welded rail (CWR) there was always the problem of the dip at the expansion-gaps between successive rails, latterly spaced in the UK at 60-ft (18 300 mm) intervals. Although passenger coaches could be constructed with relatively light axle-loads, with steam locomotives it was usually necessary to make use of the maximum loading permitted by the civil engineer to provide sufficient adhesion on the coupled axles. In the UK most main lines can take axle-loadings of 20–22 tons/tonnes, but the GWR pushed this to $22\frac{1}{2}$ tons with the 'King' class, as did the LMS with their 'Princess Royals', the extra loading accentuating the vertical discontinuities at any 'soft-spots' in the ballast. These figures are those that apply when the locomotive is at rest, and, as we have seen in Chapter 5, they are increased by hammer-blow and other inertia effects. Good springing has thus always been vital.

To begin with we will consider the springing for those axles located in the main frames themselves, as shown in Fig. 5.1, which indicates the support points for them. These are normally brackets, firmly fixed to the

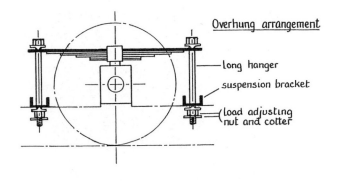

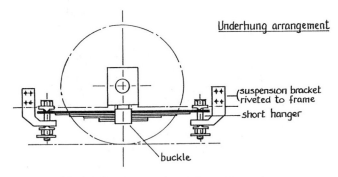

Fig. 6.4 Overhung and underhung plate springs.

bottom of the frames, to which are attached the outer ends of the springs, which are usually of the 'leaf', or laminated variety, although other types have been used, as will be discussed later. Depending on the design, such springs can be of the 'overhung' or 'underhung' variety, as shown in Fig. 6.4. The former require long 'hangers' each side, attached to the ends of springs themselves, the centres of which support the axleboxes. With the underhung type much shorter hangers are needed, but a substantial tension member is required between the buckle around the centre of the spring and the bottom of the axlebox. The choice of arrangement was determined by space considerations and the whims of the designer. An important consideration is to keep the springs in line with the frames, particularly where the forces being handled are relatively large, as in the case of the driving wheels.

Leaf springs consist of 10 to 16 separate high-tensile steel strips lying parallel to each other. They are about 5 in (125 mm) wide and $\frac{1}{2}$ in (12 mm) thick, are normally cambered in the vertical plane, and curved

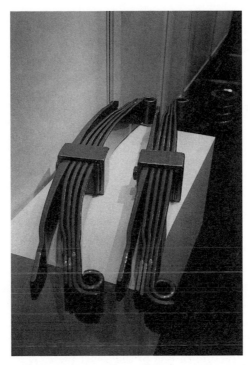

Plate 6.5 Examples of leaf-springs as used on railway locomotives and rolling-stock. The number of leaves, their thickness and curvature can be varied to provide the characteristics required for each particular axle. The bottom leaves in both these examples only come into action when the static weight has been applied.

Plate 6.6 Underhung springing on the driving axle of the unique North Eastern Railway 2-2-4T *Aerolite*, as rebuilt in 1902.

with the ends higher than the centre. Unloaded a typical locomotive spring would have a camber of up to 4 in (100 mm) before being fitted, this dimension being halved when the locomotive's weight is applied. A loaded spring thus contains a considerable amount of energy, and care always has to be taken not to release this inadvertently.

The top leaf is the longest, spanning the length between the hangers or fixing points, with the others below it being progressively shorter. As such a spring flexes, its length alters slightly, so the means adopted to secure its ends to the frame have to take this into account. As the spring flexes, the shearing action produces considerable friction between adjacent leaves, which provides an important, albeit rather arbitrary, damping effect. This reduces any sudden restoring force on the axle, and prevents it from interacting with other springs to cause a build-up of resonant rolling or pitching of the locomotive as a whole.

The top one or two leaves carry the end fixings, and these have to be robust enough to withstand the impact forces they experience in service, a break in them immediately causing the loss of springing for that axlebox. All the leaves are held in place by the buckle, and prevented from working out longitudinally by a vertical pin-rivet passing through the stack. Any fracture of one of the lower plates is not so dangerous, and will not result in the whole spring failing. If, however, the spring is allowed to remain in service in this condition, and the halves of the broken plate come out of the buckle, the other plates become loose and progressive failure occurs. Defective springs should therefore be changed as soon as possible after they have been detected.

With freight wagons, and, to some extent, coaches, the vehicles' loaded weights are very much heavier than those that are empty, making it difficult to design a springing system that gives a good ride under all conditions. On steam locomotives the only weight changes that take place are caused by variations in the fuel and water supplies, and only on tank-engine designs is the weight of these carried on the main-frames. Although such weight changes still take place with tender engines, their layout separates these from all the propulsion and adhesion forces, thus simplifying the design requirements.

In the late 1800s many locomotives were provided with helical springs, rather than the leaf variety, for their driving axles. These do not have the same inherent damping effect as the latter, but have more predictable elastic characteristics. They were presumably used at that point to make the driving wheels' contact with the rails more consistent.

Plate 6.7 One of the driving-wheel horn gaps on the Class A1 Pacific No. 60163 *Tornado* when it was under construction at Darlington. The machined faces permit the axlebox to move vertically as the wheel accommodates itself to any irregularities in the track. The unusually-shaped upper corners are a variation on those shown in Fig. 5.2 to reduce the stress concentrations in these areas. The horn stay appears to be integral with the frames, but it can be unbolted and removed to allow the axlebox and wheel-set to be inserted. The bracket below the frame is one of the pair used to attach the underhung spring for that axle, the buckle being connected to the axlebox through the gap in the centre of the horn stay.

The LNWR 2-4-0 *Hardwicke* has helical springs on both coupled axles, which are probably responsible for its lively ride! In spite of this it averaged 67 mph (108 km/h) between Crewe and Carlisle during the 1895 'Races to Aberdeen'! Helical springs also had to be fitted to the bogie axles on the GWR 'Kings', following an early derailment of one at speed. In this instance they were applied between the axleboxes and the ends of the original leaf springs, a rare example of secondary-springing on a locomotive, although most coaches are so fitted in the interests of passenger comfort. On modern diesel and electric locomotives the 'lively' performance of helical springs is moderated by a known amount using separate hydraulic dampers, an item which only became commonplace after steam locomotives were displaced from everyday commercial service.

The other type of spring which was occasionally used on steam locomotives was the 'volute', one of the more unusual installations being on some GWR branch-line tank locomotives dating back to the early part of the twentieth century. These had two nests of them for the rear coupled axle *inside* the cab, the movements of which must have been really alarming on a poor stretch of track.

Springs carrying a heavy weight such as those on steam locomotives have a limited degree of vertical flexibility. If an exceptional high- or low-spot occurs in the track the axlebox could reach the end of travel permitted by the spring, so special springing arrangements are needed if the locomotive is required to traverse track in which there are large vertical irregularities over short distances. To overcome this problem 'compensated' springing is used, which involves providing a link between those on two or more adjacent axles. This is done by means of equalizing beams, as shown in Fig. 6.5. In latter-day British designs, compensation was not widely used, but pairs of axles on the tenders of the World War 2 Ministry of Supply 'Austerity' 2-8-0s and 2-10-0s were sprung in this way. This was to enable the locomotives to cope with the

Plate 6.8 The War Department 2-8-0s and 2-10-0s built for use on the Continent at the end of World War II had to be able to operate on very poor track. The four axles on their tenders were provided with compensated springing between pairs of them.

Plate 6.9 The 4-6-4s for the Chinese Railways built by the Vulcan Foundry in 1935 had compensated springing throughout. On the trailing bogie the equalizing beam can be seen between the two axleboxes, as well as part of the angled one on the left, connecting the bogie suspension to that of the driving wheels.

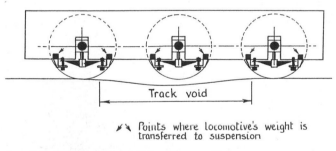

Track void

⤧ ⤢ Points where locomotive's weight is transferred to suspension

B. Suspension with equalising beams added

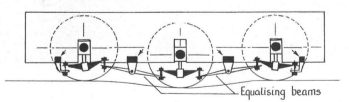

Equalising beams

Fig. 6.5 Locomotive suspensions showing orthodox and equalizing-beam layouts.

poor track conditions likely to be encountered on the mainland of Europe after the 1944 Invasion.

In some countries track standards over the vast lengths of route through difficult terrain were particularly bad, and more complicated arrangements were made to give locomotives a 'three-point suspension'. This made them effectively the same as a three-legged table, which will not rock on its feet however irregular is the surface which supports it. To achieve this the locomotive's front pony-truck or bogie has its own separate springing between it and the main frames. Behind it the springs for all the axleboxes on each side of the locomotive are compensated, which provides the equivalent of the other two 'feet'. Any rear bogie or pony-truck has to be included in this arrangement, which involves some quite long swing-links, set at an angle to the frames. Such an arrangement was fitted to the massive 4-8-4s built in 1935 by the Vulcan Foundry for the Chinese National Railways, one of which was returned to this country for display at the National Railway Museum. The 'three-point' suspension system was also used extensively in North America during the pioneering days of the transcontinental railways.

The successive vertical movements of a locomotives' coupled axles as it traverses an irregularity in the track requires a vertical pivot in each of

Plate 6.10 To provide the necessary vertical flexibility in the coupling-rods on locomotives with more than two coupled axles, a joint is needed on each rod near the bearing for the crank-pin. This illustration shows such a joint on the third driving wheel of the Vulcan-built 4-8-4 for the Chinese Railways. As this joint only has to flex through a small angle, a much smaller oil reservoir can be provided for it, compared with that for the adjacent crank-pin, which is constantly rotating while the locomotive is in motion.

the connecting rods when there are more than two coupled axles, as shown in the illustration.

Carrying the fuel and water

In long-distance commercial service a mainline steam locomotive requires considerable quantities of fuel and water to perform its duties. One of the Union Pacific's articulated 'Big Boys' could evaporate as much as 10 000 gallons (2200 litres) of water an hour, during which time the mechanical stoker would have had to feed ten tons of coal into the firebox. Fortunately for those wielding the shovels on British hand-fired steam locomotives, the fuel and water consumptions were nowhere as high as this, but, even so, the quantities were large by household standards. Although steam locomotives are now almost entirely confined to 'heritage' duties, there are now far fewer facilities for taking on more water and fuel, which can cause the organizers even greater problems.

In early 1948, just after the UK railways had been nationalized, large-scale 'Locomotive Exchange Trials' were carried out between locomotives from the previous four Grouping companies. The published results provide an interesting insight into the amounts of coal and water used by the locomotives taking part.

The trials covered three types of locomotive, hauling different types of train: express passenger, mixed-traffic, and freight. Overall, the figures in Table 6.1 were obtained, which are averages for all the different classes used on each type of train.

All the locomotives involved would have been scheduled to run at least 200 miles (125 km) without any opportunity to refuel, during which they would have required between 4 and 6 tons of coal. To this must be added that burnt in the time between leaving the depot and starting to move the train. With the classes involved in the trials, the coal capacities

Table 6.1 BR Locomotive exchange trials

Type of train	Coal consumption		Water usage	
	lb/mile	kg/km	gallons/mile	litres/km
Express passenger	44.33	12.52	37.2	105.1
Mixed-traffic	44.01	12.43	35.8	101.1
Freight	62.96	17.78	50.6	143.0

of their tenders varied between 6 and 10 tons, which provided a reasonable margin on a normal day, although in exceptional conditions a fireman could (and sometimes did) run out of coal.

However, even with a full tank of water, there were only 4000–5000 gallons (11 000–14 000 litres) available, which was only sufficient for a maximum of just over 100 miles (160 km) for some of the passenger classes, and three-quarters of this for a freight locomotive. The availability of water for a locomotive is far more critical than coal. If it runs out of fuel it can always stop and await rescue, but if the tender runs dry the crew quickly has to drop the fire.

To meet the needs of a steam railway, many opportunities had to be provided to top up water supplies *en route*. Most major stations had a water column at the departure end of each platform, and similar installations were available at the exits of loops where freight trains were regularly held awaiting 'more important' traffic to overtake. On many main lines water troughs were provided, sometimes at intervals as close as 40 miles (65 km), which enabled locomotives fitted with the necessary scoops to pick up as much as 2000 gallons (9000 litres) each time they passed over one at a speed. Scoops worked satisfactorily at speeds as low as 30 mph (50 km/h), and there were upper limits of 60 or 70 mph. (100–115 km/h) to prevent damage to the static and moving equipment. There was usually a track limit, too, as the inevitable spray made it harder for the permanent-way gangs to maintain the rail-levels on the resulting permanently-wet formation.

Some spray was always produced while taking water in this way, but the leading coach could get deluged if the scoop was not lifted in time to prevent the tender overflowing. On down East Coast Pullmans the catering staff would always take the precaution of closing the windows in the leading coach as down trains approached the troughs at Langley Junction (26 miles/42 km from the King's Cross start). At one time certain designs of tank locomotive were fitted with scoops which operated in either direction of travel, but such an arrangement was never needed with tender classes.

Water-troughs could only be sited on the level. The height of the rails was arranged to fall gently over the first stretch, which brought the bottom of the tender scoop, after it had been lowered by the fireman, down below the surface of the standing-water a short distance beyond the start of the trough. After the level centre section, a similar gentle rise lifted the scoop clear of the water before the exit end of the trough was reached, where the base rose sufficiently to contain the water. The fireman would carefully watch the tender level-gauge while taking water, and, in theory, would attempt to lift the scoop just before the tender tank overflowed, but this was not always possible if the scoop had been wound down too low. A bad overflow caused some of the water to cascade forward on to the footplate through the coal space, leaving the crew to paddle about in much of the solid contents of the tender. At some trough installations it was particularly important to raise the scoop quickly as there was a turn-out a short distance beyond the end, and this could rip off the scoop unless it had been at least partly-raised. A watch also had to be kept for Automatic Warning System ramps and sleeper crossings.

At busy periods the troughs might fail to refill completely between successive trains, resulting in the subsequent ones not being able to pick up as much water as required. If a locomotive on a non-stop train failed to achieve this for any reason, it could force the crew to stop at the next available water column. There were, accordingly, recognised whistle-codes to be given by the crew as they passed various signalboxes, indicating they needed to stop to take water. As columns were usually sited on a loop or slow line, word was passed ahead for the necessary change of track to be made. Similar arrangements were often needed for extended periods when troughs were undergoing repair or renewal.

Most of the main lines in Britain were provided with water-troughs in steam days, except those belonging to the Southern Railway (later the Southern Region). Its routes were relatively short, so it was possible to schedule trains either to take water during a stop or for locomotives to be changed. On the line from Waterloo to the West of England, Salisbury was normally the place where change-overs took place, this being a quicker operation than refilling the tender at that point.

Water-scoops are operated from the footplate by rotating a handle on the front of the tender. This lowers the front of the scoop, and sometimes also drops a pair of deflector-plates into the trough ahead of it to direct the flow of water into the scoop. The delivery pipe from the scoop rises up vertically inside the tender water-space, opening out under a half-sphere which deflects the water-jet downwards. This has to be located well clear of the normal 'filling-hole'. During each 'dip' a lot of air is rapidly displaced from the tank, and suitable vents are provided to release it. It was these which spouted streams of water if the tank was overfilled at a trough. The crew could check the water-level in the tender from an indicator on the front of it, sometimes worked by a float of some sort. A similar arrangement was usually provided on tank locomotives, although in some designs the only way to make sure of the amount remaining was to look into the filling-hole during a stop. An alternative was to provide a vertical pipe with small holes drilled into it at intervals corresponding to specific quantities of water in the tender. By turning the pipe through about 180 degrees with a handle, a valve at the bottom was opened, putting it in balance with the water in the tender. Jets promptly spouted out of those holes which were below the water-level—a simple, if messy, way of indicating how much remained. With this arrangement footplate passengers had even more chances of getting an unexpected ducking when a locomotive took water at troughs!

With a tender locomotive, the majority of the space in the tender is occupied by the water tank, with the coal-space let into it at the front. Self-contained tank locomotives carry their water on their own frames and various different arrangements have been used for this. Perhaps the most common system in later years was to provide side-tanks, mounted on the main-frames either side of the boiler. The cab limits their size at the rear, and usually also at the top, because it is necessary for the driver to be able to observe signals ahead. While it was not unknown for the bottom of side-tanks to be recessed to take the tops of driving wheels, any outside valve-gear has to kept clear for oiling and servicing. If there is any inside motion, the front of the tanks has to be sufficiently far back to permit access from the foot-framing. Space also has to be provided to reach washout plugs and mud-doors on the boiler, as well as to accommodate lubricators, sandbox fillers, and even air-brake pumps on the foot-framing. Various ways round these problems were adopted by different CMEs. It was, however, not usual to continue the side-tanks forward of the boiler itself, to avoid the unlagged smokebox heating the water, which could stop the injectors working.

Most side-tank locomotives also carry some water below the coal-space in the bunker. Whenever the water-supplies are dispersed like this, adequately-sized balance pipes are required to connect the bottoms of all of them so the water can interflow easily when they are being filled or the injectors running. Suitable filling arrangements are also needed, situated where the leather 'bag' of a water-column can easily be inserted. A steel 'flap' is usually provided to cover the opening at other times. It keeps out dirt which might clog the injectors, but is by no means water-tight. A locomotive with a full tank buffering-up somewhat too heartily can easily eject a lot of water around the sides of the lid, with sometimes embarrassing results for anyone standing on the platform alongside!

The amount of water that a tank engine can carry is also limited by the maximum axle-loading permitted. In Britain this resulted in an upper ceiling of 2500–3000 gallons (11 000–13 500 litres), which provides a severe limit on the maximum distance that can be run between refills. This is a factor which a designer must keep in mind when deciding whether to produce a tender or tank locomotive for a specified duty.

With steam locomotives these days running 'under the wires' on electrified lines it has become necessary to provide filling arrangements for water that avoid the need for people to climb on top of the tender. Pressure hoses are used instead of water-columns, and are attached to a low-level connection on the tender, the pipe from which discharges into the water-space. When a number of locomotives were converted for oil-firing for a few years after World War II, a similar arrangement was used to pipe the fuel into the special tank located in the tender coal-space.

A different water-tank arrangement was widely adopted for industrial tank-locomotives, even if it was less popular with the main-line companies. This is the saddle-tank arrangement, where it straddles the top of the boiler. The big disadvantage of this system is that the centre of gravity of the locomotive (and its stability) changes appreciably as the tank empties. For a locomotive pottering around a factory or mine this is not a great drawback, but it has important implications for fast running on a main line.

Well-tanks have occasionally been used, with the water supply located between the frames. Space is always particularly at a premium at this point, and the use of this type of water storage is complicated by the need to provide means for the axles to pass through or past the tank. In Britain the best-known design that used this arrangement was that introduced by Beattie. The final trio continued at work until the 1960s on the lightly-built and curvaceous Wenford Bridge branch in Cornwall. They were the last survivors of a class of 85, originally introduced in 1874 for the suburban services out of Waterloo.

As already mentioned, most locomotives carry their coal in a space let-in to the front of the tender or bunker, but a few, very small, tank engines have kept their supplies in an open box in front of the fireman's side of the cab, with access to it from alongside the firebox. In the main, supplies of fuel were tipped into the bunker or tender from the coaling-stage, which, in the days of commercial steam traction, existed at most locomotive depots. The larger ones had overhead bunkers, refilled by lifting loaded wagons with a hoist, and then tipping them sideways. Although these were expensive to build and maintain, they were capable of dealing with many more locomotives in a given time. In the heyday of North American steam, when locomotives used to work through in both directions between Chicago and San Francisco, at various stops *en route* they refuelled from similar installations, sometimes on the running lines.

It is important to make sure that the top of the pile of coal does not infringe the loading-gauge, as the first low bridge will otherwise send large lumps flying, perhaps through the windows of a train on the opposite track. On older designs of tenders coal-rails were used on the coal-space to prevent lumps vibrating their way off the sides, but in later years most tenders have been of the high-sided design. In other countries, such as France, a low wall of briquettes was often used for restraint, and would also form a reserve if the main supply ran out.

Part of the bottom of the tender or bunker is usually sloped to help 'bring the coal forward', thus easing the work of the fireman, but there were limits to what could be done in this way within the constraints of the loading-gauge. A few British locomotives were equipped with mechanical assistance for this. Some of the LMS Pacifics were fitted with steam-operated 'coal-pushers' for use on long journeys, a pair of cylinders at the rear of the coal space operating a plough arrangement to move the coal forward. They were operated by a simple steam valve under the control of the fireman. As mentioned earlier, most of that company's Garratts had a rotating coal bunker. This was conical in shape, with its larger end behind the cab, so, when it was rotated by a small steam engine, the contents worked their way towards the fireman. With preserved locomotives operating at times 'under the wires' on Railtrack's lines, entry to the tender is now forbidden, and consideration is being given to redesigning the coal-space to make more of the contents available, or perhaps trading-off some coal capacity for additional water-space.

With a full tender another problem can arise, as small coal cascades through the gate under the coal-doors on to the footplate, rather than remaining on the shovelling-plate. If the sizes of the coal-lumps have not been properly graded it often becomes necessary to open these doors and break up large lumps with the coal-hammer before they can be got out of the tender and through the firehole door. It is also important, but not always recognized, to design the shovelling-plate so that it is at least the same height above the footplate as the bottom of the firehole-door, because the fireman otherwise had to expend energy lifting every shovelful as it is moved from one to the other. The plate should also be inclined upwards towards the fireman, and have raised sides, to discourage the spillage of small coal on to the footplate.

A few locomotives have burnt wood as fuel, notably those operating through tropical forests. Wood provides much less heat for a given weight, and is far less easy to handle. Several decades ago on the Benguela Railway in Angola many of its steam locomotives were wood-fired, and short lengths of timber were fed into the firebox

Plate 6.11 The 1930s were the 'Streamline' age, and, when Deutsche Reichbahn wanted to supplement their high-speed diesel services with steam-hauled expresses, two massive, three-cylinder, Class 05 4-6-4s were obtained from Borsig. Their streamlined casings came down almost to rail-level, and, when at work, the motion was hidden behind a series of roller-shutters on each side. In May 1936 No. 05002 set a new record for steam of 200.4 km/h. (124.5 mph). No. 05001 was withdrawn in 1958, and is now preserved in the Nuremberg Transport Museum. It has been partially restored to its original form, the streamlined casing having been removed after World War II.

by hand, two firemen being carried on the larger locomotives for this purpose. At various places along the line there were refuelling points where the contents of the tender were refilled during a short stop.

Mention was made earlier of mechanical firing for coal-burning locomotives. This was rarely used in Britain, because locomotives were hardly ever required to operate beyond the physical ability of an experienced fireman. Only on special high-power trials were two firemen used, although in ordinary service a 'popular' driver would sometimes take over the shovel for a spell. In North America, however, a grate-area limit was laid down above which it was obligatory to fit mechanical-firing equipment. A scroll conveyor, driven by a small steam engine, brings the coal forward from the tender to the bottom of another which lifts it to the level of the firehole-door. There it is discharged on to a plate, where steam-jets, controlled by the fireman, project the lumps to the required part of the firebox. The fuel has to be uniformly sized to avoid any blockages. Limited British experience suggested that coal could not be placed on the fire in this way as

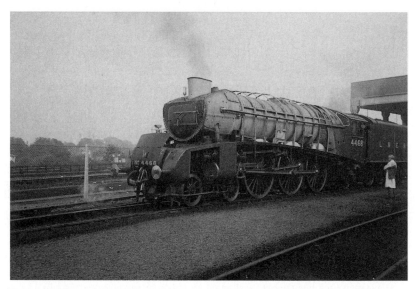

Plate 6.12 Throughout the world many streamlined locomotives had their casings removed in later years, but all of Sir Nigel Gresley's Class A4s retained theirs until withdrawn, although the deep valances over the wheels and motion were discarded during World War II in the interests of accessibility. In the 1985 photograph the world steam record-holder, *Mallard*, undergoes a steaming test. Afterwards the boiler lagging was applied as a prelude to refitting its streamlined casing for the commemorative runs the following year to mark the fiftieth-anniversary of its record.

accurately as with a fireman's shovel, the fuel consumption on an extended trial with a specially-fitted 'Merchant Navy' Pacific being higher than normal.

As previously mentioned, considerable numbers of steam locomotives, worldwide, have burnt oil. Depending on the grade used it may be necessary to apply steam-tracing to the feed pipes to ensure the fuel remains mobile at low atmospheric temperatures, but, this apart, the task of moving oil from tank to firebox is a much simpler than with solid fuel.

CHAPTER 7

The steam locomotive at work

Different duties

During the Grouping and early BR years, for operational purposes most steam-hauled trains were classified into ten categories, as shown in Fig. 7.1, each of which was identified by the position of one or two lamps

Plate 7.1 More than half the steam locomotives ever built in Britain were 0-6-0s, the last generation being typified by the Class 4Fs designed by Fowler and first built for the Midland Railway in 1911. After the 1923 Grouping more were constructed for the LMS, until there were over 770 in service. While primarily designed for freight traffic, they were frequently pressed into service on ordinary passenger trains during the warmer months, when the absence of steam-heating facilities for the carriages was acceptable, as on this charter train in September 1963.

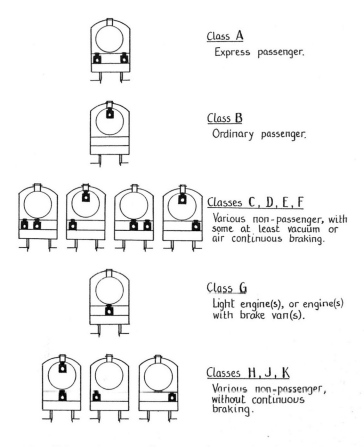

Class **A**
Express passenger.

Class **B**
Ordinary passenger.

Classes **C, D, E, F**
Various non-passenger, with some at least vacuum or air continuous braking.

Class **G**
Light engine(s), or engine(s) with brake van(s).

Classes **H, J, K**
Various non-passenger, without continuous braking.

N.B. Not used universally, and in some areas white discs substituted for lamps.

Fig. 7.1 British lamp head-codes for various classes of train.

or white discs carried on the leading end of the locomotive. These were not used universally, as in some parts of the country, notably on the Southern Railway/Region, headcodes depicted the routing of trains, rather than their category. Operationally the priority of trains was nominally in the order shown, Class A taking precedence over Class B, and so on down the table. For our purposes we have not always included all the types of train in each category, such as 'Light engine going to assist disabled train', which, like one of today's 'Thunderbirds', had top priority, and would carry Class A lamps or discs. Originally a signalman was within his rights to hold a train at a converging junction or in a loop to allow a higher category one to pass, unless specifically over-ruled by 'Control', which might take a broader view if any major traffic disruption had occurred.

Plate 7.2 On many lightly-used branch lines, steam locomotives were required to operate 'mixed trains', with one or more unbraked goods vehicles coupled on to the rear of the non-corridor passenger carriages. This illustration was taken at Boscarne Junction in North Cornwall in 1960.

Plate 7.3 One and a half million tons of imported iron ore used to be hauled every year from Tyne Dock to the steelworks at Consett, some 24 miles away and more than 850 ft (260 m) above sea level. In the late 1950s a number of BR Standard 2-10-0s were modified for this service, being fitted with Westinghouse pumps to provide the compressed air to open the side-discharge doors on the special hopper wagons. On arrival, turning a valve on the locomotive discharged some 1700 tons of ore, almost instantaneously, into the hoppers below the track. On two stages of the journey an additional locomotive was required at the rear of the train to provide the necessary tractive effort required to surmount the gradients, which were as steep as 1 in 35.

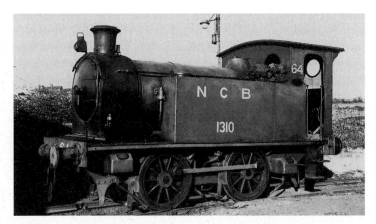

Plate 7.4 Many steam locomotives had very long lives and several owners. This 0-4-0 tank, weighing less than 23 tons, was built by the North Eastern Railway in 1891, and sold to a colliery company in Co. Durham 40 years later. In 1965 it was purchased from the National Coal Board by a group of enthusiasts, and, after restoration, has been in operation on the Middleton Railway in Leeds.

Plate 7.5 At one time it was the practice on some railways to carry re-railing jacks on each locomotive. One such example is the London, Tilbury & Southend 4-4-2T No. 80, *Thundersley*, built in 1909. On other railways re-railing ramps were provided, a practice still followed by the Cumbres & Toltec Railroad which operates in the United States. The locomotive crews there are very adept with their use when a wheel-set on one of the coaches comes off the track in the middle of the New Mexico desert!

Plate 7.6 The adaptability of steam locomotives was widely exploited by the main-line railways within the limits of track and loading-gauge. In 1874 Beattie built a class of 2-4-0 well-tanks for the London & South-Western Railway's suburban services in the London district. After three successive rebuildings, a trio of them remained at work in North Cornwall well into the 1960s, as they were the only locomotives which could cope with the curves on the lightly-constructed Wenford Bridge freight line. The relatively-small capacity of the water-tank between the frames necessitated them taking water in this sylvan setting beside the River Camel.

The choice of motive-power for different classes of train depended on various criteria, and we can now consider some of the more demanding ones as they existed in the days of steam.

Speed

Except for the war years, certain prestige British 'Express Passenger Trains' (Class A) would have been expected to reach speeds of up to 90 mph (145 km/h) on many routes, and locomotives capable of running at a minimum of 60 mph (100 km/h) would have been required for the majority of the remainder. The fastest trains would be allocated the company's largest locomotives, with driving wheels of over six feet (1830 mm) in diameter. 'Ordinary Passenger Trains' (Class B) were less demanding, but many of these would have been scheduled for speeds of up to 60 mph (100 km/h), for which locomotives with '$5\frac{1}{2}$-ft'

(1675 mm) driving wheels would have been adequate. In this country no specific maximum speeds were laid down for classes of locomotive. This was done in some continental countries, in the same way that the maximum speed permitted for each of today's diesel and electric locomotives and units is shown in each of their cabs. Such restrictions would be largely meaningless unless the locomotives were fitted with speedometers, which was not generally the case in the UK until BR days.

The 'Ordinary Passenger Train' category also included the multitude of branch-line trains which ran daily before the 'Beeching axe' and other cuts took effect. Some of these lines were subject to very modest maximum speeds, often well below 60 mph, and in many cases locomotives with driving wheels as small as $4\frac{1}{2}$ ft (1370 mm) were used without the number of revolutions per minute getting undesirably high.

While some parcels, mail, and perishable-goods trains ran almost as fast as express passenger ones, the vast majority of 'Freight Trains' (Classes H, J, and K) in the steam era were not fitted with continuous brakes, and their maximum speeds were constrained by braking distances and the running stability of the four-wheeled, short-wheelbase, wagons and vans being hauled.

Tractive effort

When allocating locomotives to particular duties it is necessary to keep in mind the maximum tractive efforts likely to be required on the journey to be made. These are determined by two factors: the weight of the train and the steepness of the gradients encountered. Loading tables for every route were provided to show the maximum loads permitted with each individual class. These took into account factors such as the adhesion weight available, as well as the locomotives' ability to exert the required tractive effort at up to the scheduled speeds required. This is governed by the rate at which the boiler can produce steam, as will be explained in a later section. On many very steep sections of line—often those with gradients greater than about 1 in 70—the commercial requirements for train weights often necessitated the use of assistant locomotives to help trains up the banks, although this inevitably required a stop at the foot of the incline to bring the banker up in rear. As an alternative, an assistant locomotive might be attached in front of the train engine over certain stretches of line, the loading tables specifying the maximum weight of train permissible with various combinations of locomotive. The tables often recognized that two locomotives were not necessarily twice as capable as a single one!

In BR days the haulage capability of each locomotive design was broadly classified by a power rating, from 0 to 9. The higher the figure, the more powerful was the locomotive. This system was the same as that originally adopted by the LMS, and the figure was given a letter suffix, 'P' or 'F', to indicate whether the locomotive was primarily intended for Passenger or Freight duties, the requirements for each being slightly different. With passenger trains the grate area is the most significant factor, but with freight the tractive effort is more important. Mixed-traffic designs with similar 'P' and 'F' ratings were suffixed with 'MT' although, in the early days of LMS usage, that classification was stated in the form '5P5F'. (The LMS also used the '5XP' classification for the three-cylinder 'Patriots' and 'Jubliees' as originally built, to indicate they were 'worth' $5\frac{1}{2}$ P, being more powerful than the two-cylinder Class 5P5F 4-6-0s.) It became usual to display these 'Power Classifications' in the form of small transfers above the locomotive's number on the sides of the cab.

Adhesion

The adhesion weight of a locomotive is also a factor that has to be taken into account when selecting one for a particular working. To some extent this was included in the calculations behind the loading tables referred to above, because in a well-proportioned locomotive the nominal tractive effort is related to the total weight on its driving-wheels. This determines the maximum tractive effort likely to be achieved at slow speeds without causing the wheels to slip. Other things being equal, this depends on the number of driving axles, a 0-4-0, for example, potentially having only half the adhesion of a 0-8-0. The adhesion weight is important enough for traction purposes, but is even more vital when it comes to stopping trains which are only partially fitted with continuous brakes or have none at all. If the locomotive is provided with a tender, the maximum braking force available is greater than with a comparable tank engine because tender axles are normally provided with brakes which can operated from the footplate, as described in the next chapter.

Length of journey

The locomotive requirements for a given type of train are also dictated by the length of journey it is required to undertake. Two factors are important in this respect—the amounts of fuel and water carried. The tender or side-tanks might fairly easily be refilled during a short stop, or from troughs in the case of classes fitted with scoops, but, in Europe, there is no quick way of replenishing a locomotive's coal supplies without uncoupling it from the train and taking it to a depot. Some North American railroads used to have coaling equipment at intervals close alongside their running lines enabling the same steam locomotive to run through for long distances on the same train—all the way from Chicago to San Francisco, for example. The coal supply requirements are thus of a somewhat longer-term nature than the water ones, many locomotives having sufficient coal capacity to complete their day's roster without the need for refuelling. Even so it was not unknown for a locomotive to run out of coal at times, usually as a result of extremely adverse atmospheric conditions.

Infrastructure restrictions

For historical and economic reasons, not every railway line was built to the same loading-gauge, and there are considerable variations in the maximum weights that can be allowed over them. A railway's civil engineers thus have to classify every line to ensure that locomotives using them do not hit any over-bridges or tunnels with tight clearances, or overload under-bridges or the track itself. The railway's Chief Civil Engineer would have a dossier of all this information, and this would be kept up to date and, hopefully, circulated to all concerned. The GWR Chief Mechanical Engineer discovered to its surprise in the 1920s that the maximum permitted axleload on that railway's main lines had been increased to $22\frac{1}{2}$ tons, but the locomotive department had not been informed.

The maximum permitted axleload is largely determined by the point-loading that the track, including switches and crossings, can support at the time it is due for renewal. From the point of view of under-bridges, it is the spread of weight that matters, referred to as 'per foot run', and this in places could debar the heaviest classes from double-heading trains, an example being the Aberdeen–Elgin line in the north of Scotland.

From 1947 the LNER used a 'Route Availability' system to classify their locomotives and lines, ranging from 'R.A.0' up to 'R.A.9'. The higher the figure the more severely restricted was the locomotive's ability to wander. This system was extended to all routes after nationalization in 1948, and eventually all BR locomotives carried the 'R.A.' number on the cab side.

Another infrastructure consideration that had to be taken into consideration when allocating a type of locomotive to a particular line was the availability—or otherwise—of a large enough turntable to enable it to be turned when it reached either end of its journey. Where there was either no turntable or one that was too small for a particular class, it was necessary to consider whether it would be safe for the locomotive to operate 'tender-first' on the return working. Visibility was usually a lot worse when running like that, and if drivers put their heads out of the cab window they might be danger of hitting them on an over-bridge or other lineside obstruction. In some places where there was no suitable turntable, a 'triangle' provided an alternative way of turning a locomotive end-for-end, but these were sometimes too sharply curved to be traversed safely by large locomotives. Known as a 'Wye' in North America, these were used more extensively that side of the Atlantic, as they were cheaper to construct in the 'wide-open' spaces of the western states. Tank locomotives are designed to be operated safely in either direction, and were consequently employed extensively on many minor branch lines, where their smaller coal and water capacities did not interfere with operational requirements.

Some branch lines, or even certain mainline services, were worked by 'push–pull' trains. In the diesel and electric era very many trains are operated in this way, but these rely on modern electric or electronic control systems to enable the driver to operate the motive power and braking system from whichever cab is being used. With steam traction, only the driver would be at the front-end when the locomotive was propelling its train, the fireman staying on the footplate to look after the fire and the water-level in the boiler. There was usually a simple bell-system between the leading cab and the locomotive, with a set of codes for the driver to give specific instructions to the fireman, such as when to open or close the regulator, or 'link-up' the valve-gear. In practice, however, the firemen got so used to the routine that they were left to get on with these operations at the right time. On the Great Western Railway, their 'Motor Trains', as they termed the push–pull workings, were provided with a mechanical link to enable the driver to operate the regulator in the locomotive's cab, and other railways used a system worked by vacuum from the locomotive's ejector for this purpose. The driver was also provided with a brake-application valve acting on the vacuum train pipe, the release relying on the action of the small ejector as described in Chapter 8.

The Railway Inspectorate has historically stipulated a maximum number of coaches (normally two) that could be propelled in this way. In the light of carefully controlled tests by the Southern Region, which showed that up to eight coaches could be propelled safely on the Waterloo–Bournemouth line, whole trains are now operated in this way. All electrically powered expresses of the East Coast Main Line in the UK have been operated for nearly a decade at speeds of 125 mph (200 km/h) with the locomotive at the north end, propelling nine passenger coaches and the leading vehicle (a driving-van trailer) in the southbound direction. On a special run in 1995, with the Secretary of State for Transport aboard, a shortened set even reached 154 mph (248 km/h) with the locomotive propelling it. At speeds of over 100mph (180 km/h), however, following an accident at Polmont, the Railway Inspectorate withdrew permission for passengers to ride in a leading, non-powered vehicle, although such an arrangement is widely authorized on the mainland of Europe at speeds as high as 300 km/h (186 mph). On the latest German Inter-City Expresses some of the first-class passengers will be able to watch the line ahead over the driver's shoulder, although the glass partition separating them will automatically go opaque if the emergency brake is applied, as it would be if a collision were imminent!

In steam days some other permanent-way layouts could also restrict the use of a particularly long locomotives. At various terminal platforms it was often necessary to be able to 'release' a locomotive so it could run-round its train for the next working. Space in some stations was very limited and there could be a maximum length of locomotive which could be accommodated between the buffer-stops and the cross-overs used to release them, so the allocation of one longer that this would upset the regular working of the services. A different example of platform-length limitations faced the so-called 'Jazz' suburban services which used to operate out of Liverpool Street station in London. As originally introduced, these used a set of four platforms, and, as soon as a train stopped, the tank locomotive was uncoupled, while another set back on to the rear coach. Four minutes later the train departed, the incoming locomotive following it into the short dead-end 'dock' at the 'country' end of the platforms, where it awaited its turn to set back on the next arriving set. Each of the four platforms was thus able to deal with a train every ten minutes, but chaos would have ensued if a locomotive was used which was too long to be accommodated in the 'dock'.

Economics

The directors and officers of a steam-operated railway had to weigh up the construction and operating costs of different-sized locomotives when deciding how many of what type were required for the service pattern they needed to optimize revenue. Larger locomotives were more expensive to build and maintain, as well as requiring more fuel, particularly when they were being lit up from cold. A quota of extra locomotives was needed, over and above those rostered for service every day, to ensure that all regular services, as well as seasonal and extra trains, could be covered. This still had to apply when some of that class of locomotives were being 'washed-out' or were undergoing shed repairs or a works overhaul, but a well-run railway would keep this 'surplus' under close review.

The steam locomotive is a versatile machine, and, given no constraints of the types described above, there are no operating reasons why a larger one should not be used on a less important service if it is available. Indeed, one of the attractions offered by a steam-operated railway was the variety of locomotive types that could turn up with the same working on different days. There were, for instance, certain locomotive rosters which were earmarked for use as 'running-in turns' when required, enabling the fitting staff to check that a locomotive just back from overhaul was ready to undertake its regular, more demanding, mainline duties. As an example, King's Cross frequently used one of its workings, normally a 4-6-0 'job', to send an 'ex-shops' Pacific on a 'leisurely' round-trip to Cambridge, where members of the university railway society used to keep an eye (or ear) on what turned up with that particular service!

On the other hand, a smaller locomotive usually could not satisfactorily take the place of a larger one on a demanding working, and substitutions of this sort were less common, except when no larger one was available, a situation that was not uncommon in an emergency. Nevertheless it was not unknown for a shunting locomotive to take over a mainline service if the normal train engine suffered a failure of some sort. Even a 0-6-0 tank should have enough tractive effort to haul a mainline train plus locomotive at low speed, say 15–20 mph (24–32 km/h) on level track, as far as the next loop where the failure could be sidetracked to clear the main line.

In today's preservation world, the locomotives used on the privately-owned lines are frequently far larger than those which were used there in the days of BR steam. Again there can be a good economic reason for such an over-provision of motive power, as the 'guest appearance' of a famous Pacific on a line normally only worked by less notable locomotives can significantly boost its revenue by enough to justify the cost of the several additional tons of coal needed to raise steam.

Shunting duties

In steam days there were numerous important locomotive workings for which none of the headcodes in Fig. 7.1 were used. Vast numbers of shunting locomotives were needed in passenger and freight yards to sort vehicles and make-up trains for dispatch,. Some would work empty passenger stock to and from the station where it began or finished its journey, for which a Class C headcode was specified. For the last type of working, relatively small six-coupled tanks were perfectly adequate, and were able to shift even the longest rake of coaches. On the other hand, some of the regular shunting operations in freight yards were very demanding and required the services of large, specially-built designs. These were needed to propel long trains of freight wagons over the steeply-inclined 'humps' used to speed up the sorting process. From 1929 the Southern Railway built eight Class Z 0-8-0Ts for this purpose, and the LNER rebuilt 13 of the former Great Central 0-8-0 tender locomotives as 0-8-0 tanks for similar use during World War II.

Even before the days of BR and the Modernisation Plan, the advantages of using diesel-electric locomotives for heavy shunting duties became apparent. To add to the benefits of the almost continuous availability provided by this type of motive power, they could be operated without a fireman. The first major replacement of steam operations in Britain was thus made with shunting duties.

Although an individual headcode for yard shunters does not appear in Fig. 7.1, in BR days diesels used to carry one red and one white lamp at either end of each buffer-beam, which provided adequate warning of movements in either direction without the constant need to switch the lamps from one end to the other whenever the locomotive changed direction.

For the sake of completeness, it should be added that Royal Trains used to carry four headlamps, often of a special ornate design, one on each of the usual four brackets at the front of the locomotive. These workings also used twin tail-lamps, and the 'stop and examine' message was only sent ahead at night if both of these oil lamps had gone out.

Matching output with demands

Unlike the engines of an ocean-going ship, which will often operate at constant output for days at end, in the course of every journey the power demands from a steam locomotive are constantly being varied, either because of speed restrictions or to cope with changing gradients. The driver has two means of adjusting the power output: the regulator opening and the cut-off used for the valve-gear. Altering either of these can bring about an immediate change in power output, and therefore the steam demand from the boiler. The effect of this on the boiler depends on its volume, as well as the magnitude of the change made. Balancing the two effects requires cooperation between the driver and fireman, particularly if the locomotive is being worked at the upper end of its power output.

As discussed in Chapter 4, for maximum efficiency a locomotive should normally be operated with a wide-open regulator. If a train that is travelling at a steady speed on the level approaches a rising gradient, the driver, to maintain the same speed, would have to increase the cut-off point of the valve-gear to admit more steam into the cylinders for every stroke. A small change in cut-off will only increase the steam requirement by a small amount. The resulting increased vacuum produced by the greater flow through blast-pipe might be enough to draw extra air through the fuel already present in the firebox, and, by burning more of it, this might be sufficient to maintain the boiler pressure. This would balance things in the short term, but, as the locomotive is working harder, in the longer term fuel will have to be put into the firebox at a greater rate to provide the additional source of heat. The boiler thus provides a 'cushion' or dynamic reservoir of energy which enables the crew to 'buffer' any short-term alterations in steam demand.

The steam reserves in the boiler at any particular time are determined by two different factors: the water-level and the steam pressure. Either can be mortgaged for short periods, but, like all loans, they have eventually to be paid back. On a climb over a summit the water level has to be carefully watched to ensure that there is no danger of exposing the top of the inner firebox when the gradient suddenly changes at the top of the bank. On the other hand, once on the down-grade less steam will be required to maintain speed, so there is no great disadvantage from filling the boiler up with cold water towards the top of the ascent, even if this knocks the pressure back.

In the extreme case, if the gradient is so steep that even full cut-off is inadequate to maintain the train's speed, there is nothing more the crew can do, assuming the boiler-pressure is at blowing-off point, making it impossible to operate that train at constant speed. In practice, the schedules for steam-hauled trains normally made allowance for speeds to vary appreciably on the uphill and downhill stretches of line. The tendency was for the locomotives to be operated closer to a constant power output rather than a constant speed.

On a down gradient, with speed tending to rise, the driver will normally alter the setting of the valve-gear to admit steam for less of the pistons' stroke, but there are limits to how far it is practicable to 'link up'. This is because, at very short cut-offs, inaccuracies in valve-setting become more obvious, and most valve gears also restrict the openings to exhaust. Excessive compression then occurs as the piston approaches the ends of its stroke, and the back-pressure wastes steam because the relief-valves on the cylinder covers open on each stroke. This also causes mechanical shocks to the motion, which are, at best, uncomfortable, and can be damaging. If a locomotive continues to accelerate on a particular down-grade with the valve-gear linked-up to the point where over-compression is about to take place, the driver will start to decrease the use of steam by partially closing the regulator.

As well as meeting the requirements of maintaining the schedule over varying gradients, the crew have constantly to keep in mind the possibility of meeting adverse signals, which, in the worst case, could immediately necessitate the shutting of the regulator, and braking to a standstill. If the firebed has been built up for a high power output, even though the blast stops, a lot of steam will still be generated with nowhere to go, except through the safety-valves. If it is possible to operate with a fairly low water-level in the boiler, there is always the possibility to put both injectors on immediately to stop the safety-valves lifting and wasting energy. It is also important for the driver or fireman to turn on the blower to maintain some vacuum in the smokebox, and thus prevent a 'blow-back' of smoke and flame into the cab through the firehole.

The steam locomotive is thus operating at its best when the driver and fireman are both aware of exactly what the other man on the footplate is doing and aiming to achieve. Many mainline drivers used to make it a regular policy to let the fireman drive for a short period every turn, while he took over the shovel. Not only did this enable the fireman to understand the control settings needed to work the train to time, but also prepared him for the day when he could seek promotion. Such a policy also effectively prevented the fireman from complaining that the driver worked him harder, physically, than he was prepared to exert himself!

Power vs speed

Steam locomotives differ very considerably from modern motive power when it comes to the development of maximum power output. The diesel engine 'prime-mover' in a diesel-electric locomotive can produce its full rated output independently of the locomotive's speed, and newly-overhauled ones are regularly tested in this way, with the locomotive stationary and its electric power being passed through static 'resistance banks'. When the generator is connected to the traction motors it is not be possible to use full output at very low speeds because of adhesion limits and the risk of overheating the electrical equipment, but even with the high-powered 'Deltics', the controller can be opened fully as soon as speed reaches 20 mph (32 km/h). To avoid overheating the generators and traction motors, the automatic controls of the diesel engines still throttle the power by a maximum of 10 per cent until a speed of about 42 mph (68 km/h) is reached.

Unlike a diesel-electric locomotive, the pistons of a steam one are directly attached to its driving wheels, and the train has to be moving at an appreciable speed before the cylinders are capable of 'consuming' all the steam capable of being produced in the boiler. Its maximum production of power—the rate of doing work—can thus be limited by either of these items, depending, for a particular design, on its speed along the track.

With ideal dry rail conditions, from quite a slow speed the driver might be able to have the reversing gear in the fully-forward position and the regulator fully open without causing the driving-wheels to slip. Even so, one of the rebuilt 'Merchant Navy' class Pacifics—the last sizeable class of British express-passenger steam locomotives for which test results are available—had to be travelling at about 20 mph to use the 38 000 lb/h of steam its boiler could produce. (See Fig. 7.2.) The corresponding horsepower produced was about 1725 hp. at 20 mph, and below that the output varied almost linearly with speed. Under these slow-running conditions the internal friction of the locomotive and its air resistance would be small, and, on level track, the drawbar

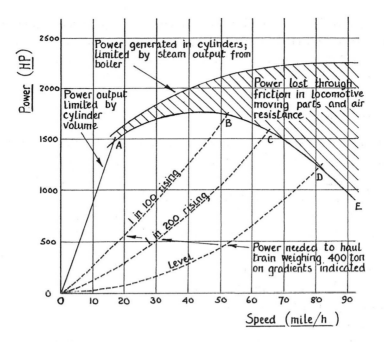

OABCDE – Power output available at drawbar to haul train.

The above graphs demonstrate the train balancing speeds
achievable – in this example for instance :

  81 mile/h   on level track (point D)
  65   do.   1 in 200 rising gradient (point C)
  51   do.   1 in 100 rising gradient (point B),

all determined by the steam output from the boiler
controlled by the cut-off selected by the driver.

Fig. 7.2 Typical locomotive power output and train resistance curves.

horsepower (DBHP) would be very close to that produced in the
cylinders, which is known as the Indicated Horsepower (IHP).

As the speed increased, a driver wanting to maintain maximum
acceleration, keeping the same steady steam rate, would start to link up
the valve gear. This would have the effect of reducing the Mean Effective
Pressure (MEP) in the cylinders, but the greater number of strokes in a
given time would still increase the IHP, but no longer linearly with the
speed. The straightline part of the power-output line thus changes to a
curve, as shown by the uppermost one in Fig. 7.2, and, with this class,
continues to rise to a speed of about 80 mph. The extra energy for this

comes from the expansion of the steam in the cylinders, the actual steam production in the boiler remaining constant.

Unfortunately not all this extra power being produced in the cylinders can be used to haul the train. The locomotive's internal friction and its air resistance both start to increase rapidly as speed rises above 20 mph, as represented by the shaded portion of Fig. 7.2. Deducting these losses from the cylinder output gives the lower power line, which shows a peak of 1750 DBHP at a speed of 45 mph for this particular class of locomotives, falling off to less than 1000 hp at 90 mph. Such a curve is typical of those for all steam locomotives.

Below this DBHP line in Fig. 7.2 are three dashed curves, showing how the power required to move a typical 400 ton train of that period varied with speed on different gradients. The points where these intersect the DBHP curve indicate what the balancing speed of the train would be on such a stretch of track with the locomotive operating at its maximum rate of steaming.

For maximum acceleration a steam locomotive driver will use full cut-off, and control any tendency to slip with the regulator. As soon as the latter has been opened fully, the driver will prepare to 'link-up' (reduce the cut-off). Some drivers did this in large steps of 10–20 per cent at a time, but other drivers would wind the reverser back slowly to maintain a roughly constant use of steam in the cylinders, trading off a reducing quantity used for each stroke with the extra revolutions of the driving wheels. This was not possible with lever reversers, because they had to be moved from notch to notch, nor with slide-valve locomotives where, as described earlier, it was necessary to close the regulator before altering the valve-settings.

Limits of performance

The maximum power output of a steam locomotive is affected by a number of different constraints, some determined by its design, and others by the conditions under which it is having to operate at the time. Given that all the power comes from the burning of the fuel, the maximum quantity that can be consumed is determined by size of the grate and/or the amount of draught produced by the blastpipe. Either of these factors can cause the limitation. Once all the oxygen in the air is being used for combustion, increasing the firing rate will not liberate more heat. On the other hand, if the blast is increased, for example by using longer cut-offs or wider regulator openings, the point can be reached where the firebed begins to be lifted by the rapid flow of air. This inevitably results in large amounts of unburnt fuel being ejected out of the chimney, with all the fire-raising hazards that implies, but little real increase in the amount of steam raised. This is the primary trade-off that has to be taken into account by a crew wanting to get maximum output from their locomotive.

This trade-off assumes that the fireman can maintain whatever firing rate is required to achieve the maximum output, which is not always the case. The sheer physical effort may be too much for even the most 'macho' of firemen, but this can be overcome by fitting mechanical stoking equipment, albeit with a lower efficiency, as mentioned earlier. On some of the high-output test runs carried out in BR days it was customary to use two firemen to keep up the necessary firing rate. It must not be overlooked that a fireman cannot spend all his time shovelling coal through the firehole door, as there are other important duties to be carried out, such as controlling the water-level, and looking for signals that are not visible from the driver's side of the cab. The amount of coal remaining in the tender or bunker can also have an effect, for two reasons. There is the important consideration whether it will be sufficient to last the rest of the journey, while, as the quantity remaining get less, it usually becomes steadily more difficult to reach from the firing-plate. The quality of the fuel is also a vital factor, both from calorific-value considerations, as well as its tendency to form ash or clinker, because either of the latter can clog the firebed, thus reducing the combustion rate.

Clearly, any dimensional factors can be altered at the design stage, but again there are limitations to what can be done to increase the size of the grate or the airflow through it. Loading-gauge and/or weight restrictions are likely to exert an upper limit on the former, but altering the blast-pipe arrangements may not be so difficult if it is necessary to provide more air, as described in Chapter 3. However, it may not make economic sense to increase the draughting on a particular design to enable a few locomotives produce high power outputs, if the rest of class is only used on less demanding duties when the overall efficiency might suffer from the modifications made.

Another operating trade-off that has to be considered is the question of water-level and boiler pressure, as described in the previous section. As with the fuel, there is the longer-term aspect of whether the quantities are sufficient to last until the next point where more can be obtained from the troughs or a line-side water-column. If the crew are trying to regain time, any forced out-of-course stop to take water will have the opposite effect from that desired, and, if they were to 'press on regardless', they could face the prospect of having to drop the fire to protect the boiler should the water supply run out completely.

There can be other limits to performance, such as the maximum speed at which the locomotive can be worked within the limits that the crew are prepared to tolerate. This is determined by several basic design factors, including the driving-wheel diameter and the degree of balancing, as well as the suspension and general riding capabilities, in addition to the general condition of the permanent way. On a particular locomotive, the condition of the motion and the steam tightness of many components are major factors which can produce significant variations between theoretically identical members of the same class.

Emergencies

There are several emergencies that can arise on the footplate of a steam locomotive, the ultimate severity of which can, in some cases, be affected by the immediate action taken by the crew.

In an earlier section the possibility of a blow-back through the firehole-door was mentioned. The simplest cause of this is the failure to turn on the blower as the locomotive goes under a low bridge or tunnel, or when the regulator is closed suddenly. A quick turn of the blower valve should deal with the problem. There are, however, more serious causes for such a happening—the failure or holing of one of the smoketubes or superheater elements in the boiler. This requires not only immediate full use of the blower, but the closing of the regulator together with an emergency brake application, because the copious escape of flames, smoke and steam could drive the crew off the footplate.

On the other hand, emergencies can arise when closing the regulator could cause more damage. As described earlier, the direction of the vertical forces on the slidebars reverses as the regulator is opened or closed. If there is a sudden burst of clattering from the motion, an emergency application of the brake should not immediately be followed by closing the regulator, as the latter might well exacerbate the problem.

There used to be other emergency conditions when it was better to keep going at all costs, such as when a loose-coupled freight train became divided on a falling gradient. A whistle-call to the guard would alert him, if needed, to the need to apply the van handbrake, but this might not, of itself, be sufficient to hold the rear portion of the train on the gradient. Under such conditions it could have been better for the locomotive to maintain the speed of the front portion to avoid it being overtaken by the rear one. The profile of the track ahead would clearly have an important effect on the ideal tactics to be adopted. Fortunately the most likely conditions for such a breakaway were in the dip between two opposed steepish gradients. On the descent the couplings would be slack at the front of the train because of the brake application being made by the locomotive. As this was released, and power applied ready for the climb ahead, the couplings would successively be tightened. If this was not done carefully, a bad snatch or 'rug' could be sufficient to pull a wagon's drawhook out by the roots. On the Glasgow & South Western Railway at Pinwherry an incident occurred when a rake of wagons separated and then ran backwards and forwards several times through the dip at the station before they came finally to a halt, while the locomotive and front portion of the train continued safely up the incline out of harm's way.

Another emergency that can arise on a steam locomotive is the overheating of a bearing, usually on one of the driving axles. This can make itself known to the crew by the smell of burning oil, although the streamlined Gresley Pacifics were fitted with a special 'stink-bomb' on the middle big-end to make sure those on the footplate were quickly made aware of any problem with that hidden component. In such circumstances power and speed needed to be reduced immediately, the train ideally being brought to a stand. If the problem has been detected in time it may be possible to continue to the next loop or station where the failed locomotive and its train are not blocking the running line. A generous dose of oil from the driver's can also help under these conditions. If the overheating is serious, the white metal in the bearing will 'run', and the resulting bright dribbles will draw attention to the site of the problem.

Servicing and maintenance

Like most mechanical devices, the steam locomotive requires attention during its working life, to keep it in good condition and enable it to carry out its intended duties. Practical experience over a century and a half saw this work being split into three separate headings:

1. *Servicing.* This includes the supply of fuel, water, lubricants, and sand, as well as cleaning work on the fire and smokebox.

2. *Running maintenance.* Attention to the material parts of the machine itself, including minor repairs.

3. *Overhaul.* This is when the locomotive is stripped down to its component parts for rehabilitation, and requires the resources of an appropriately-equipped workshop, rather than a running shed.

The split between Running Maintenance and Overhaul varied between railways and from time to time, depending on the policies laid down for the Operating and Engineering Departments of the owning company. Different views have inevitably been taken on whether to carry out as much work as possible at the running sheds, or concentrate the effort in a minimum number of Main Works where it might be possible to provide more extensive equipment which would speed up the overhaul.

Servicing

Fuel

Every locomotive needs a supply of fuel. By definition a locomotive is designed to move about, and to be used effectively it needs to take an adequate supply of fuel with it. As indicated in Chapter 6, the quantity needed depends on the duties it is required to perform from day to day. As refuelling is a slow and labourious job, and fuel supplies need to be delivered to a suitable reception point, it became customary for this operation to be carried out at depots.

The most common fuel used in Britain was coal, which could vary over a range of composition and quality, from semi-anthracite to briquettes made from compressed coal dust or slack. Semi-processed coal, in the form of coke, was also used in the early days to prevent the emission of smoke. All these materials are bulky, and dirty, so refuelling tended to involve hard physical work by a 'black gang', although mechanical equipment was provided at some major depots.

This typically took the form of a concrete hopper over the track, with a delivery system which enabled the crew to let the required amount of coal into the tender or bunker. The hopper was filled using a hoist which either lifted a complete wagon and turned it over sideways, or used a skip operating from a wagon-discharge pit at ground level. Many mainline depots were provided with nothing more than a raised track some 5–7 m (15–20 ft) high, to take the coal wagons. Space alongside enabled the fuel to be shovelled into small skips, which were then pushed and tipped by hand into the locomotives' tenders or bunkers.

Coaling equipment usually had to be provided for the supply of two different grades of coal, because that needed for express passenger work was more expensive than the lower quality material which was adequate for other duties. All types had to meet minimum requirements laid down by the railway concerned, and supplies could sometimes be hard to obtain. Industrial problems at the mines could stop production, and it was sometimes impossible to purchase what was required in the country concerned. When coal mining was mechanized, the size of the coal lumps decreased, and this caused difficulties for the railways, although electric generating stations were happy to use it, because they needed to grind it to produce the finely pulverized fuel with which their boilers were fired.

In less peaceful times the need for assured supplies to keep a country's strategic railways running at times of crisis could even colour the nation's politics. One of the French railways was so concerned about security of coal supplies that it invested in overseas mines and a fleet of colliers to transport the fuel to the home country. To economize on the use of the higher-grade fuels some railways used briquettes, made from compressed coal-dust with a suitable binder. These were used for lighting up and operations around the depot, as well as a mobile reserve. Their shape made it possible to keep them separate from the ordinary coal by stacking them at the back of the tender.

The next most common fuel used was oil, again with a range of chemical compositions and viscosities. In the main these were fluids, although some, such as heavy fuel oil, needed steam-traced piping to ensure they would flow or could be pumped into the locomotives' fuel tanks. Refuelling with a fluid was somewhat easier, as it did away with physical handling, and could be carried out from ground-level if the locomotive was fitted with a suitable hose connection on a pipe leading to the top of the tank.

Elsewhere in the world almost every combustible material has been used from time to time as fuel for steam locomotives. The majority of these have been solid materials, which present similar problems to coal when it comes to loading them on to the locomotive or its tender. In some tropical countries the railways relied on wood fuel, grown in forests alongside their tracks, and in places trains would stop by a convenient woodpile to restock the tender with logs a foot or two long (300–600 mm).

The size of a locomotive's fuel capacity has to be scaled for the duties for which it was designed and had to carry out during its most lengthy turn of duty. In this country the longest and most demanding locomotive duties were those on express passenger trains between London and Scotland, a distance of some 650 km (400 miles). There were commercial pressures for the locomotives to work through, because either there was no business need for intermediate calls, or to save the time needed to change them at an intermediate stop. A maximum of 10 tons of coal would be needed for such a journey on the Euston–Glasgow route, but the less heavily-graded line between King's Cross and Edinburgh enabled the LNER's original Pacific locomotives to get by with a capacity of eight tons. Later locomotives used on this route were provided with tenders holding nine tons, which gave an increased margin, especially after schedules had been tightened. Most of the GWR's locomotives managed with six tons, although after World War II this was increased to seven with the new design of tenders first built for the 'Counties', possibly because of the declining quality of coal then available. On the Southern, even Bulleid's Pacifics had a capacity of five tons only, but this reflected the short distances over which they operated. Smaller locomotives needed less still, and, if their turn of duties was likely to require a capacity of less than $4\frac{1}{2}$ tons, it became possible to consider the tank-engine format, which was simpler and less expensive to build. In countries where trans-continental locomotive workings were much longer, the coal capacity of tenders was much higher, some of those in the United States carrying up to 30 tons.

Water

Just as vital to the successful operation of a steam railway is a plentiful supply of water at key points on the system. In the vast majority of cases locomotives did not condense their exhaust steam, so, as with the fuel, their range of operation was limited by what they could carry. Water, however, was more vital than the fuel, because of the danger of damage to the boiler if the water level dropped too low. A locomotive running out of fuel could safely stop and await rescue, but if the water in the tank became exhausted at a point where no additional supplies were available, the crew were faced with the prospect of having to stop and drop the fire quickly to prevent damage to the firebox.

Where locomotives required to be fitted with equipment for condensing their exhaust steam, the easiest way of doing this was to divert the steam exhausted from the cylinders away from the blast-pipe into the water in their tanks, using pipes which dipped down close to the bottom. The condensation heated up the water, and, if the temperature rose too high, a point could be reached when no more condensation would take place. It was thus a temporary expedient, used on short stretches of track where there were particularly difficult conditions. The majority of these were in tunnels, such as the Inner Circle in London, where atmospheric conditions became intolerable if the steam were exhausted to the confined spaces. There were drawbacks, as the loss of blast reduced the steaming rate, and the raised temperature of the water-supply required the provision of a mechanical feed-pump to top up the boiler, because injectors will not work with hot feed water.

Other, more elaborate, condensing systems were used under particularly demanding conditions, such as operations across deserts. There was an even more specialized use in World War II, when the German supply railways behind the front lines in Russia wanted to prevent the tell-tale exhaust plumes from steam locomotives being spotted from the air. Large condensing tenders were used, with fans pulling air past numerous tubes through which the steam passed. It was also necessary to provide a steam-driven exhaust fan in the smokebox to draw sufficient air through the firebed to ensure the locomotive steamed properly.

The quantities of water used on a mainline steam railway made it uneconomic to provide locomotives with enough tank capacity to enable their supplies to last between visits to depots for refuelling. In the course of a 650-km (400-mile) journey, such as the through workings from London to Scotland, a locomotive could easily use more than 70 m^3 (15 000 gallons) of water, weighing some 70 tons/tonnes. It was therefore the normal practice to provide water in quantity at most main stopping points. (One of the fireman's priorities was to 'put the bag in' at every opportunity, as there was nothing more worrying for the crew than finding that an anticipated watering point had run dry when the water level in the locomotive's tank was already near the bottom.)

As described in Chapter 6, to cope with the long-distance runs for which the mainline railways in Great Britain were noted, numerous sets

Plate 7.7 The tender water-scoop on the GWR 4-4-0 *City of Truro* in its raised position, with a protective metal plate covering the open end on the left-hand side to prevent any debris entering it. The gap on the right, below the hinge, closes when the scoop is lowered, forming a continuous duct to carry the water up into the tender.

of water troughs were installed, where a speeding locomotive, fitted with a pick-up scoop, could lift some 10 m³ (2000 gallons) of water as it passed over them. The design trade-off between the spacing of these installations and the locomotive's tank capacity varied between railway companies, the traffic levels and commercial demands. Smaller locomotives usually had to manage with a smaller water capacity.

Another factor to be considered when planning the provision of water supplies is its rate of flow from its source, but low rates can be compensated by local storage, and lineside watering points could frequently be identified by the presence of large cylindrical or rectangular tanks. Ideally a locomotive should be able to fill up with water in the time scheduled for passenger duties at that station, but this was not always possible. The Southern's practice of changing locomotives at Salisbury was adopted because it was quicker to do that than wait for the tender to be refilled.

While the water supply for steam locomotives does not have to be of potable quality, the less impurities the better. In mountain areas the run-off from streams often provided an extremely pure supply, but it was rarely economic to pipe water any distance. At York the Ouse was

Plate 7.8 In 1955 Ivatt 2-6-2T No. 41295 takes water at Hatherleigh, North Devon. On a summer Saturday that year one of the authors was the only passenger on the train for most of the journey from Halwill to Torrington, so the line's closure in 1966 came as no surprise. When originally designed these locomotives had a shorter, wider-diameter chimney, and the less elegant design shown in the illustration was subsequently fitted to improve the steaming.

still clean enough to enable the columns to be supplied from the river over an area around the station that stretched for a mile or so in each direction. A pump-house and storage-tank were provided in the angle between the lines to Scarborough and Darlington at the north end of the station.

In parts of the world where water was very scarce, the railway had no alternative but to build long-distance pipelines. A particularly striking example occurred in the Atacama Desert in Chile, where the whole 325 km (200-mile) stretch of line between San Pedro and the Pacific coast was fed with melt water from the permanent snow-cap on two nearby volcanoes. Across the wastes of the desert the twin rails are still parallelled with a telephone line and the two, half-buried, pipelines for

Plate 7.9 One of Drummond's Class T9 4-4-0 'Greyhounds' gets the road at Halwill with a train for Bude in 1995. The large tenders provided on this class made up for the lack of water troughs on the London & South-Western Railway's routes to the west of England, and were nicknamed 'water carts'.

the water, which is now sold to the local towns since steam locomotives have been phased out.

In this country it was rarely economic for a railway to take a supply from the local waterworks, but the alternatives could be very variable in quality. In some places water treatment was used by the railway, either on the ground or in the locomotive, and some of the problems could be overcome by using a continuous blow-down from the boiler to limit the build-up of dissolved solids.

The contrasts between the best and worst water supplies were considerable. At one extreme good water might make it possible to operate a boiler for several months without washing it out, while, at the other, even twice-weekly washing was not enough to prevent the build-up of hard scale which reduced the steaming rate and necessitated a full boiler overhaul being carried out annually.

Lubrication

As described in Chapter 5, most moving parts of a locomotive require some form of lubrication, to enable them to operate freely and only suffer minimal wear during the process. The responsibility for applying oil where it is needed rests with the driver, whose oilcan was often identified as his 'tool of the trade.' He has to check everything, and ensure that all the reservoirs are topped up, before taking the locomotive from the depot, as well as en route if its particular design requires it. As already described, on the more modern locomotives some parts were grease-lubricated, which only needed to be replenished at less-frequent intervals. Greasing was the responsibility of the fitting staff at the shed, since they had the grease-guns or machines needed for the job.

As we have seen during our study of the various different components of steam locomotives, numerous different ways have been adopted to provide sufficient lubricant for non-stop journeys of several hours. The one-time dangerous practice of the driver walking out along the foot-framing while the locomotive was moving, to apply oil to some parts of its motion, would not be countenanced in today's safety-conscious environment, even if the layout made it physically possible to do this. While the driver's pre-journey 'oil round' was the most important part of his lubrication duties, there were some jobs that needed doing when the locomotive was being 'disposed' at the end of the shift. As we have seen, certain lubrication points use wicks which syphon a controlled supply of oil into a bearing. To avoid waste of oil, and prevent slippery puddles in the stabling area, it is necessary to pull these out of the reservoirs when the locomotive finishes its duties for the day.

Firebox and smokebox cleaning

In the course of a day's work, a considerable amount of ash and clinker can build up in the firebed, and ideally should be removed before the locomotive is stabled. This is usually the responsibility of the fireman who is on the locomotive when it comes into the depot, although in some places separate disposal crews were provided to undertake the work.

As described in Chapter 2, some steam locomotives have an opening section in the firebars to enable the remains of the fire, plus ash and clinker, to be pushed into the ashpan using the rake and long tools carried on the locomotive, while other, later designs, are fitted with rocking grates. Disposing of the ashes is a dirty dusty job, and thus has to be carried out in specific areas to avoid interfering with other, cleaner, activities, either in the shed itself or those going on in the neighbourhood. Normally at a depot there were special ash-disposal pits, sometimes filled with water which would quench any hot embers remaining from the firebox.

If the type of coal being used has an ash with a low fusion temperature, the resulting fused clinker can attach itself to the firebars, which makes it very difficult for the fireman to remove, even using the long pricker or 'slice' provided for the purpose. In some cases it is necessary for someone to go inside the firebox, despite the boiler still being very hot, to knock off the clinker. Because it is desirable to site the ash disposal work well away from the offices or where any mechanical work was carried out, this meant the crew had to carry out the job with the blower turned on to keep the firebox 'habitable', but still had to ensure that sufficient steam pressure still remained in the boiler to move the locomotive to the stabling sidings after the job was complete. A crew that needed the services of the shed pilot to make the move would not be popular.

Ashes accumulated in the ashpan(s) and smokebox, as well as the firebox. Locomotives with wide fireboxes usually have three ashpans, one centrally mounted, with the others outside the frames, but normally there is just the one between the frames. Emptying these requires a lot of raking after the catch to release the door has been opened, although that is not always easy as the heat could warp the fittings. Modern ashpans were made hopper-shaped to make them at least partially self-emptying. One of the more significant ways in which lineside fires can be caused in dry weather is by hot cinders bouncing out of the ashpan, and this was why, during the steam era, particular efforts were made by the permanent-way maintenance gangs to keep the linesides clear of long grass and other foliage which could easily be set on fire as it ripened or dried out.

Many locomotives have self-cleaning smokeboxes, which are designed to discharge most of the 'char' through the chimney when the locomotive is steaming. Even when these are fitted, some of the larger material still remains, and has to be removed by shovelling it out carefully over the bottom lip against which the door closes. Inevitably some gets split onto the front buffer-beam, and a conscientious fireman would sweep this clear, as it could blow back in the faces of the next crew to take the locomotive out into traffic.

Sand

The arrangements to provide sand under the locomotive's driving wheels to increase adhesion have already been described, and the sandboxes provided have to be kept filled with material which will flow easily through the pipes. Most depots had sand-drying equipment to aid this, and it was part of the crew's servicing duties to top up the boxes before taking a locomotive out on the road.

Cleaning

Although steam locomotives often operated with their paint- and bright-work very dirty, particularly in the later days of main-line steam, railways used to employ cleaners to ensure that those on passenger workings at least looked clean. When a locomotive was allocated to one or two crews, they often took pride in its appearance, and did some cleaning themselves. In Edwardian and Victorian days the standards of cleanliness required were much higher, and at some stations an inspector at the train's starting point might pass a cloth over the paintwork to check that its cleanliness was up to standard. Stories are also told about crews who, after polishing the huge brass domes on Dean's passenger locomotives in the depot, covered them up with a sack, which would only be removed when they had backed on to their train ready to depart. Less obviously, but practically more important for the efficient and safe operation of the locomotive is that the working parts should be kept clean enough for them to be visually inspected for loose items or fractures.

Running maintenance

This consists of remedial work, which, as a rule, should not detain a locomotive for more than a few hours, but which does require specific facilities. These may be available at its home base, or at a nearby one referred to as a 'concentration depot'.

Boiler washing

The most repetitive form of running maintenance is boiler washing. As explained earlier, boilers concentrate a variety of foreign matter, its nature depending on the chemical content of the water that has been used in service. As long as any solid matter thrown out in this process remains in suspension, it will eventually sink to the lowest part of the water space above the foundation ring, between the inner and outer fireboxes. This can be removed by 'blowing down' through a manual valve positioned low down on the outer box. Using the residual pressure in the boiler the outflow of water carries the sludge away with it into the depot's drains. (This blow-down arrangement should not be confused

Plate 7.10 Running-sheds for steam locomotives were of two types. Most were of the 'straight-through' type with parallel tracks inside a building with doors at both ends, access pits between the rails being provided for at least some of their length. The last of these major depots to be built in Britain was at Thornaby, on Teesside, and, when completed in 1958, was designed to accommodate diesel traction as well. It had 12 straight tracks for steam locomotives in addition to the 24-stall round-house (see below)

Plate 7.11 On large steam depots the 'round-house' layout was frequently adopted, as illustrated by this photograph of the one at Upperby, Carlisle. An LMS Class 5MT 4-6-0 stands on the turntable, ready to move out of the depot after receiving attention on one of the radial tracks. In contrast to the remaining turntable at the National Railway Museum in York, the one at Upperby was open to the sky, with only the separate stalls being under cover.

Plate 7.12 The wet ash-pits at York in September 1947. In spite of the dirt and the steam discharging from the open blow-off cocks, the grids over the pits can just be made out to the left of the 'Austerity' 2-8-0, which is still carrying its War Department number and Westinghouse air pump on the side of the smokebox. In 'wet' pits the ash dropped into water. This reduced the dust nuisance, but required some form of mechanical discharge system, usually a mobile crane with a 'grab', which lifted the ash into wagons for ultimate disposal.

with a continuous blow-down valve which would be located just below the operating water-level, where it discharges small quantities of water whenever the regulator is open, to keep down the level of soluble salts in the boiler.)

Many of the impurities, however, form scale—insoluble compounds which often have a negative solubility coefficient. This means their solubility decreases as the temperature rises, which gives them a tendency to attach themselves to the hottest parts of the boiler. These are the firebox crown, its sideplates and stays, and, to a lesser extent, the boiler tubes and flues. As described in Chapter 3, scale has poor heat conductivity, so any such deposit acts at an insulator, cutting down the heat transfer. This reduces the ability to raise steam and can also cause overheating because it hinders the cooling effect of the water, the result being to make the metal waste away on the fire-side.

Washing is carried out after removing various strategically-placed washout plugs and mudhole doors. A high-pressure water hose is inserted, and, with the aid of 'descaling irons', as much as possible of the scale is removed. This is a difficult task, but the boilermen become adept at peering into nooks and crannies to dislodge most of the deposits, which are then washed out of the mudhole doors. Some scale can never be reached or is attached too firmly to be dislodged, and it can only be removed by opening up the boiler during a general overhaul at one of the Main Works.

The older and less well-equipped depots were only equipped to use cold water for this work, but elsewhere increasing use was made of storage systems which utilised some of the heat remaining in the hot boiler when the locomotive arrived. This was blown down into a holding tank, from which it could be used for the washing process. Any left-over at the end could be used to refill the boiler ready for raising steam again. Hot water is better for washing out purposes, as it is more effective at removing scale and its use causes less thermal stress to the hot boiler structure.

Piston and valve (P&V) examination

Piston and piston-valve rings are easily damaged. Broken rings do not necessarily fail the locomotive, but, by allowing live steam to blow straight through to exhaust, they are clearly wasting energy and reducing the locomotive's power output. Rings, and the grooves in which they work, can also become clogged with carbonised oil and dirt, and even by smokebox char which has come the 'wrong way' down the blast pipe. This contamination can prevent the rings from following the cylinder or steam-chest bores accurately. If they stick 'out' they become broken, and if they are 'in' they cannot form a proper seal against steam leakage as described above, with similar adverse effects on performance. It is, therefore, good practice to 'pull' the pistons at regular intervals and clean them thoroughly.

Running repairs

Unfortunately most in-service problems do not occur tidily at consistent intervals, but have to be dealt with as they arise— immediately if they could threaten safety or the ability to perform reasonably satisfactorily. Alternatively the work might be deferred until, for example, the locomotive was due to be stopped for a boiler washout or a P&V examination.

Most defects come to light either in a report from a driver on a 'Repair Slip' or from a routine check by an examining fitter or boilersmith during a depot visit. The variety of work is very great, and can involve at some time or other practically any part of the locomotive—which certainly tests the versatility and skills of the depot staff. This adds to the interest of depot activity, and compensates, in part, for the harsh conditions under which most work is done.

Some railways have made a practice of allowing their depots to do quite large repairs by providing them with, for example, lathes, power presses, and boring machines, so that jobs such as rebushing side-rods or remetalling axleboxes could be tackled. Other companies insisted on what was little more than a component-exchange policy, with parts requiring repair being sent back to Main Works for replacement with a reconditioned item. The relative merits of the two systems have been debated at length without either coming out as favourite. This is perhaps understandable, bearing in mind the real differences between railways is their geographical shape and size, their prosperity, and the scope and amount of standardization within their locomotive fleets.

Overhauls

The steam locomotive is fundamentally a robust machine, but deterioration does take place over a period of time, in the following ways:

Wear between rubbing parts

This is limited by effective lubrication, but nevertheless occurs in the working environment of locomotives, where dirt abounds and some is certain to enter.

Work hardening

This is again a phenomenon which results from movement and vibration, and particularly affects parts such as pipes fabricated from copper, which can also become brittle.

Fatigue

Caused by repeated reversals of stress, which can lead to fractures.

Wasting and distortion

Loss of material by chemical attack, particularly when hot. This particularly affects boiler and firebox plates if they are overheated in the presence of acid gases.

Corrosion

Oxidation of mild-steel parts in the presence of water, coal, and ash. This is a special problem with water tanks, coal bunkers and smokeboxes.

Accumulation of dirt and other foreign matter

This removal work is normally scheduled in depots, as described above, but this still leaves many components, such as pipes and valves, where deposits gradually build up and affect performance.

The various forms of deterioration can be monitored, and when any of them reach a stage when safety and/or efficient operation appear to be at risk, the locomotive is given a careful inspection by the depot's technical staff. The results are reported to the railways' Shopping Control or equivalent organization, accompanied by a proposal for the locomotive to be called into Main Works for overhaul. Although not all the components will require urgent attention at the same time, the policy of most railways is that, when a locomotive is sent to a works, it is worth dealing with all items of equipment which are unlikely to remain in satisfactory condition until the next routine overhaul. In this way the number of separate visits to works is kept under control, as these are expensive and make the locomotive unavailable for revenue-earning operations.

In practice many administrations find it convenient to define three categories of shopping:

General repairs

Complete stripping down to individual components, including the removal of the boiler from the frames. All parts are then overhauled before being refitted.

Intermediate repairs

The overhaul is limited to the main moving parts, and most other small components. The boiler is not removed from the frames.

Casual repairs

Work outside the normal pattern of overhauls, which may be needed because of a derailment or collision 'incident', or involving work which the depot cannot undertake.

In general, the objective is to restore all components to an 'as new' condition, or, if this is impracticable, to replace them with new items. In this way the people responsible for running the trains can expect that a locomotive returning from overhaul will be able to cover a similar distance or run for a similar length of time before the next works visit becomes necessary. Wear of the mechanical parts takes place in proportion to the distance run, whereas it is steaming time which determines the deterioration of the boiler and its associated fittings.

The time needed to repair a locomotive's individual components varies enormously. It will be economic for a large works involved with the overhauls of large classes of standard designs to have stocks of spare items, the quantities of each being roughly in proportion to the time taken for their overhaul. Spare boilers were frequently provided for numerically large classes of locomotive, and in these cases it was rare for one undergoing a general overhaul to depart with the same boiler it had on arrival. Many of the major motion components of locomotives were normally stamped with its original running number, and these would be restamped if moved to a different locomotive.

Over the years some interesting puzzles have arisen with certain preserved locomotives, on which components have been found, not just with several different numbers, but also numbers from more than one design class. Smaller components were freely interchanged, and many

Plate 7.13 An example of locomotives exchanging parts during overhaul. In BR days, when the paint on N15 0-2-2T No. 69179 became abraded on its side-tanks, the earlier number of another of the same class (No. 9180) became visible, showing they had at one time been fitted to this sister locomotive.

were not stamped with the running number of a locomotive. In some cases items would be numbered in separate series which enabled the works to keep track of their condition or record test performance after being overhauled.

It is usually considered that the identity of a locomotive remains with its main frames, but several of the BR works kept a spare set of frames for certain more numerous classes, and this would be used if one of the locomotives came in with frames that needed a lot of time-consuming attention, perhaps because of major fractures. The spares would then be 'stepped-up' in just the same way as happened with boilers during general overhauls. There are on record other, higher-profile, changes of identity, either temporary or permanent. LMS No. 6229 *Duchess of Hamilton* became No. 6220 *Coronation* for its North American tour in 1939, and the GWR 4-6-0s *Bristol Castle* and *Windsor Castle* exchanged identities permanently when the former had to be used for the funeral of King George VI at a time when its sister locomotive was undergoing a major overhaul. This practice was in fact widespread, and a locomotive's identity was effectively only nominal, like Len Hutton's cricket-bat which was reputed to have had three new blades and four handles! It may come as a surprise to some enthusiasts, but a locomotive's running number (and name if carried) often only provided a short-term identity. Any well-managed Main Works took full advantage of standardization to minimize its stocks of spare parts.

When a locomotive entered a Main Works for overhaul, the first operation was to remove all water, coal, ash, and smokebox-char remaining. It was then moved to the stripping shop to be dismantled into its various components. This work was always concentrated in one particular area, as it was by far the filthiest operation in the whole factory. As each component was taken off it was 'boshed' (immersed in a bath of caustic soda solution) to remove all the remaining grease to aid the task of scraping off most of the solid dirt remaining. Any components containing aluminium bypassed this process, because that metal, which was fortunately not used frequently on steam locomotives, is attacked by such caustic solutions.

Main frames

If the main frames did not require any major repairs they were then removed to the erecting area, where the locomotive was progressively built up again, using the Work's stock of reconditioned or new components. Every removed item was careful inspected by the Initial Examiners, to determine if it was repairable, and, if so, what work was needed to 'make it good',

In spite of careful design, stress concentrations still occurred in places, plate frames being prone to suffer fatigue fractures, particularly in the upper corners of the horn-gaps, and at the brackets to which the springs were attached. These were located by cleaning the critical areas thoroughly and applying a coat of matt white paint. Left for a few hours, any cracks showed up as black lines where the traces of oil in left them stained the paint. If the cracks were small, repairs could be made by welding after they had been gouged out, but such treatment is usually only temporary. A better solution, albeit a more expensive one, was to cut out a whole section of the affected plate and replace it with an insert. The welds holding this in place could be located in lower-stress areas, and the locations where the cracks had occurred were polished to remove any 'stress-raisers' which might initiate a recurrence of the problem. The use of such techniques clearly demands a high standard of skill by the welder undertaking them.

Problems also arose at the points where cylinder castings faced on to the plate frame. As long as the securing rivets remain tight there is no problem, but if any slackness develops, the cylinder starts to move slightly at every stroke. Not only does this allow steam to escape, but fretting occurs on the two faces, which it is extremely difficult to repair. Often the cure again was to weld a new section of plate into the main frame at the affected point.

Collisions and 'rough shunts' in traffic can distort a frame assembly, preventing the horn gaps on the two sides from lining up with one another. Any such distortion is transferred to the axleboxes and axles, which, in turn, wear badly and are inclined to run hot. Forcing the frames into line hydraulically is not satisfactory, nor is it suitable to recut extra-wide horn-gaps which are properly aligned. The best technique is to machine the axleboxes off-centre so that the axles run truly at right-angles to the centre-line of the locomotive (See the upper diagram in Fig. 7.3.) For locomotives which have pre-assembled roller-bearing axleboxes, the realignment is carried out by inserting packing of the appropriate thickness between the horn-blocks and the bolted-on horn cheeks. (As shown in the lower diagram in Fig. 7.3.)

1. - With plain bearing axleboxes

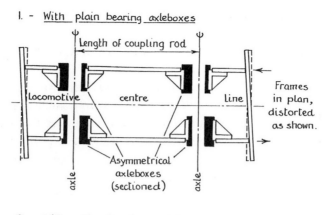

2. - With roller bearing axleboxes

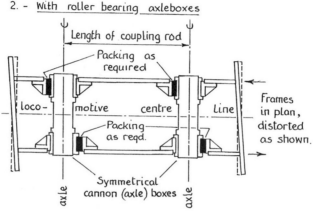

Fig. 7.3 Locating axles in a distorted frame assembly.

Cylinders, steam chests, pistons, and valves

Between overhauls, the pistons and valves of a steam locomotive may well have oscillated through more than 20 million cycles, so it is inevitable that significant wear will have taken place, in spite of efficient lubrication systems and the routine P&V examinations at depots. Steam leakages will have built up progressively with the mileage run, and wear will not be uniform around or along the bore. One reason for this is that the piston-speed varies throughout the stroke, being determined by the angularity of the crank. Irregular wear can also be caused by worn or damaged rings, lack of uniform lubrication, and the effects of the dead-weight or misalignment of the piston and its rod.

To restore components to good working condition, machining will be necessary. Portable machines are inserted into the bores of the cylinders and steam chests, and, of necessity, their diameters will have to be increased to make them truly cylindrical. After a number of successive rebores of this sort it may be necessary to insert a liner to replace the machined-out metal. The restoration of pistons and piston-valves to circular shape also involves machining, but they become smaller as a result, which makes them unusable in their original cylinders and steam-chests. A works with a large turnover of nominally-standard components can reduce the amount of scrapping by establishing a 'cascade' system, with new pistons being used in old cylinders, and old ones fitted into new or relined bores. The process is controlled by specifying a series of step-diameters for both cylinders and pistons, and storing the components in distinct groups according to their actual size. When the diameter of a piston is altered, the grooves for the piston-rings have also to be recut to the appropriate depth.

Motion and axleboxes

The philosophy used when designing surfaces that impact on one another, as described in Chapter 5, means that, at an overhaul, nothing more than a modest regrind will be needed to restore the harder metal surface, while it will be possible for the other, softer, one to be replaced or built up during the same visit to Works. The white-metal on the flat bearing-surfaces of crossheads and axleboxes can easily be removed by heating. A new pad is then cast in its place, and machined to the required size and thickness. The same material in the bearings surrounding the journals on the axles can be restored to 'as new' condition in the same way. Motion-pins are case-hardened, so can normally be reused, the coupling- and connecting-rod brasses being more easily renewed.

Wheels and axles

The main wearing components with these are the tyres, which become 'hollow' in the tread, and acquire thin flanges, as shown in Fig. 5.12. Machining on a wheel lathe will, up to a point, restore an acceptable tread profile, but it is often necessary to remove additional metal to obtain flanges that have the full thickness. (A thin flange might 'split the points'.)

Eventually new tyres are needed, the limit to turning down the old ones being the minimum thickness at the outer edge. (Because the tyres are shrunk on, when the thickness of metal gets too thin there is no longer sufficient tension to ensure they remain firmly held on to the wheel.) When tyres need to be replaced, the old ones are removed by cutting them through with an oxy-gas cutter, and new ones are pre-heated and shrunk on. It is necessary for all the wheels which are to be used as a 'coupled-set' on a locomotive to turned to the same tread diameter. This is a more demanding specification than ensuring that the two wheels on every axle are exactly the same size, and this can require the removal of yet more metal than that needed to produce a satisfactory profile. If this is not done, the axleboxes and coupling-rods will be subjected to excessive stresses.

Axle journals and side-rod pins can usually be brought back to good condition by grinding. Replacement will only be needed if heavy wear has taken place, or there has been surface damage which grinding cannot remove. It is also important to check that the crank-pins on the left- and right-hand wheels are truly 90 degrees out-of-phase, to avoid excessive loadings on the coupling-rod bushes. One particular requirement for driving wheel and axle assemblies is for them to be correctly 'balanced', as described in Chapter 5.

Springs

As described in Chapter 6, multi-plate leaf springs are used for suspension on steam locomotives, and undergo continual flexing when the locomotive is working, although the use of continuously-welded track will have eliminated the disruptions caused by rail-joints every 20 yards (18 m). The plates are highly stressed, as the top face of each is in tension and the lower one in compression. The magnitude of these stresses is indeterminate, but is greatest where the plate emerges from the spring-buckle at each end. Constant rubbing at this point causes the plates to wear, which makes them work loose in the buckle and slide laterally. This, in turn, makes 'nicks' in the plates at exactly those points where they are most highly stressed. These conditions are ideal for initiating random plate fractures, and, when one of these occurs, the stresses on the remainder are increased, starting a chain-reaction.

The only remedy for a broken spring is for it to be replaced immediately, which is task within the capabilities of most depots. As a rule the spring is changed for a spare, and the faulty one sent to the works for repair. This process begins by forcing the stack of plates out of the buckle with a purpose-built hydraulic press. After this all the rust and scale is removed from the individual plates so they can be examined visually for any damage to their surfaces or edges which could act as a stress-raiser and initiate a future fracture. Any suspect plates must not be reused. A new assembly of plates is then built up, a new buckle heated and shrunk around it.

Fireboxes, boilers, tubes, flues, and superheater elements

During the overhaul of these components it is necessary to look for a very different form of deterioration, the causes of which are excessive heat, chemical attack, erosion from particles being carried at great speed in the flue-gas stream, and cracking which arises from the cycles of expansion and contraction as each part is alternately heated and cools.

The most extreme conditions occur in the firebox itself. The plates are subjected to intense convected and radiant heat on one side, but the actual temperature they reach depends on how effectively the water on the other side keeps them cool by removing the heat. This, in turn, is governed by the amount of scale on the water-side, and during a works overhaul, the consequences of poor depot washing-out and the effects of hard water come home to roost—often at considerable expense! If any wasted areas are small they can be patched, but more often the damage is so widespread that a substantial area of plate has to be cut-out completely, and a new piece welded in place, a process which has to be carried out in an inert-gas atmosphere if the firebox is made of copper, as it usually is in Britain.

Firebox stays are subjected to tension forces as the boiler pressure tries to force the inner and outer firebox shells apart, but they can also suffer shear forces as the shells expand and contract. Broken stays have to be drilled out, the holes in the plates retapped and bushed, and new stays fitted. The expansion and contraction movements can also cause stress fractures to start at stay-holes and in the firebox corners where the plates have been bent to shape during manufacture. Treatment is again *in situ* welding or, in bad cases, replacement of the affected part of the plate.

The main parts of the boiler (the outer firebox and drum) do not experience the same extreme temperatures, but are subject to mechanical stresses and can develop fatigue cracking. Welding, this time of steel, is a viable repair technique, subject to strict quality control.

Smoke tubes and flues deteriorate in two ways. The tube ends next to the firebox are continually abraded by the particles of hard, hot ash being carried by the exhaust gases, and these can, if they are very hot, build up deposits—known as 'birds nests' if they grow to any size—leading to local corrosion. The tubes and one end of the flues are only held in place by the expansion of their ends in the tubeplates, and these joints often leak, the escaping water eroding the tubes. The usual works procedure is to remove all flues and tubes at a matter of routine when a boiler is overhauled, which helps to dislodge persistent scale. They are not necessarily discarded, but have their ends cut off and new ones butt-welded on.

Superheater elements suffer the same erosion as the tubes and flues, with most of the damage occurring on the U-bends that face the stream of char particles. The bends are manufactured with thicker walls than the main parts of the elements, so can readily be built-up to thickness by electric welding.

Smokeboxes

These are not the most glamorous parts of a typical boiler assembly, but they nevertheless require careful attention during an overhaul. The acid char which collects inside them can be a menace when it is hot and dry, but, when the boiler cools, the presence of water makes it even more corrosive. Water collects by condensation on hygroscopic particles, or comes from leakage at the tube ends, while rain can enter via the chimney. (If locomotives were stored out-of-use for a few weeks, it was standard practice to cover the chimney with waterproof material, keeping it in place with a flat plate held down by a couple of bricks.) The combination of char and water forms acids which corrode the smokebox plating, particularly in nooks and crannies around the base of the blastpipe and rivet-heads. When this has occurred the only satisfactory remedy is to replate the affected areas.

Air can leak around a badly-fitting or improperly-secured smokebox door, causing the char to burn. This can both burn away some of the interior plating, and distort the door itself, which then admits yet more air. During an overhaul it is thus important to ensure that the smokebox door is made reliably airtight.

Preparation for service

At the end of a major overhaul the external appearance of a locomotive may look even worse than it did when it entered the works. There will be bright metal where welds have been ground smooth, and rusty patches caused by damage to old paintwork. The dark, mottled red colour of annealed copper pipes will catch the eye, and there will be a plethora of painted or chalked identification numbers on many components, together with records of particular dimensions. All this is superficial, and the appearance of the locomotive will then be restored by external repainting, numbering, and, if its public image is important, lining out. To get the best finish the locomotive is usually moved to the Paint Shop, where the atmosphere can be kept cleaner than in the average engineering workshop.

From the engineering point of view it is even more important to check that the locomotive is fit for service. Some of this work is normally done at an earlier stage, such as the hydraulic and steam-pressure testing carried out on the boiler if this item has undergone a major overhaul. Finally it is the turn of the rest of the locomotive, which is first steamed and then examined while standing over a pit to enable all parts to be observed while being tested operationally. Particular attention is paid to the braking system, which must be in full working order before the locomotive is driven away. The locomotive is weighed and its springs adjusted to ensure that each wheel carries the correct share of the total load. A short, light-engine, trial run follows, with a halt being made in a loop somewhere to enable the driver to feel that none of the working parts has any tendency to overheat. If all is well, the locomotive can be returned to traffic after any residual defects have been dealt with—and there always seem to be one or two needing attention even after the most careful overhaul! Where possible it will be first scheduled on a light-duty ('running-in') turn to allow the odd tight bearing to bed in, after which it enters normal traffic—as a virtually new machine.

It was vitally important to return overhauled locomotives to traffic as quickly as possible, and many works used 'production-line' techniques. Crewe had the most developed form of this in Britain, with six parallel 'Belts' being provided. In the main any locomotive could be overhauled on any of them, although the Pacifics and Garratts were normally restricted to one particular Belt. Figure 7.4 shows the sequence of work as it was carried out in 1952. The locomotive, split from its tender, entered the Erecting Shop via a traverser, and was positioned in one of

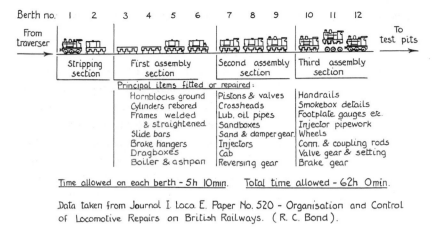

Time allowed on each berth - 5h 10min.   Total time allowed - 62h 0min.

Data taken from Journal I. Loco. E. Paper No. 520 - Organisation and Control of Locomotive Repairs on British Railways. (R. C. Bond).

Fig. 7.4 Typical sequence for classified repairs, as carried out on belt system at Crewe Works.

the two stripping berths, where, after the main motion parts were removed, it was lifted off its wheels, which were sent to the Wheel Shop for attention. There was space alongside for temporary storage of large items like cabs, and each pair of Belts had an empty track between them, which could be used for the wagons needed to transfer boilers and other major components for attention in their own specialized area of the Works.

After the locomotive had been stripped, it was moved on to one of the four berths in the First Assembly stage, where it started to receive reconditioned components, including a replacement boiler, if needed. This process continued in the Second Assembly stage, where most other components would be added.. In Final Assembly the locomotive would be re-wheeled, and, the motion reassembled. When all this work was finished, the locomotive left the shop at the opposite end on its own wheels, to be reunited with a tender, tested, and painted. On the particular Belt illustrated there were berths for 12 locomotives at a given time, and only 62 working hours of normal time were allowed for each of them to pass through the Erecting Shop, although overtime and night-shifts might be worked if necessary. The aim was to get the work on each particular locomotive completed in seven working days. At that time the works operated a 44-hour working week. A massive planning operation was needed to ensure that all the components needed for re-assembly arrived back at the right place on the Belt exactly when they were needed, and this was backed up by acres of other shops where the refurbishing work was carried out.

In 1951 the maintenance and depreciation costs for BR locomotives were getting on for £28million, at a time when it had some 20 000 of them on its books. With steam locomotives having long lives and low first-costs, the depreciation was likely to have represented a fairly small proportion of this total. Locomotive running expenses that year cost a further £89million, out of BR's total working expenses of nearly £338million. To obtain a closer comparison with today's money values, the above figures should be increased by a factor of just over 16, which represents the changes that took place between 1951 and 1999.

Longer-term considerations

The servicing and overhaul pattern described above is applicable to the locomotive fleet of a commercial railway seeking to maintain the same level of activities for the foreseeable future. The sequence may be broken if a particular class of locomotive proves to be poorly designed, becomes technically obsolescent, or is no longer needed to meet the railway's traffic requirements. It may then be necessary to undertake a major rebuilding of a particular class, or scrap them all after obtaining more modern replacements. If none of these more drastic circumstances apply, the process of restoring each locomotive to 'nearly new' condition from time to time ensures that its motive-power fleet is available to maintain the railway's ability to meet its commercial requirements almost indefinitely. During the age of steam, many individual locomotives throughout the world, with a well-organized back-up of this sort, have been able to make a vital contribution to the success of their owner's business for upwards of half a century.

Today's steam locomotives are operated under very different conditions, although all the types of maintenance work described above still have to be carried out. There is no longer any separately-financed Main Works where they can be sent when overhauls are needed, and lengthy fund-raising is often needed before the work can even be started. While there are now many jobs which can only be carried out by specialized contractors, either on- or off-site, much of the overhaul work is usually provided by teams of dedicated volunteers. Even then, appropriate professional certification is essential to meet 'Health & Safety' requirements both in the workshop and out on the line.

Throughout the world many highly specialized designs of steam locomotives have been used

In many places steam is still used on rack railways, and some of their unusual features are shown in these illustrations

Plate 7.14 Examples of different types of pinions and racks which have been used on steam locomotives on mountain railways in Switzerland.

Plate 7.15 A crank-axle from a Swiss steam locomotive which only operates on rack-equipped track. The connecting-rods are attached to the outside cranks in the normal way, but the final drive is through the central pinion, and the carrying wheels are free to rotate on the axle. As a result the grooved brake-drums are attached to the pinion, while lubricators are provided to aid the rotation of the conventional wheels on the axle. The gear wheel drives the speed-governor.

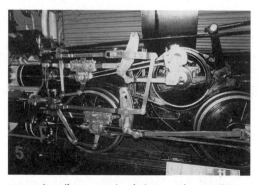

Plate 7.16 Some mountain railways require their steam locomotives to operate as conventional adhesion machines, as well as on rack-equipped sections. As a result they have separate cylinders and drives for each form of traction, the upper cylinder in the illustration driving the pinion via gearing. The external hand-brake is only required to stop the pinion rotating on adhesion stretches, the counter-pressure system being used when descending the steep rack-equipped sections.

Plate 7.17 The steep gradients on rack-and-pinion mountain railways are well illustrated by this view of the Brienze Rothorn Bahn in Switzerland, which is inclined at 1 in 4 (25 per cent). (Courtesy Brienze Rothorn Bahn).

Plate 7.18 No. 4 *Snowdon*, one of the Swiss-built locomotives on the Snowdon Mountain Railway in North Wales. The cylinders are mounted in line with the nameplate, and drive the pinions by means of the massive rocking-lever, an arrangement which provides a degree of mechanical advantage.

Articulated locomotives with the boiler suspended between two power units were widely used on lines where the topography necessitated continuous track curvature.

Plate 7.19 The first Garratt locomotive ever built, on display in the National Railway Museum at York. It has a 0–4–0+0–4–0 wheel arrangement, and was used on a narrow-gauge line in Tasmania. As it is a compound, the cylinders are mounted on the inner ends of the bogies, to minimize the length of the connecting steam pipe. There is a clear difference in size between the high-pressure cylinder under the cab compared with the low-pressure one below the smokebox.

Plate 7.20 One of the less common types of articulated locomotive was the Kitson-Meyer. This example was built for use in Chile on a line which penetrated high into the Andes, and was therefore fitted with a snowplough. In addition it has a moveable cowl on the chimney, which deflected the blast away from the crowns of tunnels when the locomotive was working hard uphill. It is hinged down forwards when operating in the open. There is a steam-powered generator behind the chimney, a powerful headlight being necessary at night to enable the driver to spot any rocks which might have fallen on the track.

Plate 7.21 The Shay locomotive was designed to operate on temporary tracks laid on the ground during logging activities in a forest. Its three cylinders were mounted vertically alongside the firebox, and drove a longitudinal shaft running the full length of the locomotive. Splines and universal joints provided connections with the bogies, each axle of which was driven by bevel-gears. To improve the lateral balance, the boiler was off-set to the left to match the weight of the cylinders and drive-shaft.

CHAPTER 8

Brakes

Braking systems

One of the surprising things about the early steam locomotives was that many of them were not provided with *any* brakes. In that respect, however, they did not differ from the four-legged contemporary alternative form of motive-power, which was not able to provide much in the way of braking effort to supplement what, if any, was fitted the vehicles they hauled. Well into the twentieth century, too, it was not unknown for horses to bolt, dragging their load at a high speed through the streets, so the idea of a runaway train did not concern the railway pioneers unduly. In the early days of the steam locomotive, when George Stephenson was asked what would happen if *Rocket* came across a cow on the line, he is reputed to have replied 'It would be so much the worse for the coo'! However, had there been investigative journalism in those days, he might have had occasion to regret this statement when that locomotive fatally ran down the President of the Board of Trade at the opening of the Liverpool & Manchester Railway in 1830. (Railways in the UK are nevertheless still required to provide fencing through the countryside that is 'stock-proof'.)

In spite of the early development of significant speeds on the railways, inadequate braking continued to cause accidents until quite late in the nineteenth century, for which technical difficulties and lack of expenditure were both to blame. Simple handbrakes were fitted on the locomotive or its tender, where the driver and fireman could apply them, and similar equipment was provided in the guards' vans, although it could only be used when a guard or travelling porter was riding in the vehicle concerned. This latter arrangement developed into the 'chain brake', where a friction clutch on one of the axles wound a chain on to a drum, the tension applying the brakes on several adjacent vehicles. By 1880 this system had become the most reliable available. With considerable reliance being placed on the action of the guard(s) along the train, braking distances were still relatively lengthy. Even with the use of whistle-codes from the footplate, action required for unexpected out-of-course stops or slowings might fail to happen for a crucial short time.

As the steam locomotive was the only primary source of power in a train, it was obviously desirable to develop some form of powered braking system controlled from this point. A steam brake used on the locomotive itself, and possibly also on the tender, could not, however, be effectively extended along the train, because condensation would prevent the brake force developing until the whole system warmed up, causing an unacceptable delay. The two alternative options which developed used air, either in compressed form, or as a partial vacuum.

In both cases a continuous train-pipe is needed, approximately 1–2 inches in diameter (25–50 mm), joined by flexible connections between vehicles, to which each of the brake-cylinders is connected. An air compressor would pressurize a reservoir on the locomotive, and, when the brake needed applying, a valve would enable the train-pipe to be 'charged', together with the brake cylinders, thus slowing the train. The vacuum system operated in reverse, with atmospheric pressure moving the piston in each brake cylinder after a vacuum had been created in the train-pipe.

Both these arrangements were known as 'simple' systems, and both would fail if continuity was lost, particularly if a train became divided as a result of a coupling breaking, and, in any case, they were very slow-acting. The alternative was to make the arrangement 'automatic', which would be 'fail-safe' and apply the brake immediately if air was admitted to a vacuum-brake system, or allowed to escape from the compressed-air version. Such an arrangement clearly also enables the brake to be applied by a valve anywhere on the train, should the need arise, thus increasing the safety factor still further.

In 1875 the Royal Commission on Railway Accidents arranged a series of brake trials at Newark, but the choice of systems was not clear-cut. The compulsory use of an automatic system only became mandatory after the major disaster at Armagh in 1889. On this occasion, a train fitted with a simple brake system was divided after it had stalled on a steep gradient, to enable the two sections to taken separately to the summit, and the rear part ran back down the bank. In Britain the automatic vacuum brake was more widely used in the days of steam traction than the alternative compressed-air system, often known as the

Westinghouse brake, from the name of the company that developed the technology, and still provides much of this equipment.

After this very brief outline of the development of train braking in this country, we will now look at the details of each system as it was applied to steam locomotives.

Handbrakes

Considerable forces need to be applied between the brake-blocks and wheels of a locomotive to slow it down because the coefficient of friction is low. Some form of mechanical-advantage is thus needed to enable the required forces to be generated by human muscles. In most cases a screw-thread is used for this purpose, the driver or fireman winding a handle round to move the nut along the thread, the brake linkage being attached to the nut (see Fig. 8.1). Even with such an arrangement a lot of force is needed, and the friction in the brake rigging also has to be overcome. On modern locomotives the handbrake handle is often arranged to turn in a vertical plane to avoid it occupying too much space on the footplate, the necessary provision of bevel-gears also adding to the effort needed when the brake is being applied or released. Friction and mechanical-disadvantage are, of course, helpful in preventing the brake self-releasing, and all that is needed in some designs is a chain with a loop which is put over the handle, this being sufficient to prevent

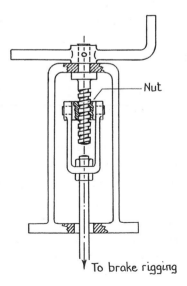

Fig. 8.1 Handbrake handle and screw.

it moving through vibration. By contrast, in a guard's van the horizontal handbrake wheel is usually fitted with a pawl-and-ratchet system to hold it after it has been applied. It must be emphasized that *all* steam locomotives require a handbrake to secure them, because any powered braking system is rendered useless when the boiler-pressure disappears after the fire has gone out, or the reservoirs are devoid of compressed air.

Steam brakes

The next obvious form of braking to use is one powered by steam, which is available at boiler-pressure whenever the locomotive is in operational condition. If the valve-gear on a locomotive enables it to be quickly reversed, doing this and then opening the regulator will provide a measure of retardation as the cylinders try to work 'backwards'. Such an action is only to be relied on in an emergency, as it is likely to draw solid particles from the smokebox into the cylinders and valve-gear, and is not easy to control, possibly causing the driving wheels either to slide on the rails or rotate backwards. Both of these reduce the braking effect, and the first will also cause undesirable 'flats' on the tyres.

A few, specialized steam locomotives still use their cylinders for braking in another way. This is the counter-pressure system, when the valve-gear operates in the opposite direction to travel, enabling the pistons to compress air admitted during the 'suction' stroke. It is discharged through a control-valve, the setting of which can be altered by the driver to provide the degree of braking required. To cool the cylinders a small bleed of water is injected into them, which is turned into steam by the heat generated. The main use of this system is on rack-railways, and there is a tell-tale small plume of vapour from one corner of the cab when it is in use. Two of the North Eastern Railway class S 4-6-0s were successively so-equipped from 1934 until 1951, for use in tests with a dynamometer car. It could provide an infinitely variable resistance to simulate different lengths of train, making it the equivalent of what we refer to today as a mobile load-bank.

The more usual way for steam to be used for braking, even with the quite low boiler pressures in the early days, is by admitting it to a cylinder containing a piston which is attached to suitable brake-rigging. However, as the brake is not in continuous use, problems arise each time steam enters a cold cylinder. This initially causes the steam to condense, so reducing its pressure, and thus the braking effort. To overcome this the driver has to keep the application valve open until the brake cylinder has warmed up. Arrangements are also needed to avoid the cylinder filling with condensate, and thus rendering the system useless, because any further supply of steam would then condense rapidly in the feed pipe. Accordingly cylinders are fitted with drain valves, which allow any liquid to escape, but close as soon as live steam reaches them. Many British locomotives used such a system to provide the braking forces for themselves and their tenders. When one so-equipped is being operated as a light-engine it is advisable, if time permits, to warm up the brake cylinder before using the brake 'in anger'. The brake-valve also has to be able to release the brake quickly, which involves letting the steam escape to atmosphere through a pipe which discharges under the cab, where it does not cause any hazards. When continuous brakes had been developed, it became usual to provide a combination-valve which applies the locomotive's steam brake whenever a significant application is made of the train's vacuum or air brake.

The tender is close enough to the boiler to make it practicable use a steam brake for its wheels as well, with its own cylinder fed by a flexible pipe from the locomotive's brake valve. Unfortunately, if this pipe broke, or a forgetful fitter neglected to recouple it after a locomotive and tender had been 'parted', *both* brakes would fail. Webb used an ingenious system which split the force from a single cylinder, mounted on the locomotive, to operate the brakes on the tender as well as the locomotive. Unfortunately again, if either half of the rigging broke, the whole system failed, and this equipment was quickly replaced after he had retired, albeit not until the age of 67. With other systems a braking cylinder on the locomotive can successfully operate brakes on the tender, as long as suitable rigging is provided to minimize the loss of brake-power on the locomotive if it should become separated from its tender.

Simple vacuum brakes

The next easiest use of steam for braking is by means of the production of a partial vacuum, which can easily be done with a steam ejector, as described in Chapter 3. Steam from the boiler enters a converging cone and entrains air from the annulus around it, which is connected to the train-pipe. In its initial form the vacuum would be created to apply the brakes on the locomotive (and tender, if provided), the force on each brake piston being generated by the differential pressure between atmospheric and that in the closed end of its cylinder. Clearly such a

Plate 8.1 The steam ejectors for the 'simple' vacuum brake on North Eastern Railway 2-4-0 No. 910.

system could easily be extended along the train, and the 'simple' vacuum-powered continuous-brake was used for a some time. The former North Eastern Railway 2-4-0 No. 910 in the National Collection, dating from 1875, retains this arrangement, a pair of large ejectors alongside the smokebox being needed to apply the brake quickly by removing as much air as possible in a reasonably short time.

Simple air brakes

Even if it is possible to create a 'perfect' vacuum, the maximum differential pressure available is only about 14.7 lb/in^2 (1.0 bar), whereas it became relatively easy to compress air with a suitable steam-operated pump to 90–100 lb/in^2 (about 6–7 bar). This means the same braking force can be obtained with much smaller brake-cylinders and/or the provision of brake-rigging with reduced leverage. Simple air brake systems were thus favoured by some railways for use on their locomotives and trains, although the pump was a more complicated item of equipment to build and maintain than a vacuum ejector.

Both 'simple' systems shared the disadvantage of becoming useless if the train, or the brake-pipe, parted. Accordingly 'automatic' vacuum and air brakes were invented, the former being somewhat simpler. It will

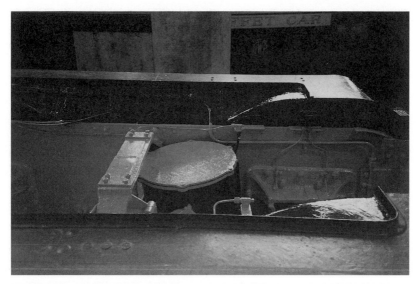

Plate 8.2 The top of the locomotive's vacuum-brake cylinder on the LNER Class V2 No. 4771 *Green Arrow*, seen while the boiler was removed for overhaul. It is situated off-centre between the second and third driving axle.

be described first because it was used more extensively than the air-brake in Britain during the mainline steam era.

Automatic vacuum brakes

The automatic operation is obtained by effectively holding the brakes 'off' by means of the vacuum, thus ensuring that the brakes are applied along the full length of the train if air is admitted to any part of the system, either in a controlled fashion by the driver or guard, or because the train has split into two portions. It also enabled the railways to provide a 'communication system', whereby passengers could partially apply the brake to alert the crew to any untoward dangerous happening.

The mechanism for achieving this is part of every vacuum-brake cylinder, which contains a large-diameter piston that divides it into two chambers. As shown in Fig. 8.2, both chambers are connected to the train-pipe, the upper one via some form of non-return valve or sealing piston-ring (different companies used varying designs for these fitments). When the vacuum is first created, the air pressure in the whole system is reduced to whatever is the working vacuum used. As soon as air is admitted to the train-pipe to apply the brakes, some of it flows into the bottom chamber, but the non-return system (the 'ball

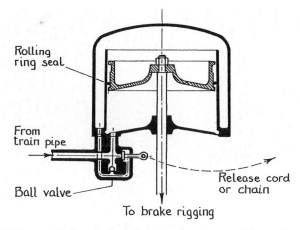

Fig. 8.2 Vacuum-brake cylinder with release valve operated by cord or chain.

valve' in Fig. 8.2, or the piston-ring) seals itself, and prevents the air reaching the upper chamber. A differential pressure is thus generated across the piston, moving it upwards and applying the brakes, the force produced being proportional to the pressure-difference across the piston. When the full vacuum is restored in the train pipe, this difference disappears, and the brakes drop-off as gravity acts on the weight of the piston and its connecting linkage.

Usually two differently-sized ejectors are fitted to each locomotive, the 'small' one operating all the time to overcome the various inevitable small leaks throughout the system and so maintain the vacuum. The 'large' one is normally only used to recreate the vacuum to release the brakes quickly after they have been applied to stop or slow the train, or to exhaust the system initially. Such a system easily maintains a vacuum of '21 inches of mercury', which was the differential used operationally on most British main-lines, and is based on the fact that, with a 'normal' atmospheric pressure of about 14.7 lb/in^2 (1.0 bar), a perfect vacuum would support a column of mercury 29.9 in high. The reading shown by one of the pointers on the gauge in the cab indicates the vacuum initially created in the upper ends of the locomotive's brake cylinders and vacuum reservoir, in inches of mercury. With a vacuum of 21 in, this works out at 10.3 lb/in^2 (0.7 bar) below atmospheric. The other pointer indicates the (vacuum) pressure in the train-pipe, so the difference between the two shows the amount of braking currently being applied.

Plate 8.3 The vacuum-brake pump on the preserved Great Western heavy-freight 2-8-0, No. 2818 is attached to the foot-framing on the right-hand side, in line with the second coupled wheel. The piston in driven by a bracket attached to the crosshead.

The Great Western Railway used a somewhat higher vacuum of 25 in of mercury with its steam locomotives. This corresponds to a working differential of 12.3 lb/in^2 (0.84 bar), which, at first sight, apparently increases the braking pressure available by 20 per cent, but, as we will see when we discuss the operation of the brake cylinders, the benefit can be appreciably greater still. Such a vacuum is not easily maintained by a 'small' steam ejector, so the Great Western fitted each of its locomotives with a multiple-jet ejector, and also with a vacuum pump, driven by one of the cylinder crossheads, which maintained the vacuum in the train-pipe while the train was moving. The large ejector was provided to speed-up the 'blow-off' of the brakes after an application, and to create the vacuum when the train was standing. It was also usual on the locomotive to provide a vacuum reservoir or 'chamber', which was connected to the system on the ejector or pump side of the brake valve. This gave the driver a finer control of the pressure when applying and releasing the brake, and also formed a reference pressure for the 'proportional valve' used to apply the steam-brake at the same time on any locomotive so fitted.

The driver's brake valve provides a means of admitting air to the vacuum system in a controlled fashion, which causes the brakes to be applied, and has two extreme positions, labelled on the BR standard locomotives as 'On' and 'Off'. In the first case the valve connects the train-pipe to the atmosphere via a variable restriction, permitting air progressively to destroy the vacuum in the system along the train to apply the brakes. When the handle is moved to the 'Off' position, the vacuum-pump or ejector, which has continued to be connected to the train-pipe, is able to remove the air and release the brake. With such a system it requires skill to hold a constant partial braking effort.

Even if the ejectors could produce a perfect vacuum, the maximum braking force that can be produced is relatively limited, even with brake cylinders as large as 24 in (610 mm) in diameter. The brake-rigging is thus arranged to increase the leverage, but that also increases the travel of the piston in the brake cylinder. As that moves upwards it increases the pressure in its 'closed' end (the 'upper chamber' referred to earlier) which, in turn, diminishes the maximum brake force that can be applied to the wheels.

Working on the BR standard of 10.3 lb/in^2 of vacuum, the absolute pressure in the top chamber under running conditions is:

$$14.7 - 10.3 = 4.4 \text{ lb/in}^2.$$

If the brake is then fully applied so the pressure on the lower side of the piston rises to atmospheric, the maximum differential pressure across the piston becomes 10.3 lb/in^2. However, if, as a result of the piston's resulting movement as the linkage takes up its slack, the volume of the top chamber is halved, the absolute pressure in it will double to 8.8 lb/in^2. This will reduce the differential to

$$14.7 - 8.8 = 5.9 \text{ lb/in}^2.$$

This is only 57 per cent of the 10.3 lb/in^2 it would have been if the piston had not moved. The brake force available has thus been reduced by more than 40 per cent.

On the other hand, if the cylinder was on a Great Western train, the initial differential would have been 12.3 lb/in^2, which, when the brake is fully released, gives an absolute pressure in the top chamber of

$$14.7 - 12.3 = 2.4 \text{ lb/in}^2.$$

If its volume similarly decreases by 50 per cent when the brakes are applied fully, the absolute pressure will only rise to 4.8 lb/in^2, making the differential across the piston

$$14.7 - 4.8 = 9.9 \text{ lb/in}^2.$$

This is a reduction of only 20 per cent on the theoretical maximum. The benefits of such a smaller reduction in the available braking effort was clearly considered by Swindon to be worth the complication of providing a crosshead vacuum pump, as well as a multiple-jet ejector, and increasing the leakages into the system.

All these calculations are based on a nominal atmospheric pressure of 29.9 in. of mercury, but, as we know from the meteorological reports, this can actually vary quite considerably over the range 28–31 in. When the brake is fully released, the difference between atmospheric pressure and the vacuum in the train-pipe is controlled to a constant figure by the ejector's vacuum-limiting valve. As a result, the absolute pressure in the system is higher during a meteorological 'High'. This means that there is also a higher pressure in the upper chambers of the brake cylinders in such conditions, which causes a proportionately larger reduction in the brake force as the piston moves upwards.

Whatever system is used, better braking will result if the travel of the brake piston is reduced and if a larger space is provided above the piston. Because of the mechanical linkages, the former is affected by the amount of movement made by the blocks before they come into full contact with the wheels. It is important therefore to take up any slack in the braking system that may develop from wear on the blocks. Provision is always made for the fitters to undertake such adjustments at convenient times, but a set of stock may only be scheduled to receive such attention once a week. Most of the East Coast steam-hauled Pullmans in Britain only operated on Mondays to Fridays, and clearly it made sense for them to undergo their brake-adjustments at weekends. As a result it used to be said by the drivers that the brake was much better on a Monday morning than it had been on the previous Friday night. The alternative was to fit automatic slack-adjusters in the brake-rigging, but these were not generally used in Britain during the steam era.

There are limits to the amount of extra space that can be provided above the piston in a vacuum-brake cylinder, so a separate vacuum reservoir is usually connected to this side of the vessel. On many locomotives, the brake-equipment manufacturers got round the pressure-rise problem in a different way. When the brake-valve is opened, as well as admitting air to the train-pipe, it connects the small ejector or air pump to the upper-chamber of the brake-cylinders on the locomotive and tender. This maintains the full differential pressure across the pistons in its brake cylinder(s), regardless of how far they have moved. In theory this benefit could have been extended along the train, but only by providing a second train-pipe. As we will see, when BR switched to air-braking in the 1970s, they adopted a twin-pipe air system, but there were other reasons for that change.

When a vehicle is detached from a vacuum-braked train, the severance of the joint between the two connecting hoses will inevitably cause its brakes to be fully applied. This could be a disadvantage if it then needed to be moved by some form of motive-power which did not have the means of creating a vacuum, and was able to rely on its own brakes for the slow-speed shunting movements required. Even when it was possible to reconnect the vacuum pipes, if the second locomotive's vacuum-limiting valve happened to be set at a higher (absolute) pressure, the brakes could still not be fully released. The worst difficulties would arise when another company's locomotive took over a train which had arrived behind one of GWR origin.

To overcome this difficulty, release valves are fitted to each vacuum-brake cylinder, which can be used to equalize the pressures above and below the piston, as shown in Fig. 8.2. These are normally actuated by a cord or small chain, the outer end of which is attached to the vehicle's solebar. A white-painted star on this marks its position, and the shunter or guard responsible for 'pulling the strings' can walk along beside the train and easily locate where the release cords are situated.

On a long, vacuum-braked train it will require quite an appreciable time for any brake application initiated by the driver to become fully operational on the rear vehicle, as the air required to move the brake-pistons has to travel all the way along the train-pipe from the locomotive, a distance of over 200 yards in the case of a lengthy passenger train. During the steam era in Britain there were relatively few freight trains provided with continuous brakes, and the 100-wagon coal trains were certainly not among those so fitted!

When passenger-train speeds started to rise in Britain between the two world wars there were places where speeds had to be restricted because of close signal spacings, given the lag with braking applications along the train. To overcome this the 'direct admission' system was widely adopted. A special valve was provided between the train-pipe and each cylinder, which sensed any reduction in vacuum created by the driver, and admitted supplementary air from the atmosphere directly into the brake cylinder. (See Fig. 8.3.)

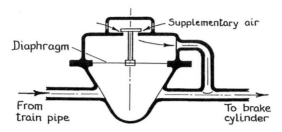

Fig. 8.3 Diagram showing operating principle of direct-admission valve.

A further development was introduced on the 1930s 'Streamliners', which admitted supplementary air into the train-pipe itself, but this had to be limited or it could result in an increasingly severe brake-application towards the rear of the train as more of the vacuum was progressively destroyed by too much air being admitted. Various trials were needed to develop this system, the most notable being in 1938 when one particular test was used as the excuse to work the LNER Pacific *Mallard* up to its world-record speed of 126 mph (203 km/h). The Westinghouse Brake Company's test staff on the train were only told of the changed plans after starting the day's running, but, although then offered the opportunity of completing their journey by other means, to a man they remained aboard to participate.

Automatic air brakes

Automatic air brakes for trains operate at higher pressure-differentials than the vacuum variety, with air initially compressed to 90–100 lb/in^2 (6–7 bar) above atmospheric. This enables comparable brake forces to be obtained with much smaller cylinders, but considerably more equipment is needed to operate the system. On the locomotive an air-compressor is required, usually known as the 'Westinghouse Pump', and mounted above the running-plate, often close to the smokebox to shorten the exhaust steam pipe which usually discharges into the chimney. Sometimes a separate pipe is used, but that makes the operation of the pump even noisier. Another location that has been used is the front-plate of the cab, the main criterion always being to enable it to be kept within the loading-gauge.

A normal pump has its steam and air cylinders in line, one above the other, and connected by a common piston-rod. Only a simple valve-gear is required for the steam cylinder, while the air one can operate quite

Plate 8.4 The Westinghouse brake pump on the preserved London, Brighton & South Coast 0-4-2 *Gladstone*. The steam cylinder is at the top, with its supply coming from the main on/off valve in the cab. Exhaust steam is discharged through the larger-diameter pipe on the right. The simple non-return valves for the delivery air are alongside the lower, air, cylinder, which is this case is not fitted with cooling fins.

happily with nothing more than a pair of non-return valves, comparable in principle to a bicycle pump. (See Fig. 3.10.) On some very large locomotives, capable of hauling extremely lengthy trains, such as those in North America, very large pumps are required. These are sometimes of the 'cross-compound' design, with the high-pressure steam cylinder connected to the high-pressure air one, and the two low-pressure ones sharing a common piston-rod. (The British-built 4-8-4 for the Chinese railways, now on display at the National Railway Museum, has one ordinary and one cross-compound brake-pump mounted on opposite sides of its front buffer-beam.)

The air cylinders on most pumps are provided with fins for cooling, like those on an air-cooled motor-cycle motor. By contrast the steam cylinder is lagged to maintain its efficiency. Air reservoirs are needed on the locomotive, and in this country it was customary to hide them away underneath the boiler or cab, but in some countries they were far more visible, as were the serpentine lengths of piping provided to cool the air leaving the pump. This cooling caused the water vapour taken in from the atmosphere to separate out, enabling it to be discharged through a suitable 'trap'.

The operation of one of these air pumps is controlled automatically by the pressure in the delivery reservoir. As soon as this falls below a particular setting the steam supply is turned on to set it operating. When a locomotive is standing on a stationary train the pump may only made one double stroke once every quarter of a minute or so if there are not many leaks from the brake system. As soon as air is taken from the reservoir to release the brakes, the pump is likely to 'clatter' away hard for up to half a minute to restore the pressure.

While a 'straight' air brake is often used on locomotives, such a system does not meet the 'automatic' requirements along the train. To achieve the same fail-safe requirements as obtained with the automatic vacuum system, a somewhat more complicated arrangement is needed with the compressed-air brake. The vital new component is the so-called 'triple-valve', one of which is connected to the train-pipe on each vehicle provided with a brake cylinder. A small (auxiliary) air reservoir is also provided alongside. As shown in the upper diagram in Fig. 8.4, when the train-pipe is pressurized to its normal running pressure of 70 lb/in^2 (5 bar), each triple-valve connects it to its auxiliary reservoir, which becomes charged with air at the same pressure. As soon as there is any reduction of pressure in the pipe, air from the auxiliary reservoir forces the valve spindle to the left, isolating itself from the train-pipe, and connecting itself instead to the cylinder. The pressure in the latter will build up in proportion to the pressure decrease in the train-pipe, thus applying the brake by the appropriate amount.

When the driver releases the brake by increasing the pressure in the train-pipe again, the triple valve moves to reconnect the reservoir to the train-pipe, and, at the same time, exhausts the air from the brake-cylinder to atmosphere. The latter produces a marked explosive 'hiss', and, where such a system is installed, a series of these noises can be heard occurring in quick succession on each vehicle along a train standing in a station when the driver gets ready to move the train.

Immediately the brake has been released in this way, the pressure in the auxiliary reservoir is lower than it was before the brake was applied.

1. BRAKE FULLY RELEASED

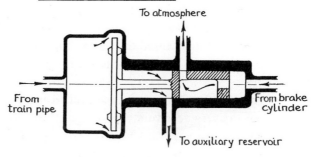

2. BRAKE FULLY APPLIED

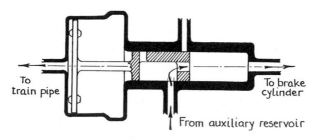

Fig. 8.4 Diagram showing operating principle of Westinghouse triple-valve.

It is only slowly restored to full line-pressure as the additional air is pumped into the system by the pump on the locomotive. This cannot take place instantaneously, and, if a further brake application is made before the pressure has fully recovered, the brake power available will decrease still further, and, by too-quick repetition it can become exhausted. Drivers are taught, therefore, not to make frequent application and release actions.

The original design of triple-valve also had the disadvantage that it did not allow the brakes to be progressively released, as the brake-cylinder pressure is discharged immediately the valve is reversed by an increase of pressure in the train pipe. A more advanced form of valve, called a 'distributor', now enables *progressive* reductions, as well as increases, to be made in the brake force. This gives more precise control of the braking, as well as conserving compressed-air supplies.

The need to avoid operating with reduced pressure in the cylinder reservoirs can at times cause operational difficulties. There is a site in Virginia, USA, where coal trains a mile-and-a-half long (2.4 km.) may have to stop to recharge their reservoirs at the top of a long descent. While this is being done, the automatic brake is in its 'release' state, so the train is held by applying the handbrakes on a number of the leading wagons to supplement the straight-air-brakes on the group of locomotives at the front. When the whole brake system is up to pressure, a task which can take over twenty minutes, two of the crew have to go back along the train to release the handbrakes. To keep the train stationary until these brakesmen have completed the job and climbed back on the locomotives, about 20 lb/in^2 (1.4 bar) of pressure has to be applied with the train brake. When this is eased off to let the train start moving under gravity, that amount of available brake-power is lost. This results in 'a lot of pounds being left behind up the mountain' as the crews describe it.

On long, steady descents when varying brake forces are needed, 'retaining valves' on a number of wagons nearest the locomotive(s) can be applied by hand when the train is stationary, which stop the triple-valves discharging the brake on those vehicles. A second stop is needed at the bottom of the bank to reset them, in the same way as was necessary when handbrakes were 'pinned down' on freight trains without continuous brakes before they descended steep gradients in the UK during the steam era.

To avoid these problems when air braking was adopted in Britain, a twin-pipe system was introduced, which also enables the brakes on long trains to be released more rapidly. The additional pipe is connected directly to the brake-reservoirs on each vehicle, which enables the full working pressure in them to be maintained regardless of what is happening in the control train-pipe. The two train-pipes must be kept separate, so the couplings on the flexible hoses between vehicles are painted in different colours (red and yellow) and only pipes with similarly-coloured ones may be joined.

These pipes and connections have to contain a much higher differential pressure than those on the vacuum brake, and a totally different design is needed. In addition, an isolation cock is necessary at each end of each vehicle, in contrast to the open ends of the vacuum connections, which only require placing on a 'dummy', where the vacuum automatically keeps them in place and sealed. It is thus vital to ensure that all the cocks on both air-brake pipes are open along the length of the train, always excepting those on the extreme ends.

Plate 8.5 The London, Tilbury & Southend 4-4-2T No. 80, *Thundersley*, as preserved and now currently exhibited at Bressingham Steam Museum, is fitted with vacuum *and* air braking equipment. The differences between the hose connections on the front buffer-beam are very obvious, with the cock on the air system (left), while the vacuum hose is just placed on the thimble. The hose below the buffer-beam is for the steam-heating system.

Whenever the composition of a train is changed, a member of staff always has to collaborate with the driver in carrying out a brake-continuity check, to make sure that the continuous system is fully operative before the train starts. This is needed with the automatic vacuum-brake system to ensure that all pipes are connected, but is even more important with the air brake, because of the presence of the cocks.

Even though these checks have been carried out, mishaps could from time-to-time occur. During the 'Deltic' era in Britain there was a notable occasion when one of the cocks was closed by an impact with an object, probably ballast, thrown up from the line somewhere between York and Darlington. When the driver braked for the stop at the latter, the train did not slow as much as expected, and only came to a halt a considerable distance north of the station after one of the restaurant-car crew had operated the emergency brake on a coach in the rear of the closed cock. As a result, the isolating cocks were fitted with catch-handles, which have to be operated by hand before the cock can be moved. Whenever such a cock is closed it also releases the air in the adjacent flexible-pipe, to facilitate the subsequent breaking of the connection with the next vehicle.

This mention of the passenger alarm serves as a reminder that this has long been a requirement for all passenger trains. Although emergency-application handles are provided on today's air-braked stock, in steam days a different operating arrangement was used on both air- and vacuum-braked trains. A chain was threaded through a small tube running the length of each vehicle, with gaps in each compartment where a passenger could get a grip on it to apply a pull in an emergency. This action rotated a cross-shaft at the end of the vehicle which opened a small valve communicating with the train-pipe, and so partially applied the brake as air was let in or out. The driver could overcome the change in train-pipe pressure, if necessary, by using the large ejector or the full-release position with the air brake. This enabled the train to be brought to a *controlled* stop, because there are many places, such as tunnels or high viaducts, where it would not be desirable for the train to be halted while the cause was investigated. This was particularly important with non-corridor coaches, where access to compartments was only available from the line-side. For this reason its official name was the 'Passenger Communication System'. The cross-shaft had oval or round discs on each end, enabling the *fireman* to determine quickly in which coach the chain had been pulled. (In the days of manual signalling, the first duty of the guard at such times was to go back along the track to protect the rear of the train by placing detonators.)

It will be realized from the descriptions of these braking systems that various different ones were used on the railways of the United Kingdom during the steam era. At the time of the 1923 Grouping some of the constituent railways used air but the majority worked with vacuum. In the main, vacuum became the standard for the Big Four companies, although pockets of air-braking remained, and subsequent passenger electrification using multiple-unit trains resulted in a rapid spread of air equipment.

These developments mainly took place in specific areas, but problems arose elsewhere with through running (which became more common) as on the East Coast main line. While the Great Northern and North

British Railways had used the vacuum system, the North Eastern was an air-braked railway. By and large it was easier to provide dual-braking equipment on locomotives rather than the coaching-stock, if only because most trains consisted of more than one passenger vehicle behind a single locomotive. As new coaching-stock was built the proportion of air-braked equipment decreased, thus reducing the operational complications. A different policy was adopted on the Great Eastern, which had also been an air-braked railway. The superior performance of the air system had made a large contribution to the successful introduction of their London suburban services, and this remained in use until the 'Jazz' services were replaced by electrics after World War II. For many years the clatter of Westinghouse pumps remained a very characteristic feature of the suburban platforms at Liverpool Street station.

Braking mechanisms

Although a large proportion of today's trains are equipped with 'high-tech' disc brakes, throughout the steam era braking was achieved almost entirely by cast-iron brake-blocks being pressed on to the treads of the wheels. This applied equally with the hauled vehicles as it did with locomotives, but, with the latter, it was customary only to provide braking equipment on their driving axles, and those on their tenders. There were two good reasons for this, the first being the difficulty of fitting the equipment to small-diameter wheels mounted on a separate moveable frame. Equally important was the fact that the axle-loads on the coupled axles of most steam locomotives were much higher than those on any bogies or pony-trucks. For example, a Great Western 'King' 4-6-0 had a total of $21\frac{1}{2}$ tons on its bogie, and $22\frac{1}{2}$ tons on each of its driving axles, while on an LMS 'Princess Coronation' Pacific each coupled axle has a loading of about $22\frac{1}{4}$ tons, with the bogie carrying $21\frac{1}{2}$ and the rear truck just under 17 tons.

In later years brake-shoes have been made from cast-iron, although in the nineteenth century it was common for wooden ones to be fitted. The North Eastern Railway 2-4-0 No. 910 in the National Collection, dating from 1875, is still fitted with this earlier type of brake-block, which is very much thicker and deeper than the cast-iron variety. Another National Collection locomotive, LNWR 2-4-0 *Hardwicke*, built in 1892, has wooden brake-blocks on its tender. In spite of this it averaged more

Plate 8.6 The North Eastern Railway 'Long-Boilered' 0-6-0 No. 1275, dating from 1874, was fitted with wooden brake-blocks on its tender.

than 67 mph between Crewe and Carlisle during the 1895 'Races to the North'.

Generally speaking, the coefficient of friction between a cast-iron brake-block and the steel tyre on the wheel will be of the same order as that between the wheel and the rail. Ultimately, therefore, the maximum braking force available is determined by two factors: the coefficient of friction between tyre and rail, and the total weight carried by the braked axles. With a clean, dry rail this coefficient is of the order of 0.25, which is usually referred to as an 'adhesion factor' of 25 per cent. To achieve such braking forces on each axle it is necessary to apply a force comparable to the static weight carried by it, which, in British practice, can be up to $22\frac{1}{2}$ tons. With up to five driven axles on a large freight locomotive this requires a total force of appreciably more than 100 tons. This forms the final limitation on the maximum retardation from the brakes, equally as it does when the locomotive is exerting its tractive effort. In the latter instance, loss of adhesion causes the wheels to spin uncontrollably, whereas with excessive braking they 'lock-up' and skid along the track, which is liable to wear 'flats' on the tyres, especially as the coefficient of friction rises as the relative speed between the tyre and brake-block falls.

Plate 8.7 The brake-block on one of the driving axles of the Great Western 4-6-0 *Lode Star*, showing the adjuster provided to keep its face aligned with the wheel-rim. The safety-chain is to prevent any chance of the cross-beam assembly, which includes an equalizing-link, falling off and causing a derailment.

Having decided the brake forces needed, the brake-cylinder area required depends on the pressure of the steam or air used to actuate it. Finding space for this particular item on a steam locomotive is not easy. As a rule, only a single cylinder can be accommodated, which is why many designers used steam brakes on their vacuum-fitted locomotives. Vacuum-brake cylinders are always massive affairs, and also suffer from the constraint that they have to be mounted vertically.

The mechanisms to transmit the braking forces to each axle not only have to be robust, but there must not be any undue frictional losses, the overall task being made harder by the length of the coupled wheelbase of most latter-day steam locomotives. This factor, together with clearance and weight considerations, nearly always dictates that *tension* rods are used to connect the brake cylinder(s) with the brake-blocks, the additional size and weight of the components capable of transmitting a comparable *thrust* without buckling being unacceptable.

Brake equipment, as well as being robust enough to exert the necessary radial force on the rotating wheels, has to be capable of withstanding the resulting forces produced in the plane of the wheel when the blocks are forced into contact with the rapidly-rotating tyre. The design also has to cope regardless of the direction in which the locomotive is travelling. (Before the development of power-assisted brakes on cars, designers used to provide better servo assistance when they were moving forwards, but this was to reduce stopping distances, rather than to avoid the braking equipment becoming detached, a very different situation from that with the brakes on a steam locomotive.) A locomotive's brake-hangers are thus substantial affairs, with equally robust pivots attached to the main-frames. To stop any out-of-balance forces across the locomotive, it is usual to connect the hangers for the two wheels on each axle with a substantial cross-beam, linked at their bottom ends with an appropriately sized pin. As we will see later, there are two alternative methods of transmitting the braking forces from the cylinder(s) to these beams.

As is the case when locomotives are producing power from their cylinders, complex forces result when the wheels are being braked. As the rotation of the wheels is opposed by the brakes, the resulting retardation forces are transmitted by the axles to the axleboxes, from which they are transferred to the locomotive as a whole. For the reasons given above, the longitudinal forces applied to the wheels by the brake-blocks are comparable in magnitude to the vertical ones caused by the locomotive's weight, so, if the locomotive is going forwards and the brake-blocks are applied behind the wheels, some of the locomotive's weight is actually carried on the brake-hangers rather than the springs! Conversely, if the brake-blocks are mounted ahead of the wheels, the locomotive is pulled down harder on its springs during braking. The weight transmitted to the track by the wheels nevertheless remains unchanged.

The practice of mounting the brake-blocks so they made contact with the wheels in one of their lower quadrants also ensures that they readily 'drop-off' by gravity when the brake is released. The blocks are secured to the hanger with a horizontal pin, which permits a limited amount of movement in the plane of the wheel and so maximizes the contact surface between the two surfaces, regardless of the evenness of wear. A few designers provided a secondary, spring-loaded, attachment to ensure that one end of the block did not drag on the wheel when the brake was released.

Some locomotives have been provided with pairs of blocks on each wheel, one in front and the other behind the line of the axle. This has the advantage that the forces from the brake-blocks are more balanced, but the retardation force remains unbalanced. In the normal arrangement with the pairs of blocks making contact with the lower quadrants of the wheels, the upward component of the thrusts of the blocks actually increases the compression of the main springs, although it does not take any weight off the treads of the braked wheels. On his Pacifics, Bulleid located the brake-blocks on the upper-front and lower-rear quadrants of the driving wheels by means of a swing-lever mounted on the hangers, thus balancing the braking thrusts diagonally across the wheels, with some of the actual braking effort being transmitted to the locomotive's frame via the hanger-pins and the brake pull-rods.

As already mentioned, the brake-blocks are normally mounted on vertical hangers, free to rotate in a fore-and-aft direction about their upper ends, which are supported by pivots attached to the main-frames. Because of the appreciable stresses these have to resist, they are of substantial construction. The brake cylinders are normally mounted in a suitable space between the frames, and linkages have to be provided from them to the hangers. Vacuum-brake cylinders operate at low pressures, so are always massive affairs, and also have to be mounted vertically, so cranks are needed to transfer the brake forces to the pull-

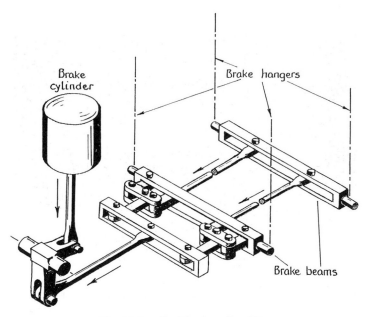

Fig. 8.5 Equalized brake pull-rodding.

Steam brake equipment on Great Eastern 0-6-0 No. 8217 as exhibited at the National Railway Museum

Plate 8.8 The steam-brake cylinder can be seen mounted horizontally under the floor of the cab, behind the trailing axle. It acts on the top end of a vertical equalizing-link, which is normally connected to the brake rodding for the tender as well as the locomotive. The single rod to apply the brakes on the locomotive's three axles can be seen extending forward under the ashpan, with equalizing links at each of the first two brake-hangers.

Plate 8.9 The unoccupied pin on the link directly operated by the brake-cylinder is normally connected to the crank on the cross-beam for the brakes on the leading axle of the tender, and the force is then applied to the other axles on that vehicle by mechanisms of the type shown in Fig. 8.5.

rods which run horizontally along the length of the locomotive. Steam and air brake cylinders may be mounted vertically or horizontally, according to the space available.

Broadly-speaking there are two different ways in which to arrange the brake-rodding. A single rod can be used to connect with the centres of the separate cross-beams, or alternatively a pair of rods can be provided outside the frames, connecting the ends of the beams, and passing either inside, or outside the wheels. It is important to ensure that variations in brake-block wear do not cause significant differences in the braking forces applied to each axle, and many locomotives are provided with a simple lever-system in the rodding to equalize these forces. (See Fig. 8.5.)

Because steam- and air-brake cylinders are relatively small, it is sometimes possible to arrange for them to act directly on the brake-hangers. A particularly neat arrangement was adopted on Deeley's Midland 'Compounds', as shown in the Fig. 8.6. The steam brake-cylinders are mounted between the hangers for the pair of coupled wheels on each side. The reaction produced on the brake cylinders provides the force on the blocks on the opposite side of the wheel to that from the pistons. Additional attachments to the two ends operate extended rodding running inside and outside the driving wheels to connect with the brake-hangers on the outer sides of both pairs of wheels. To prevent the risk of derailment should the brake cylinders become detached, an emergency chain attaches these to the frames, a feature also used with the cross-beams on some designs.

Minimizing the rigid wheelbase of a locomotive is desirable for several reasons, and this necessitates making the 'gap' between the tyres of adjacent coupled wheels as small as possible. The Ivatt Atlantics on the

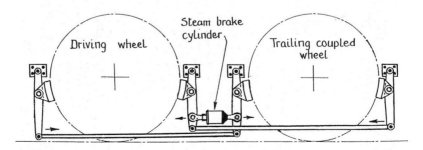

N. B. Safety chains not shown.

Fig. 8.6 Opposed-thrust brake-rigging on Midland Railway 'Compound' locomotive.

Plate 8.10 Part of the steam-brake equipment on the driving wheels of a Midland 'Compound'. The full operating mechanism is shown in Fig. 8.6.

Great Northern/LNER had coupled wheels 6 ft. 8 in. (2,032 mm.) in diameter, and their axles were spaced only 6 ft 10 in (2083 mm) apart, so, even in the absence of any clearances between the axleboxes and frames, the adjacent wheels, each rotating in an opposite direction at

Plate 8.11 The braking system for this 1872 Black Hawthorn industrial shunter was simple but effective, to judge from the wear on the brake-block.

line speed, had their flanges almost touching. This was perhaps an extreme case, but it shows how little room could be available to fit the brake blocks and their hangers.

Brake-blocks often reached quite a high temperature in service, as shown by the discoloration close to the rubbing surface, and it was not too unusual for there to be signs of incipient melting at the edges of the blocks. In the dire conditions of a runaway train on a steep gradient the ineffectual full application of the locomotive's brakes would produce a spectacular ring of sparks around the periphery of every coupled wheel. Clearly, it was advisable to use a material for the brake-blocks which would wear preferentially to the tyres, and care had to be taken to ensure that in normal service any heating effects from braking were not sufficient to cause the tyre to expand and come loose on the wheel-centre. As a result, metal brake-blocks wear quite quickly, and at most steam locomotive depots a substantial pile of spare blocks, carefully stacked in rectangular form, would usually be found, located within easy reach of the servicing tracks. An important design feature with all steam locomotives is the ease with which brake-blocks can be changed, reducing the length of time it is kept out of service.

CHAPTER 9

Designing a steam locomotive

Most steam locomotives were designed by the organization that operated them, and, during the twentieth century in Britain, the railway companies also constructed the majority of those used on their own main lines. This contrasted fundamentally with the situation in some other countries, where the state railway was specifically barred from building its own locomotives. Between 1923 and 1948 in Britain, all the four Grouping companies constructed the vast majority of the locomotives they required, continuing the practice adopted by the larger pre grouping railways during the nineteenth century.

The Great Western Railway works at Swindon had opened in 1843, originally for repairs, but within three years the advantages of using the facilities for new construction were obvious, and the Wiltshire railway town sprung up around it. In 1960 it was this works which built the last steam locomotive for British Railways—the 2-10-0 *Evening Star*, now on display at the National Railway Museum in York. Further north, Crewe works was founded by the Grand Junction Railway at much the same time, and, again, subsequently added the construction of new locomotives to the other activities carried out there. In a notable demonstration of mass production, in 1891 it assembled and steamed a 0-6-0 locomotive in $25\frac{1}{2}$ hours, but the Great Eastern at Stratford Works beat this three years later. They achieved a similar feat with one of Holden's 0-6-0 freight locomotives in no more than 9 hours 47 minutes, using a total of 137 men and boys.

As a result of the pioneering development of steam traction in Britain, a large independent railway industry also sprang up, its traditional main markets being overseas, particularly in the former British Empire, which, in the declining years of steam became the Commonwealth. The Crown Commissioners had a major responsibility for such procurement, and developed a degree of standardization in and between

Plate 9.1 In 1941, 137 years after Trevithick trundled his rudimentary steam locomotive down the Penydarren tramway, the designers of the American Locomotive Company produced what many consider was the ultimate steam locomotive design—the 530-ton 4–8+8–4 'Big Boy' for the Union Pacific Railroad in the United States of America. There were eventually 25 members of the class, and they were noted for their performance climbing Sherman Hill at the head of long freight trains on their way through the Rocky Mountains. All were withdrawn by mid-1962, diesel-electric locomotives in multiple being far less costly to operate. Although not the largest locomotives in the world, they came to epitomize the zenith of steam traction, and no less than eight of the class were preserved, but none of them has been returned to steaming—yet!

some of the countries concerned, which also required a broad design input at the specification stage of an order.

Before the development of road transport, many domestic factories and other types of heavy industry had their own internal railway systems, on which their own shunting locomotives moved the wagons to and from the main lines. Some of these small tank locomotives were purchased second-hand from the mainline companies, but the majority were manufactured by private industry, and various standard designs were more or less available 'off the shelf'.

Having outlined the range of locomotive construction that took place during the steam era, we will concentrate our more detailed examination of the design process to the practices which were followed by the mainline railway companies, as this was most closely connected with day-to-day operational matters, providing an important feedback.

The Chief Mechanical Engineer (CME) was one of the most senior officers of a mainline railway, but rarely, if ever, was a member of the company's board. Remits, like titles, varied between companies, but in most cases, with the exception of the LMS (the largest private railway company to operate in Britain), he was not only responsible for the design of new locomotives, but also for their servicing, maintenance, and overall performance in traffic, including the all-important costs. While local locomotive superintendents would work closely with the area operating manager on a day-to-day basis, technically they would report in the first instance to the CME's organization. In this way information about the locomotives' performance in traffic could flow back up the hierarchy to the design teams, while instructions and details of any changes, together with the reasons for them, were intended to follow the same route in the opposite direction to inform the depot and footplate staff.

Because of this widespread remit, which usually also covered the mechanical aspects of the company's rolling-stock, as well as the mechanical plant and machinery in depots and stations, the appointment of a CME could be made from men with quite diverse backgrounds. Some had been primarily involved in workshop management, while others had specialized in design or operational aspects. There was considerable interchange between companies, and sometimes a CME was appointed from outside industry. Stanier, one of the most successful of the Grouping CMEs, was notably head-hunted by the LMS from the Great Western in 1932, and Bulleid was originally a Doncaster man.

From the above it will be seen that the design and construction of new classes of locomotive were not usually the *primary* tasks of the CME, whose main occupation was managing a very large heavy-engineering activity. This was particularly the case with one new to the office, as his assistant staff kept the locomotive activities operating, albeit still following the policies and standards initiated by his predecessor. On the other hand, there were undoubtedly instances when the performance (in its widest sense) of a particular railway's motive power had fallen well behind the current state of technology, in which case the new incumbent might well be told that his first job was to produce new designs as quickly as possible to bring the railway's performance—and image—up to date.

New classes of locomotives could become necessary for several reasons, the most pressing usually being a perceived growth in traffic, which made it impossible for existing designs to keep time with the heavier loads required by the commercial staff to meet passenger or freight demands. (It should not be forgotten that during the first half of this century the railways obtained roughly two-thirds of their revenue from freight.) One way round this problem was to double-head the heaviest trains, and, although that was expensive in crews and coal, at times it was used quite widely. As one verse of some nineteenth-century doggerel had it:

M is for Midland, with engines galore

They've two on each train, but hanker for more.

However, the ability to change such a situation did not depend solely on the CME and his design team. It might not be possible to accommodate longer locomotives on some of the turntables, and the increase in weight might be more than some of the weaker underbridges could withstand. It was thus vital for the CME to keep in close touch with his civil engineering counterpart. In a notable 'incident' one Scottish CME had a whole new locomotive class completely barred from the company's lines.

Weight, as well as length, width, and height, were all critical constraints that had to be respected when designing a new locomotive. A draughtsman could easily keep within the dimensional limits on his drawing-board, but the only way to estimate the weight was to work out the volume of every part, multiply this by the specific gravity of the metal it was to be made from, and then sum the total of all the parts. In the days of computer-aided design it is only too easy to forget the long and tedious work involved in the steam age at this stage of design. Today, with three-dimensional drawings of a component on screen, it is only necessary to enter a figure for the specific gravity and press a key to have the weight printed out virtually instantly.

A well-organized drawing office would consequently have records of the weights of all previous components used on its locomotives, which would enable the required figures to be taken 'from the book' if the old design was reused. In the case of castings the wooden patterns for the existing designs were probably also available in the foundry, and the cost of having new ones made, as well as the time needed, would be saved if they were reused for the new locomotive. It was ultimately the responsibility of the CME to decide which line of action to take, and in many drawing offices it was customary for him to 'sign-off' each completed drawing before it was passed to the works for action. As a result there was a constant dialogue between the draughtsmen and the CME, or his senior assistants, who would normally make frequent 'rounds' of the drawing office, discussing progress, as well as providing decisions where these were required.

Nowadays engineering drawings are held in digital form, but in the steam era hand-drawn originals were needed for every component and assembly. Originally these were traced on to coated linen, enabling copies to be produced in the form of 'blueprints', which could often be remarkably difficult to read, especially when alterations had been made to the original! In latter-day practice plastics sheets replaced the linen, and, together with the use of the dyeline reproduction process, legibility and availability improved immensely. Vast numbers of drawings were needed for each design, and one of the authors recalls the difficulties of housing the one-million-plus in the National Railway Museum when they were sent on from the Museum of British Transport at Clapham in 1975.

Although railway works were remarkably self-sufficient, they still needed to purchase materials from outside, and, in later years, some specialized equipment, like brake systems, was similarly 'bought in'. The CME would thus receive many offers from suppliers, which had to be evaluated to determine their real worth to the railway. Similarly, the deliberations of the various professional bodies, particularly those of the Institution of Locomotive Engineers, needed to be studied to ensure that the railway kept up to date with developing technology.

In addition to increases in traffic, there were, from time to time, other reasons for designing a new class of locomotives. It might be necessary to introduce new designs to improve efficiency and reduce the fuel bill. Superheating was clearly one such development, and, while it was possible to provide this equipment on some existing designs, maximum benefits might necessitate the development of new designs.

From the Rainhill Trials of 1829 onwards, various practical investigations were carried out to obtain specific information on various designs of steam locomotives or features applied to them, but it was only at the end of the nineteenth century that full scientific testing on trains began, following pioneering work in Russia and North America. One of the techniques required the maintenance of a constant speed regardless of the gradients, and a second 'controlling' locomotive was used for this purpose. As mentioned in Chapter 8 two of Wilson Worsell's North Eastern Railway Class S 4-6-0s were successively so modified, being fitted with counter-pressure braking like rack-locomotives, and the second of them long outlived the rest of its class, although little use was made of it during its latter years. With the development of electric traction techniques it became possible to use Mobile Load Bank vehicles for the same purpose, generators on their axles producing current which was dissipated in roof-mounted resistors.

Although road testing became a highly-developed technique, several static test plants were constructed throughout the world, following that built in 1891 by Professor Goss at Purdue University in the United States. Churchward installed one at Swindon in 1904, but it could only absorb about 500 hp until extended in the 1930s. There was a much larger facility at Vitry in France, and Gresley sent the first of his Class P2 2-8-2s, *Cock o' the North*, there for tests in 1934/35. As early as 1927 he had advocated the construction of a similar facility in Britain, and plans for it were developed as a joint LMS/LNER project in the late 1930s. World War II delayed construction, so it was not until 1948 that the extensive testing plant at Rugby was completed, the Class A4 Pacific *Sir Nigel Gresley* appropriately being demonstrated on the rollers at the official opening, as a posthumous tribute to him. The two static facilities in Britain, together with the development of controlled road testing, enabled the performance of several important classes of steam locomotive in Britain to be significantly improved. Examples included improvements with the valve-events and alterations to the dimensions of chimneys, blast-pipes, and firebox dampers. All this took place before the change to diesel and electric motive-power.

Behind the scenes, too, there were continual reviews of design detail, the specifications for materials, and maintenance practices. These were aimed at improving the availability of locomotives for traffic, their reliability and running costs. This was unspectacular work which often went unobserved or unappreciated by outside observers, but was nevertheless a vital part of the locomotive management activity. One example of this was the switch made by the LMS from wide piston-rings to the later multiple, split-ring design, which markedly cut down steam losses as a locomotive's mileage built up after each overhaul. This type of work was a continuous process, helped by the movements of engineering staff between operating depots and drawing offices. Those companies with more than one of the latter also usually benefited from the good-natured rivalry between them, emphasizing the point that locomotive design was not always an autocratic process.

Fashion (or perhaps trendiness) also came into it at times, particularly in the 1930s when road transport started to develop as a serious competitor. 'Streamlining' was adopted as a worldwide marketing tool, together with the introduction of trains scheduled to run at far higher speeds than had hitherto been the practice. The extent to which this was adopted varied between railways, the most successful in this country being Sir Nigel Gresley's Class A4 Pacifics for the LNER. Not only does one of them (*Mallard*) still hold the world speed record for steam locomotives, but their day-to-day running with the high-speed East Coast expresses set new standards of performance in this country. The LMS, rivalling them for Anglo-Scottish traffic, produced their streamlined 'Princess Coronation' class, which was something of an add-on to a traditionally conceived locomotive, and did not have anything like the same stylish appeal, although they were streets ahead of the contemporary Great Western offering. The latter's semi-streamlined *King Henry VII* and *Manorbier Castle* were modified by little more than the addition of a disfiguring hemisphere attached to the smokebox door! In the fullness of time the A4s were the only streamliners to retain their basic shape, which was an integral part of their design and also helped to lift the locomotives' exhaust, thus improving the driver's visibility. On the other railways the streamlining was ultimately removed, the few advantages that it provided failing to outweigh its nuisance value during servicing and maintenance.

There was clearly an incentive for any incoming CME to leave his mark on the locomotive fleet of the railway, or produce a design which made the headlines. There are instances when considerable benefits resulted from the construction of even a single steam locomotive produced for 'shop-window' reasons. One of the more interesting of these was the Great Eastern 'Decapod', built in 1902. At the turn of the century other interests had put forward Parliamentary Bills for competitive electric railways in the area served very effectively, although not profitably, by that company's steam-hauled services out of Liverpool Street station in London. To counter this threat, the Great Eastern wanted to demonstrate that the same rate of acceleration could be achieved with steam, so Holden built a massive 0-10-0 tank at Stratford Works. So large was the boiler and grate that four safety-valves were fitted, but historical examination of the tests runs suggest that it might have been necessary for these to have been 'screwed down' to lift the nominal boiler pressure sufficiently to obtain the required performance! (For a single trial with a brand-new locomotive this would not present an unacceptable risk if carried out within the design limits of the boiler.) These demonstrations persuaded Parliament not to pass the rival Bills, so this one-off locomotive achieved its purpose of heading-off electrification, even though it never went into regular service. In 1920 the Great Eastern was able to introduce an extensive suburban commuter service (the Jazz Trains) based on Liverpool Street station. This was referred to as 'The Last Word in Steam-operated Suburban Services', and, in *The Oxford Companion to British Railway History*, Professor Jack Simmons called it 'the finest of its kind, worked entirely by steam, anywhere in the world'. Nevertheless, 30 years on, commuters were very relieved when the first of the Liverpool Street lines (to Shenfield) was electrified after World War II.

Once it had been decided that a new class of steam locomotive was needed by a railway, a specification had to be worked out for it. In some cases the 'incremental approach' was adopted, by extending each of the critical dimensions of an existing design by perhaps ten per cent. This would minimize the number of new design calculations, and enable advantage to be taken of the good features of the earlier design, while strengthening those parts which had proved troublesome in service. Such a progression can often be traced in locomotive families, a notable example being the 4-6-0s of the Great Western—the 'Stars', 'Castles', and 'Kings'—their introduction being spread over 20 years. On many other railways there were numerous examples of a design being developed in this way for just a second generation.

However, such a philosophy would not always give sufficient extra haulage capacity for a proposed new service or duty, and could also inhibit the introduction of new desirable features. Ideally the CME would then allocate sufficient of the drawing-office resources to the more extensive task of starting from scratch. After listing the performance demanded from the new locomotives, the tractive effort required at the proposed running speed could then be determined, either from experience or by carrying out suitable dynamometer tests. By extrapolating from this, the necessary nominal tractive effort could be calculated. As described in Chapter 5, this is determined by boiler-pressure, cylinder-volume, and driving-wheel diameter. These variables can be juggled within limits to reach an acceptable set of figures. For example, the cylinder diameter might be limited by loading-gauge considerations, in which case the next easiest alternative might be to raise the boiler-pressure, although that would almost always increase the locomotive's weight.

If higher speeds were to be required with the new trains compared with those already operating, there would be little scope for using smaller driving-wheels, but the use of a more efficient valve-gear would counter the fall-off of tractive-effort with speed. Estimates also had to be made of the ability of the proposed firebox and boiler to generate the required amounts of steam. Numerous combination of factors thus had to be examined before a decision could be reached by the CME. Optimization was needed at almost every stage of the process, many of the decisions actually made having a vital effect on the locomotive's subsequent performance. Other constraints had also to be taken into account, such as axle-loadings (including hammer-blow), and the all-up and adhesion weights, together with the need for carrying axles to give the necessary guidance. It will easily be seen how the adoption of standard designs, if only for components, could considerably speed up these stages of the design process.

Another significant factor that had to be taken into account was the expected number of locomotives in the class. Given the design effort needed when starting from scratch, if only a handful of a new design was required for some particular line, it might be more economic to dust off the drawings for an old class and make the minimum number of changes needed to meet the new requirements. When the Eastern and North-Eastern Regions needed some more small 0-6-0 tank locomotives shortly after nationalization in 1948, a batch of Class J72s was built at Darlington, the original design going back to 1898.

While the basic design process was similar in the railway industry, as a self-standing commercial enterprise they had to 'push' their products. They thus advertised extensively in professional periodicals, and, when an order was being negotiated, they would try to interest the client in various 'add-ons' which had not previously been contemplated by the domestic railways. The latter never wanted to spend their own money on items which produced doubtful returns, whereas it might be easier to persuade a colonial railway (or its government) that it needed to keep up with modern trends. A corollary to this was that British-designed locomotives were far less cluttered with external equipment than those

Plate 9.2 Although steam locomotives are no longer used in day-to-day commercial service anywhere in the world, in many countries there is still great interest in the occasional 'Heritage' operation on main lines. In addition there are numerous tourist railways throughout the world, many of which are run by preservation societies. Even in Japan, the country which pioneered high-speed railways, during the summer it is possible to change out of the 300 km/h Shinkansen at Ogori, and travel by steam train to Tuwano. A special stop is made *en route* where passengers can safely wander over the tracks to take photographs. This one of eight such seasonal services operated by the mainline and 'private' railway companies in Japan.

of many other countries, which contributed considerably to their classic appearance and retention of traditional design features.

After both World Wars considerable numbers of heavy freight locomotives, built during hostilities for the government by private industry, became available and found their way into the mainline companies' fleets. World War I saw no less than 521 of Robinson's 2-8-0s being constructed for service with the Royal Engineers' Railway Operating Division. These were almost identical with those he designed for the Great Central in 1911, and were used behind the British Army's lines in France and elsewhere. Some were purchased by our domestic companies shortly after the end of the war, but the main disposal of them did not take place until the mid- to late-1920s, the LNER buying no less than 273, while 100 went to the GWR and 75 to the LMS, mainly at reduced prices.

At the beginning of World War II the government placed orders with private industry for 240 of the LMS-designed Class 8F 2-8-0s. In 1942 the policy changed, and a new design was developed, requiring less manpower to build, and economizing in the use of certain scarce materials and processes, the locomotives later becoming known as the 'Austerities'. No less than 935 of these were built by the North British Locomotive Company and the Vulcan Foundry, 350 of them being lent to the country's mainlines until needed overseas. After the end of hostilities most were returned to the UK, and 732 were purchased by the newly-formed British Railways in 1948, together with 75 of the 2-10-0 version. Although the latter mainly worked in Scotland, the others saw service over most of those other parts of the BR system where such locomotives were permitted. Again, the newly nationalized railway system obtained the locomotives at well below the price paid for them by the government during World War II.

At times, however, our domestic railways had to turn to the country's private manufacturers to construct locomotives for them when it became necessary to replace a large proportion of their existing stock in a short period. One instance of this occurred after World War II, when the LNER required a large number of Thompson's Class B1s to revitalize their stud of mixed-traffic locomotive, which had been used intensively during the six years of war, when no new ones were built. Within the timescale required, their works at Darlington and Gorton were only able to construct 70 of them, while the North British Locomotive Works was responsible for no less than 290, with another 50 coming from the Vulcan Foundry. These external contractors worked from the railway's original drawings and specifications. All except the final 40 of the North British batch were constructed in just under $2\frac{1}{2}$ years, which provides a clear indication of that company's manufacturing capabilities at that time.

Although actual figures are not available, it would have been highly likely that the unit price paid for them by the LNER would have been appreciably higher than that 'charged' by one of the company's own works. This was a commonplace happening in such circumstances, and explained the railways' reluctance to use outside contractors unless the situation could not be avoided. It was sometimes claimed by the contractors that the difference was far from real, because, although the railway workshops were good at recording the manpower-hours and material costs incurred on an individual locomotive, it was alleged that they did not allocate the true overheads. In fact, the sums used were undoubtedly less than the corresponding ones at an external works, because the main activity of a railway's workshops was the overhaul of existing locomotives, and only a minor proportion of its resources was devoted to building new ones. The share of total overheads applicable to the new build was thus smaller than that incurred in a factory devoted entirely to construction work.

In the diesel and electric era, the vast majority of the motive power in this country has been purchased from outside industry, and, since the privatization of the railways, the locomotives, as well as most of the passenger rolling-stock, are owned by one of the Rolling-Stock Leasing Companies (ROSCOs), and leased to the Train Operating Companies. In some cases, too, outside contractors maintain the stock, and are contracted to make the required number of trains available daily for service—a situation far removed from that which applied on the railways of this country in the days of steam.

To sum up the whole aspect of design, there seems to be little doubt that the first-class work that emanated from the railways of this country was a vital factor in the retention of steam traction in Britain for so many years. Such locomotives provide the backbone of the motive power on today's heritage railways, all of whose steam locomotives are more than 40 years old.

Index